PROF. KEITH HOLLINSHEAD

CHANGI AIRPORT —

SINGAPORE — TERMINAL 2

THURS. 6/2/2014

CONFUCIUS
THE SAGE
ON THE ROAD

KEY:

CT = CHINESE TERM

CON = CONFUCIUS DEFINED/
     DELINEATED }

     e.g., p. 214

MAN = MANKIND —— HUMAN TRAITS

2011

This book is edited and designed by the Editorial Committee of *Cultural China* series

Managing Directors: Wang Youbu, Xu Naiqing
Editorial Director: Wu Ying
Editors: Wu Ying, Parker Barnes

Text by Qian Ning
Translation by Perry W. Ma, Frederick Young

Interior and Cover Design: Wang Wei

ISBN: 978-1-60220-229-0

Address any comments about *Confucius: The Sage on the Road* to:

Better Link Press
99 Park Ave
New York, NY 10016
USA

or

Shanghai Press and Publishing Development Company
F 7 Donghu Road, Shanghai, China (200031)
Email: comments_betterlinkpress@hotmail.com

Printed in China by Shenzhen Donnelley Printing Co., Ltd.

3 5 7 9 10 8 6 4 2

CONFUCIUS
THE SAGE
ON THE ROAD

QIAN NING

N/B:

ODD CHAPTERS → CONFUCIUS
TRAVELS // CONFUCIUS

EVEN CHAPTERS → WHIMSY //
ZHONGNI

Better Link Press

2011

N-YORK

Contents

Introduction

[PERRY W. MU.]

To most modern Westerners, Confucius is already a familiar name. While his fame is on a par with that of Jesus and Muhammad, *The Analects of Confucius*, Confucius' major work, historically has not been as widely read as the works of his two contemporaries, Lao-tzu's *Classic of the Way and Virtue* and Sun-tzu's *Art of War*. Even less was known about Confucius' unique life, his challenging pursuit of a political career and his pious doctrines of benevolence. KCØ. If Lao-tzu and Sun-tzu challenged the world with their wisdom and wit, Confucius is noteworthy for his instructions on morality and stalwart belief. Living at a time now known as the "Warring States" period (also called the Chinese Renaissance), Confucius, along with his teachings, appeared as a beacon of insight that would fundamentally alter the course of Chinese history.

At the time of his life, the war-torn feudal states nurtured rival schools of thought and ultimately gave rise to Confucianism. During Confucius's own era, China was divided into twelve regions under the Zhou emperor, the territories warring amongst each other for control over the land. The lack of a strong central power set the stage for a wide variety of competing doctrines which sought to extend influence over the kingdoms. In addition to Lao-tzu and Sun-tzu, scholars such as Mencius, Chuang-tzu and Qu Yuan all became dominant figures of philosophy and literature who few could outshine in the following twenty centuries of Chinese history. Among them, Confucius' unique legacy left behind three particularly noteworthy points of dedication and perspective.

First, Confucianism's success as a philosophy is built on the lofty principles and goals that Confucius set for himself during his own lifetime. His family lineage was not remarkable. An illegitimate child left behind by a warrior father, Confucius grew up with his mother in a common, poor community in the state of Lu, in central China. He had a striking physique, at a height of six feet three, that made him stand out among his fellow men, and the top of his head was slightly sunken in the center, earning him the given name Qiu, meaning "mound". His childhood was spent playing games with the tools and utensils of ceremonial processes and rituals, which constituted his early studies of the distant, decaying liturgy of the Zhou dynasty. There is a scanty record of his early life, which may indicated he was mostly self-taught in classical learning. He worked in several odd jobs such as a warehouse keeper and lower-level cattle official. However, his grand political ambitions, to "restrain oneself and restore the Zhou rites" and "fearlessly push ahead in disseminating benevolence even with disregard for the dignity of the teacher," most likely took shape as he plunged into society by traveling and managing schools. Being opposed to the hostilities of warlords, and mourning the socially wrecked and unethical state of politics and family life, Confucius aspired to bring order to the land. Setting his aim high, Confucius pursued a career fraught with adversity, one quite different from those of most other scholars of his day. Lao-tzu is thought to have once said to Confucius, "Intelligent and knowledgeable men die early because they reveal others' weaknesses." But Confucius brushed aside these cautionary words. His ethical and intellectual ideals forced him to strive for fundamental social reforms. And his chosen career path was as formidable as it was compelling.

Second, Confucius' life reflected both his steadfast belief and tireless effort to achieve his goals. Laws of nature are similar: hydrostatic pressure increases as one descends deeper into the ocean, and air becomes thin as one climbs higher on a mountain. Lao-tzu's wisdom was confirmed when Confucius traveled extensively from his home state of Lu to many other regions, including the states of Wei, Song, Chen, Cai, Qi and Chu, and he never fully succeeded in impressing his doctrine of "rule by benevolence" upon any of reigning dukes. In the state of Wei, an aged Duke Ling was neither physically nor intellectually able to keep a tight rein on his kingdom, let alone grasp Confucius' calls for reform. Duke Jing of Qi yielded to the pressure of his prime minister, Yan Ying, who felt Confucius were little more than superficial ideals, lacking practical results, and so he rejected Confucius' ideas. In Chu, Duke Zhao took the advice of his official, Yin Zixi, and took back his promise to provide Confucius with land to serve as a testing ground for his political reforms.

Yet destiny did not completely shut the door on the sage's pursuit of a career as a government official. He once worked as a magistrate in the town of Zhongdu in Lu. But that brief stint, though a soothing moment in a long chain of failures, ended abruptly, and his hopes dashed as he witnessed the corruption and sensual indulgence of the reigning Duke. In the following years, a series of misfortunes struck Confucius one after another: the harshness of his travels with his students, along with the cold weather, bouts of starvation, and life-threatening encounters with both beasts in the wilderness and political foes like Huan Tui, the defense minister of Song. He even once admitted that a stranger's characterization of him as "a stray dog" was in fact "quite true". In facing adversity, Confucius often stumbled but always got back on his feet with the same steady confidence and an even stronger sense of optimism. "Only in the dead of winter do we see the qualities of the pine and the cypress," he remarked as he portrayed an ideal model for himself. One should "stand tall in belief, dedicated to learning, and adhere to the Great Way until his death." "It is easier to capture the chief commander of an army than to shatter a man's will." Nothing can give an honorable person more comfort than "dying as a gentleman, with a good reputation to be left behind." While the mountain was tall and treacherous, Confucius was an unshakable mountaineer.

Third, Confucius' ideas on benevolence represent a broad and profound vision of how to organize and run the affairs of both government and family. While lacking the formal study on logic and sciences championed by ancient Greek philosophers, the canon of Confucianism forms a comprehensive system of ethics in ancient China's history of thought and emphasizes moral cultivation. If

12

the *Classic of the Way and Virtue* and *Art of War* describe strategies for achieving life goals, the *Analects* claims those goals can only be realized using integrity in order to unite all lands and people, so that society can live in peace and the family can be kept in order. The Great Way of benevolence he describes soaks into every fiber of the social hierarchy, from government down to households, and provides rules of civility and behavior that govern social life and conversation. He says, "The monarch should behave like a monarch, the subject like a subject, the father like a father and the son like a son." His theory is to be approached from certain basic perspectives, emphasizing righteous worthiness and individual conduct. He holds that "good behavior serves better than an instruction or order." Particular stress is placed on defining the difference between a *junzi* (a morally superior man) and a small man, "a *junzi* is concerned with his reputation while a small man seeks profits." Such ideas, articulated through his effort to return order to society and revive the civility found in the early Zhou dynasty, focus on what he claims to be central point of philosophy: to create a land under heaven that is one community. This Chinese version of Utopia, distinctly articulated in the *Book of Rites*, imagines a society in which what is under heaven is for all, one helps and is helped by others, and peace and harmony prevail. To achieve this goal, Confucius opened schools, teaching over three thousand disciples and training seventy-two scholars, well-versed in the Six Arts (rites, music, archery, calligraphy, charioteering, mathematics). He wrote the *Spring and Autumn* on the history of Lu and collated and annotated the *Book of Songs*, *Book of Documents*, *Book of Rites*, *Records*

13

of Music, and *Book of Changes*. Through his teaching and writing, Confucius firmly planted his ideas of benevolence into the minds of dukes and vagrants alike and drastically changed the political and social development of China's ancient dynasties.

The author of *Confucius: The Sage on the Road*, Qian Ning, grew up in Beijing. He went to the People's University of China in Beijing in the late 1970s and early 1980s and obtained a B.A. and M.A. in Chinese literature. Upon graduation he worked as a cultural reporter at the *People's Daily* from 1986-89 before becoming a Michigan Journalist Fellow at the University of Michigan for a year. In 1996 he published his first book in Chinese, entitled *Chinese Students Encounter America*, which became an immediate bestseller in the country. The English translation of the book, published by the University of Washington Press, appeared in 2002. His second book, *Li Si*, published in 2004, is a novel about a Prime Minister of the state of Qin in the period of Warring States.

I met Qian Ning a couple of times in Beijing from 2008-2009 while engaged in translating *Confucius: The Sage on the Road*. I was deeply impressed by his passion for the study of the Chinese classics as well as his insights into contemporary intellectual and cultural trends in China. Having lived through China's painful eras of fundamentalism and isolation during the 1960s and 1970s, as well as the blessings of economic reform and openness of the 1980s and 1990s, Mr. Qian remains focused in an era of constant change, brimming with promises of affluence—from Starbucks and high-end athletic clubs to iPhones, iPods, Skype and Facebook. His pursuit of a literary career represents a reconsideration of

China's cultural relics by today's younger generations. It is also part of a greater response to certain political movements, which started as early 1919, that sought to vilify and discredit Confucius as an icon of decadent conservatism. The message he imparts to readers through his book is clear: that the glitz and glamour of high-technology and modern society cannot achieve much without the spirit of hope for the future and perseverance that Confucius epitomized in his own life.

Confucius: The Sage on the Road utilizes two distinct features of fictional creation: graphic characterization and historical events expressed in contemporary prose. First, based solely on the two sources, *Records of the Historian* by Sima Qian and the *Analects*, the novel evolves over two parallel story lines: The odd-numbered chapters on Confucius' travel to twelve states and regions and the even-numbered chapters, entitled with names of people, that recount major events in his life in a biographical manner. With an attentive imagination the author lifts, from scanty biographical accounts, a vivid figure of Confucius who is distinguished from those around him—family members, disciples, dukes, officials, scholars, musicians, farmers, tramps, rascals, highway men, gentlemen and common men. On this fictional canvas he portrays other characters in the same stroke of realism such as disciples Yan Yuan, Zilu and Ran Qiu. However, the character of Nanzi, wife of Duke Ling of Wei, makes a deep impression the development of plot. Only briefly mentioned in one paragraph in Sima Qian's work, Nanzi is depicted in *Confucius: The Sage on the Road* as a stunning beauty and passionate person with lingering sentiments, who sustains a longstanding romantic interest with Confucius. She is depicted to be the sensual temptress that tests the limits of Confucius' will and wisdom.

The reader can also appreciate the light hearted approach to a complex historical narrative with contemporary concepts. In the odd numbered chapters, the author narrates the events in a formal, straightforward manner, focusing on the accurate recount of the tale. This is contrasted with his whimsical tone in the even-number chapters, that are studded with humor, modern concepts and linguistic usage, blurring the line between history and reality. The parallel scenes on the sage's travel and his biography are further emphasized with strong expression that shuttles between the past and the present.

The translation of *Confucius: The Sage on the Road* is the product of a two-year sustained effort. The project originated in the spring of 2007 in a collaboration between Frederick Young and me. Fred translated the prologue, chapters 1, 2, 3 and the first part of chapter 14 and I continued translating the rest of the book. I greatly appreciate Fred's initial endeavor in setting up a consistent formal and straightforward style of writing, and his list of "Confucius-specific terminology and jargon" that he supplied me with, as well as editing my translation of chapters 21 and 22, which definitely helped me immensely.

In the Chinese text the odd number chapters give the year of the reign of a particular duke concerned in the parentheses to the chapter title, while the even number chapters indicate the event in Confucius' story. But in the English text a B.C. year to the title was added to the even number chapters in an effort to create more synchrony in the story-line. The names of the characters in the book may appear unnecessary. In the Chinese text the name of Confucius is generally used in the odd number chapters, while Zhongni is used in the even number chapters. Other characters are referred to either with the full name like Yan Yuan and Zeng Dian, or only with the styled name like Zilu who has a surname Zhong and a given name You. The book's faithful translation of these names might have caused some confusion to the reader. Fortunately a character list is appended by the author. I apologize for not being able to come up with a better way to get over this hurdle in reading.

It has always amused me and challenged my imagination when I had to put a contemporary colloquial Chinese expression into the historical context. Usage of this kind is sprinkled over the Chinese text like "jiaqiang jingwei" (tightening up the security), "bianyi" (a plainclothes police officer), and "renzheng tequ" (the rule of benevolence special zone), "bianzheng guanxin" (dialectical relations), "youban youyan" (clear expression and orderly behavior), "jingying" (the intellectual elite). Certainly those, who are familiar with Chinese political events of the second half of the twentieth century, would find an apt and delightful rhetorical quotation by Mao Zedong that "Corruption and waste are very serious crimes" expressed similarly by Yan Ying, prime minister of Qi, proclaims on his own integrity during his conversation with Confucius in chapter 16. In chapter 12, Lao-tzu speaks to Confucius about the pivotal role that the Great Way will play in history and indomitably predicts the upcoming events in the following seven hundred years such the Chu-Han War and Three Kingdoms. For all these expressions and others we tried our best to come up with English equivalents, in addition to providing notes, that would at once make sense and assist the author in conveying and infusing historical context with modern concepts and humor. *←* 2010

This year marks the 2560th anniversary of Confucius' birthday. While alive, the sage was not accepted by his society: His beliefs were met with the curse of ridicule and prejudice and his life was crippled with harsh conditions and setback. He became famous only after his death and was idolized by Chinese rulers for eighteen centuries. Though a major part of the twentieth century witnessed his abdication from a position of worship in Chinese culture, ostensibly from the May 4th Movement, a new age of Confucian Renaissance is now dawning as research institutes and colleges flourish all over the world. The quest of humanity will advance into new frontiers at the speed of light, and society will continue in its rollercoaster journey with its new discoveries of the past. But one of Confucius' legacies will remain as eternal as the Earth's orbit around the sun: His great dream and courage to make it come true.

Perry W. Ma

January 2010

Prologue Mount Niqiu
(551 BC)

It was the second day of the second month, at dusk on a day commonly referred to as "Dragon Raises its Head Day", on a hill a few miles southeast of the capital of the state of Lu, that the sound of a young woman shrieking was heard.

The shriek was at once sudden and urgent, soft and intermittent, at the same time both high and low in pitch, combining both panic and anger, full of pain and excitement, cutting sharply across the stillness of the wilderness. In the twilight, the heavy, utterly boundless setting was abruptly shattered like glass.

The sound came from a small hill on the side of the road. It was not a tall hill, growing right out of rising and falling range of hills, though due to its steep pitch and lush growth, it had an imposing, majestic nature.

Amidst the flickering shadows of leaves and branches, the bare upper torso of a man could be seen vaguely.

"With the blessing of heaven above, you'll bear me a son", said the man, lifting his sinewy, muscular torso. This was a man advanced in years, with a dark, swarthy complexion and graying temples, but also possessing a strong physique and a fierce, imposing air.

He pulled a dark brown robe from the ground, covering his shoulders. This was the combat robe of a general, embroidered with a tiger and panther and fully adorned with plates of armor.

On the grassy patch in the forest, on a section of stamped down branches and leaves lay a coat of leather mail with a young woman reclining upon it. Her long hair was disheveled, clothing scattered about, her body bare, a body not yet fully formed, rolled up like an unopened flower blossom, delicate and fragile. Grass and leaves stuck to her satin white skin, and she was covered in mud and clay.

She covered her face with both hands, crying softly, with a hidden bitterness, as though her screams had completely consumed all of her physical energy.

At this time of year, after sunset the woods gradually grew chillier. A few days before, it had rained, and an assortment of unidentified wildflowers had sporadically and spontaneously blossomed as a result. Thick evening mist appeared in all directions, gathering like a heavy fog, and, almost unnoticeably, the sky darkened.

"How could heaven above bless us?" Her cries grew progressively louder, and she started to weep with grief. "What did we do? Could heaven possibly bless us?"

"Heaven willing," the man said, "it will let you bear a son for me. If you have a child, I'll marry you." Then the man stood tall, tied his robe, put his coat of chainmail back on, straightened his hat, turned his head, and looked down at the hill below. At the base of the hill was a large road leading to the capital. On the side of the road, tied to a tree, was a horse.

Today there had been a temple fair in the town, and he had gone to offer incense, to worship heaven and honor his ancestors, hoping and praying that he would have a son. During temple fairs people came from all over to cavort and court future spouses, men and women, singing and dancing, doing all manner of wild acts in the surrounding woods. If all this was in order to continue the family line, the ancestors would be happy, and by all rights, heaven shouldn't condemn them.

"Should we be struck down by thunder and lightning after carrying on like this?" she asked, weeping uncontrollably and breathlessly.

The man replied impatiently, "How can that be? If there should be any disaster or calamity, let me bear the brunt of it."

Before his voice trailed off, a blinding, bright white light appeared on the summit, a flash that shot into the sky, right into the stars, transforming the dim dusk sky into a burst of daylight, surrounding objects in all directions were suddenly visible, as though carved or etched, coming clearly into view. Next, an enormous sound, like a thunderbolt, or muffled thunder, emanated from deep in the ground and exploded into the open, roared, and rolled away. Heaven and earth seemed shocked and dumbstruck, firmly locked in place, and then quaked with a powerful rumble. In the space of a moment, mountains rocked and the valley cracked open, stones shattered, boulders crumbled, rivers and streams rose into the air, heaven and earth turned upside down, and it seemed that everything on earth would be destroyed at that split second.

"Heavens! This is it !" the young girl cried out, crawling on the ground, kneeling, with her head lowered and eyes closed, with both hands clasped on her bosom, praying silently. Her face was covered with the trails of her tears, but did not show the least bit of panic; on the contrary, she even appeared somewhat serene, as though what she had been hoping for a long time had finally come to pass.

The man stood there, speechless and dumbfounded, his face full of fright and wearing a startled expression. His knees grew soft and he kneeled on the ground.

The earth shook violently, as though it would never cease until the sky would fall and the earth cave in.

Amidst of darkness, the young girl suddenly shouted to the heavens: "Heaven, if you want, do away with both of us, but whatever you do, please spare my son!"

Her scream rose into the sky, as though light blending into the darkness, disappearing into the vast expanse of night.

In the space of a moment, the mountain range's quaking ceased, and, just like that, the whole expanse came to a rest. Everything in all four directions suddenly returned to darkness and silence.

The man, shocked and startled, grabbed the girl, her clothes disheveled, and hurriedly ran out of the forest, falling, crashing, rushing all the way down the hill.

Having reached the foot of the hill, the man turned around to look at the small mountain behind him. All he saw was a reddish-brown pillar of smoke at the summit, rising straight up into the heavens, swirling and twisting as it rose, transforming into countless illusions, as if a pillar or a column, a unicorn or a phoenix, gradually vanishing in the great emptiness above. On the peak, trees were ablaze and boulders laid bare, casting a ghostly white glow into the deep night.

"What is this hill?" the man asked into the darkness, with trepidation in his voice.

"Niqiu." the girl replied.

Many, many years later, a seventy-year-old Confucius, in his home in the state of Lu, while revising the *Annals of Spring and Autumn*, came upon the following record:

The 21st year of Duke Xiang's reign: Spring, first month of the king, an earthquake in the state of Lu, on Mount Niqiu, fifty miles southeast of the capital. The skies jumped and stones shattered, the hill quaked and earth shook, fires scorched its summit, with all trees destroyed. After this time, the boulders of this hill remained revealed, with no trace of earth.

Following this account was a long passage, all about the local legends surrounding this event. Confucius thought about it over and over, and deleted the section. After deleting the passage, he originally intended to add a few lines but found that his inkwell was dry and he couldn't add even a single word. He shouted out for assistance, but both inside and out, not a single disciple replied. He sighed in resignation and put down his pen. After this, a few other events occurred, and the *Annals of Spring and Autumn* was compiled no further.

Chapter 1 Lu
(Spring and Autumn Period, 13th Year of Duke Ding of Lu's Reign, 497 BC)

Confucius was sitting up straight in the upper hall, looking like a small mountain, unmoved and majestic, his glance fixed straight ahead, with a frozen look and distant expression on his face.

In the lower hall, beneath him, his disciples waited. Horse carts outside the door stood at the ready, awaiting orders, ready to leave at a moment's notice.

The hall was quiet and still, with a sad, gloomy atmosphere. Dozens of disciples filled the room, dressed in scholarly dress: ceremonial hats, dark clothing, with a jade pendant and sword tied by a belt around the waist. The assembled disciples appeared nervous, all focusing on Confucius who sat motionless at the front of the hall, all of them with expressions that revealed their unease, bewilderment, and anxiety. At the front stood Yan Yuan, of diminutive physique, with a seemingly frail, weak appearance, standing sideways, clutching a writing tablet in his hands as usual, ever ready to record every word uttered by Confucius. Next to him stood Zilu, a burly figure with an imposing, tall frame, red-faced with a black beard, bulging nose and wide lips, his left hand grasping a sword and right hand clenched into a fist. His manner was bold and striking, and while an indignant expression revealed his extreme impatience, he restrained himself, as though swallowing the words on the tip of his tongue. Next to Zilu stood Zigong, tall and slight, with a pallid, fair complexion, looking as though he was the son of an aristocrat or an official, wearing shiny new silk garments, head held high and constantly looking up at the roof, with an aloof, almost haughty countenance.

In the next row stood the older, more seasoned disciples of Confucius: There was Yan Lu, Yan Yuan's elderly father, the earliest of Confucius' disciples. Zeng Dian was there, standing beside his son Zeng Shen along with Gongye Chang, youthful yet experienced and prudent, he was also Confucius' son-in-law. Slightly further back were the younger disciples, including Fan Chi, Zixia, Zizhang, Ziyou, as well as Zeng Shen, Gongxi Hua, and Yan Ke. Finally, in the last row stood Sima Niu, Gao Chai, Gongbo Liao—while hiding in the corner was Zai Yu, furtively yawning, with a half-asleep appearance, catching a few winks.

Outside the official residence, ten horse-carts were lined up, evenly spaced, each fully loaded with goods. Some carried grain and rice, some with bundles of clothing and bedding, other with daily necessities and household items, while the carts in back were packed with crates of bamboo strips filled with scholarship and knowledge, exceptionally heavy, burdening the pack mules, who snorted and hissed under the heavy weight, as though they were protesting this injustice in their lives.

It was already noon. Everyone was packed and had been ready to leave for the past two hours.

"Master, let's get going!" It was Zilu speaking. Of all the disciples, he was the bravest and also the coarsest. "What are we waiting for?"

"Ahh, Just wait." Confucius muttered, as if he had just been startled awake. "Wait a bit longer."

What was Confucius waiting for after all? Of all the disciples assembled there, no one seemed to know.

He was waiting for meat, sacrificial meat, for the Duke of Lu to present him with sacrificial meat.

Sacrificial meat is a type of salted meat, but not just any ordinary salted meat. It is used exclusively during ceremonies, as an offering to the gods and for the enjoyment of the ancestors. This kind of meat has to be top grade, sliced to perfection and preserved for an especially long time.

Was he really waiting for sacrificial meat? In fact no, in reality he was waiting for the Duke of Lu to quickly wise up and comprehend his misstep.

Today was a special holiday for offering a sacrifice to Heaven and Earth, and the Duke of Lu was supposed to travel to the southern outskirts of the city to attend the Sacrifice to Heaven ceremony. Following the ceremony, according to custom, after going through the motions of offering those sacrificial meat products to Heaven, the meat then would be divided and bestowed upon all officials to enjoy. If the Duke of Lu actually attended the ceremony, the sacrificial meat would be delivered, proving that the Duke of Lu was still thinking about Confucius; and if the Duke of Lu still thought about him, this in turn would demonstrate that the State of Lu still held promise.

"So long as the sacrificial meat is delivered, no matter how much, even a small morsel would be fine," Confucius mumbled, as if talking to himself, also as if addressing the disciples assembled below.

He looked ahead, his gaze appearing to extend beyond the room, outside the entire hall and outer wall, as if staring at some faraway place. All of a sudden, he seemed to appear in the midst of that sacrificial ceremony. This was a recurring image in his dreams—a hundred officials bedecked in ceremonial apparel, with serious expressions on their faces, lined up in a long procession, orderly and silently walking ahead along the long, long stone steps, methodically making their way up. Walking at the head of the procession was the master of ceremony, an honest and sincere figure with a proper air, striding in slow, measured steps, leading the throng, every three steps a bow with hands clasped, every five steps prostrating to the knees. The masses, rising and descending, advancing and retreating, pausing in rhythm, was an orderly and magnificent sight to behold. The stone steps led up to a peak where a towering temple had been erected. Among the clouds and mist, the temple's gates opened, revealing huge columns. Between the columns stood a lofty sacrificial altar. In front of the altar all manner of bronze sacrificial vessels were arranged, carved with the image of *taotie*, a mythical ferocious beast. Incense smoke swirled about, strains of music sounded a low melody, and it appeared as though *taotie* had come to life ... On the altar, those performing the memorial ceremony sat up straight, faces hidden in the shadows, rendering it impossible to clearly distinguish their faces.

The sunlight was brilliant yet silent, pouring from the heavens in a torrent, as though filtered through light gauze, radiant although lacking any sense of warmth. Far away in the distance in all directions were fields, a straight river, tidily arranged city wall and moat, the masses living and working in peace and happiness ... This vision before him was both familiar and soothing. It was the Zhou dynasty that had penetrated his mind, with a feeling of déjà vu, as though he had lived there in a previous life.

Over and over he dreamed as though he was back in the Zhou dynasty. His aspiration, his life's work, was for the splendor of Zhou to flourish once again on the Plains of Central China.

Today was his one hundredth day in power, and it may as well have been his last. He was not wearing the traditional embroidered dark robes of the Imperial Court, and also was not wearing the parted four blossom style hat of the Chief Justice, but rather was decked out in the garb of the *Ru*[1] scholar with wide sleeves and a broad sash, square headdress and hair tied back.

Three months earlier, he was enlisted by Duke Lu as Chief Justice, serving as acting Deputy Prime Minister, to govern the state of Lu. For

---

[1] *Ru* is commonly translated as "Confucian scholar"; here it refers to the scholarly attire worn at the time and popularized by Confucius and his disciples.

years he had cultivated his moral character and kept his house in order; but he never had a chance to realize his full ambition—preside over state affairs and govern the land—until now when he was 56 years old. He had waited for this moment all his life. On the day he had been appointed, his face beamed with satisfaction, overflowing with joy, to the extent that he was incapable of concealing his happiness. Even the gatekeeper could tell that he was clearly elated, nearly overwhelmed with joy, and joked, "*junzi* (morally superior person) is neither fearful of disaster nor delighted by good fortune. How come the Master is so clearly unable to conceal his joy?" Never one to kid around, Confucius could not resist the opportunity to joke with the gatekeeper. "You're not wrong. Since I'm all smiles now, well, maybe that shows just how amiable I am after all?"

On the first day of his rule, he issued several decrees. One concerned the economics of the market, all the pigs and sheep had to be sold at actual prices, and all bargaining was forbidden. The second edict related to the moral governance of the state. All men and women had to walk separately in the street, with no handholding whatsoever. Then there was another law about foreign affairs. All guests visiting the state, regardless of whether they were invited or came of their own accord, had to be officially received by the local authorities with good food and drinks and then escorted upon departure. As soon as these edicts were promulgated, the people of Lu all laughed and said that his governance was on a par with managing a country market, patrolling the streets with the eyes of a neighborhood watch committee, and his ability on foreign affairs was like that of a travel agent or tour guide, regulating pigs and sheep, watching over men and women, even trying to humor foreign guests. These jokes came from a character named Shao Zhengmao. This Shao Zhengmao was hypocritical and malicious, a charlatan with erroneous, unfounded teachings who established a teaching forum, and as a result corrupted quite a few youngsters. He had Shao Zhengmao arrested and

Confucius' subordinates asked whether or not Shao Zhengmao ought to be executed. Confucius replied, "How could we possibly kill him for the sake of politics? He should be educated instead." He maintained that to kill without teaching would constitute cruel, unjust killing, which was the conduct of a tyrant. Unfortunately, this Shao Zhengmao refused to submit to re-education and while in prison he committed suicide by smashing himself against a wall. Afterwards, rumor had it that he had Shao Zhengmao put to death. Confucius believed that these rumors eventually would disappear, and so he did not attempt to defend himself. As it turns out, later generations recorded this into the annals of history, making it into a rumor that would never go away. Fortunately, soon following the death of Shao Zhengmao, the perplexing, strange remarks ceased and the people of Lu laughed about Confucius no longer.

No one seemed to understand his aim: On the surface, promulgating those edicts seemed strange, disjointed, all of them unrelated to each other. However behind these decrees was a deep sense of governance. Using morality as a basis for governance, putting people's minds in order, basing everything on ceremonies, standardizing speech and conduct: this was the great path of governing a country. His single-minded goal was to transform Lu into a humane, just state, a land where the rites were practiced, with Lu serving as a model for the rest of the land. Neighboring heads of state would feel ashamed and put an end to their conquest of other lands and instead resume the ancient rites and music.

If that wasn't possible, how could the splendor of the Zhou dynasty ever be restored?

The Zhou dynasty, the very thought of it intoxicated him, made him yearn for it. Now *that* was a society that had been thought out by sages, based on divine principles, conforming to human nature, with everything in order and in harmony: There was a generational hierarchy, for respect of one's elders. The formal rites were practiced with rigor. Leaders and their subjects lived in harmony, without any distinction between one's family and one's country. Fathers and mothers were treated with filial piety and brothers never quarreled. Husbands and wives respected one another, and there was fraternal love amongst all children. If valuables dropped on the street, no one would dare pocket them; neither thieves nor poor ever entered peoples' homes ... there was equality throughout the land, and Great Harmony prevailed.

This is how it should have been in the world always, and how it should be now. This was the Great Way.

The only thing was, the Duke of Lu still hadn't delivered the sacrificial meat.

On the surface, politics in Lu were simple and straightforward, but in reality they were quite complicated. Although by name Lu was governed by the Duke of Lu, there were in fact three clans which governed Lu. These three clans were Jisun, Mengsun, and Shusun. The three clans were the descendants of Duke Huan of Lu, in other words, relatives of the reigning Duke of Lu. After the Duke became the King of Lu, the three clans took turns in governing the state, with the polity resembling something like that of a political consultative conference in our days.

At this time, Ji Huanzi of the clan Jisun was in power. Ji Huanzi was over fifty and had held the reins of power for several years, through years of hardship, though his inherent intemperance and love of drinking had not changed one bit. A few days earlier, the King of the neighboring state of Qi, harboring ulterior motives, delivered eighty dancing girls from Qi along with 120 fancy show horses, saying he recognized that Duke Lu constantly worried about the affairs of state and the welfare of his subjects and no doubt had too much on his mind, so he wanted the Duke to take it easy and enjoy himself. In order to demonstrate just how special this gift was, the dancing girls and show horses staged performances just outside the Southern High Gate of Lu's city walls for ten days straight. All of a sudden, Lu was transformed into a ghost town, without a soul on the streets. Instead, all the citizens of Lu crowded at the city gate to gawk at the performances. The Qi dancing girls all wore diaphanous, thin silk skirts and performed racy, enticing striptease dances. Meanwhile, the splendid show horses raced in circles around the crowd. At first, Ji Huanzi sneaked over to the performances clad in plainclothes, attempting to blend in with the masses; but then he became so inebriated by what he had seen, he returned to the spectacle several times. Finally, after a few visits, he was frustrated because he had not been able to get close enough to the action; dressed in plainclothes, the spectators wouldn't budge and let him pass to get to the front of the crowd. Furthermore, he was short and so couldn't get a good view. Finally he had Duke Lu accompany him and, under the pretenses of observing the rites, requested a special private performance. After seeing the show, Duke Lu also became infatuated with the spectale and watched it continuously for three days, completely disregarding the affairs of the state.

Today was the day of sacrifice. Confucius had a hard time believing that Duke Lu had completely ignored the Sacrifice to Heaven on account of the girls of Qi dancing a striptease and spectacular piebald horses. If the sacrificial meat was delivered, then that meant that Duke Lu had, in fact, attended the sacrificial ceremony; if the Duke had attended the ceremony, then that meant the Duke was an enlightened leader after all. And if the good Duke was indeed an enlightened leader, then he wouldn't be preoccupied with dancing girls and show horses and instead would focus on the affairs of the state and society.

By now, noon had come and gone, and Duke Lu's sacrificial meat still had not been delivered.

In the hall, one could have heard a pin drop. All that was audible was the buzzing of flies flying around and the occasional whinny of a pack horse outside.

All of a sudden, the clanging sound of a jade pendant sounded along with the rushed clatter of footsteps approaching. Confucius' disciple Ran Qiu dashed in, sweating profusely, his face bright red.

"Has the sacrificial meat been delivered?" Confucius arose, asking impatiently.

"No sacrificial meat. Duke Lu didn't even attend the sacrificial ceremony," the typically reserved, but now clearly flustered, Ran Qiu blurted out. "He's over at the Southern High Gate, checking out the Qi girls' striptease, and there are these piebald horses running circles ..."

"What?! He didn't attend the ceremony," Confucius sat down dejectedly, so angry that his face glowed red, "He didn't even attend the sacrificial ceremony, didn't even attend the ceremony."

"But those Qi girls were gorgeous!" Ran Qiu gasped, then exclaimed, "Eighty of them, all with sexy bodies, dancing like you'd never believe, practically wearing nothing, they were just draped in skimpy thin silk, you could see everything ..."

"QIU! ..." Confucius used his formal given name, with a stern tone.

Ran Qiu hastily covered his mouth, knowing full well that he was far too excited and also had said far too much. He was young, only twenty, but was one of the earliest followers of Confucius, and also one of the most senior. Besides being exceptionally bright, with a quick mind, he learned quickly: Apart from the six classical arts[1], he also knew how to play the *qin*, play chess, write calligraphy, paint, and also played every kind of wind, string, and percussion instrument and could sing. What's more, he also knew how to get things done, and was one of Confucius' favorite students. He was working at the Ji Mansion and knew his way around official circles.

"What else did you see?" Confucius' tone had softened somewhat and he asked impassively, as though he could have cared less what had happened.

"The Duke of Lu was sitting up there on top of the city wall, all touchy-feely with two Qi girls, drinking a lot of wine, and he said that he

---

[1] The six classical arts are the six kinds of skills that a Confucian scholar must learn. These are rites, music, archery, charioteering, writing and arithmetic.

would reschedule the sacrificial ceremony for some other day."

"What else?" Confucius asked.

"Also, court minister Jisun was there. He had a girl, too, and said to Duke Lu ..."

"What did he say?"

Ran Qiu hesitated, his voice lowering, "He said, uh, he said, don't worry about the Prime Minister, he said that you were a bookworm and had no idea about what it meant to have a good time with pretty girls."

Confucius' face glowed red again.

"And those horses," Ran Qiu added, looking at Confucius, "they were incredible, each one was so shiny, with patterns, brightly colored, not sure if that was natural ..."

"It was definitely painted on," guessed one of the students below.

Confucius had already stopped listening to what Ran Qiu had to say, with his voice trailing off as though far away, occasionally returning. He slowly rose, took one look at his students who were standing respectfully below, paused, and then muttered softly, "Let's get going."

He knew he should leave, and that all he could do, was to leave. In order to restore the prestige of the Duke of Lu, he had already insulted three clans—Jisun, Mengsun, and Shusun—and now he had lost the trust of the Duke of Lu. Lu was not a place to stay.

He left his seat and slowly walked over to the doorway of the hall. At that moment, his disciples were astonished to note just how much Confucius seemed to age within a single moment. His steps seemed unstable, and he was stooped over, with a lost, distant expression on his face, with all his physical energy vanishing in that very moment.

As he reached the doorway, Confucius stood still, turned around and asked Ran Qiu, "Did you really see all that? Up on the Southern High City Gate?"

"Yes, Master, I saw it with my own eyes."

It was late autumn, with the sunlight too gloomy to leave shadows on the ground. The wind whistled, bare branches whipped about, fallen leaves swirled,and dust rose and then fell again.

Confucius boarded the carriage, supporting himself with the handrail and stood up straight, as always, standing as straight as an arrow.

"Let's go ..."

At the reins, driving for Confucius, was Zilu. He bellowed, urging the horses to get underway, a single cry. His cry extended from the first carriage all the way to the last.

"Thwack!" came the sound of the whip, and two shaft horses dashed forth, spokes and hubs whirring along. The carriages were on the move.

"Master, which way are we going?" inquired Zilu.

Confucius stood tall and upright, speechless. All he knew was that it was time to go, though he had no idea where to.

"When there is the Great Way, then one should serve; when a country has no Great Way, then one should leave," he sighed, as though responding to Zilu, as well as comforting himself, "Of all the dukes and princes, sooner or later there will be one who employs me. And when they do use me, in just one year I can restore order to the state, and in three years, I can make it into a model state!"

"Master, where the hell are we going?" Zilu asked again. The carriages had reached a crossroads.

Confucius gazed at Zilu, and immediately understood; Zilu was asking which way to go. As though at a loss, looking in every direction, he sighed, and instructed, "Go west!"

The horses and carriages, in a cacophony of people shouting, horses whinnying, and wooden wheels clacking, rambled west.

Just as the entourage was about to reach the Western Gate, Confucius cried, "Stop!"

Zilu, taken aback, grasped the reins, halting the horses.

"Go east." Confucius said, "Leave through the Eastern Gate."

Zilu didn't think twice, turned the horses around, and immediately proceeded east. The procession of carriages followed, also heading east.

The procession left through the Eastern Gate, proceeding nearly twenty miles, and stopped in front of a barren hill. Though the hill was barren along its ridge, it stood next to the river, hemmed in by water.

Confucius dismounted and ascended the hill. On its peak, grass grew along the path, with scattered trees springing up but desolate as far as the eye could see. On the northern foot of the hill was a tomb.

He walked up to the grave, knelt down, kowtowed, prostrated himself on the ground. After a while, he rose to his feet, declaring, "Father, Mother, I'm leaving."

Chapter 2 Father and Mother
(The Chronicles: Confucius[1] at the Age of 7)

"Mom, do I have a father?" Yan-*shi* heard the child ask, giving her a shock.

In the dusk shadows of the small house, a little, bean-shaped lamp shone. Under the lamp, Zhongni molded a small *ding*[2] out of clay. After he had finished molding the vessel, he used a sharp stick to carve the character "qiu" underneath the *ding*.

"Qiu" was his given name.

The small table by the wall was filled with all sorts of sacrificial vessels molded out of clay. There were sacrificial vessels of all different sizes and shapes. The shadows of these sacrificial vessels trailed the flickering of the candlelight on the mud walls, changing the shapes into all manner of ghosts and spirits, almost like an animated cartoon.

"Of course you have a father." She was by the window, weaving cotton cloth. The loom clacked, stopped with a snap, and then resumed its clacking. "He died. You were still small then."

She gazed over at this child, feeling distress in her heart. He took the *ding* that he had just molded out of clay and

---

[1] Confucius is the anglicized version of Kong Fuzi or Kong Fu-tsu, which literally means the Master Kong, a respectful form of address for Kong Qiu or Kong Zhongni.

[2] *Ding*: Tripod sacrificial vessel used in temples for burning incense.

carefully placed it on the altar, also placing small bits of broken stone, large peach-size pieces and smaller date-size ones in the middle of a platter, as if they were sacrificial offerings. She knew that he was worshipping his father, and she sighed to herself.

From the moment he was born, this child had given her grief. He had a large head with a bulge on top that had a depression like that of a pit. By now he was seven and it seemed as though his fontanel had still not knit together, which made her worry that his brain might have some sort of congenital deformity.

What made her worry even more was that the child was a loner. Although his behavior and manner were not overly abnormal, it still seemed like he was still somewhat irregular. Ever since he was little, he rarely spoke, and even his crying had a slight rhythm to it, only three or four cries at a time, never any excessive sobbing. He never liked to play outside, but rather preferred to stay inside and play alone, always the same game, which was worship. When he was five, she brought him to see a sacrificial ceremony in the nearby village. She couldn't have possibly imagined that he would be so taken in by what he saw, to the extent that everyday at home he would practice the exact same ceremony. He molded countless sacrificial vessels out of clay, and would place them on an altar, after which he would imitate each style of sacrificial rite, kneeling, rising, kneeling again, worshipping heaven and worshipping earth, worshipping the gods and worshipping the ancestors.

She knew that eventually he would ask about his father. One day, she saw a group of children surround him in a nearby lane, abusing him with chants of "if you have a dad and no mom, there's an orphan in the family; if you have a mom and no dad, then you're a wild squash in the field." From that day on, he never again played with the neighborhood kids.

Kids without fathers had it rough.

The loom in Yan-*shi*'s hands clacked back and forth progressively slower. She had just turned 23 and her tender appearance, which ought to have been glowing with youthfulness, had instead become pale and sallow.

Outside the window a new crescent moon shone. From far away came the sound of a dog barking. The low, undersized house sat at the end of a narrow lane. This lane was located on the outskirts of the capital, outside the city wall, and because it was situated adjacent to the watchtower gate, it was known as the Watchtower Neighborhood. Four years earlier, she brought three year-old Zhongni here all by herself, leaving her hometown and moving within the city limits.

"Where is daddy buried?" Zhongni asked as he filled the sacrificial stand and vessels with water, as though making offerings of sacrificial wine.

"I don't know," replied Yan-*shi*. "How come you're asking about this?"

Zhongni raised his head, looking at his mother with bright, glowing eyes:

"When you die, then where should I bury you?"

The loom's shuttle became jammed and the loom "thwacked" to a sudden halt. Yan-*shi* froze, felt a faint twinge in her heart and for a moment was unable to speak. She glanced over at Zhongni and tears gushed from her eyes. Ultimately this was what seven year-olds had on their minds.

The boy's father had died five years earlier, and no one had told her where he had been buried, or where his grave was. On the day that he died, she and Zhongni had been kicked out of his household, with his father's clan not acknowledging the two of them as kin.

She thought back to that day in early spring. It had been some time ago, and as memories of that day had grown hazy and distant over time, all she had left were a handful of jumbled recollections. Those magnificent, marvelous impressions had gradually faded and in their place she felt a kind of bleak, desolate dreariness, like rain and fog, scattered in all four directions, vague and indistinct, concealed deep in her heart.

She recalled that day was the second day of the second month, the holiday known as "Dragon Raises its Head" day. According to tradition, on that day the heavenly dragons awakened, raising their heads and ascending into heaven, rising into the clouds to make rain, and from that day on, spring returned to the land and all of nature came back to life.

Her youth began on that day, and would also end on that day.

She remembered that magnificent spring light, the sunshine seemed almost to shower down from the heavens. The mountains and fields burned with the red of peach blossoms and brimmed with the green of willow trees. The freshness after the morning rain carried the aroma of grass and the scent of moist earth. Far away the azure sky had a smear of deep, dark green, which were the rising peaks and ridges of the Phoenix Mountains.

She was a country girl, standing in the yard of her own home, in the midst of ducks and chickens running all over the place, with a beaming smile as she watched the carts and people come and go outside her yard. Due east on the main road was the capital, where she had never been. That year she was sixteen, and she even had her own name, which was Zhengzai.

This place was not far from Zouyi (southeast of today's Qufu in Shangdong Province), which was part of the State of Lu's Changping, roughly one hundred *li*[1] from the capital.

---

[1] *li* is the Chinese unit of length; one *li* is equivalent to one-half of a present-day kilometer.

He rode up on a large horse, galloping in from the west, wearing a suit of armor, with an imposing manner, an awesome sight to behold. As the horse dashed in front of her, its front hooves rose abruptly, and raising its head, let out a long whinny, startling her. He reined in the galloping horse, smiling at her, and she returned his smile, not knowing why but all of a sudden feeling happy for no apparent reason. He inquired; did she want to go to the capital for a good time? After all, today was the temple fair! She didn't think twice about it, just nodded her head, and in that instant a gust of spring breeze blew by, and she covered her face with her hand. Why on earth did she agree to go with him that day? She herself was not too sure. Maybe she liked the might and grandeur of how he rode that fine steed, maybe she wanted to see what the temple fair in the capital was all about, or maybe the brilliance of that spring day was just too tantalizing for her.

She didn't even have time to tell her parents. Her father was of the gentry class, well known in the prefecture, and her upbringing had been strict. She thought to herself, I'll just go for a moment, and then come right back home.

She rode on his horse, seated in front of him. The horse hurtled down the main road, with the wind whooshing in her ears and trees on both sides of the road whizzing past. Her skirt flew upward, her body flew upward, and her heart also flew upward.

She could feel his hulking chest as she was encircled by his burly arms and could feel the warmth emanating from his strong frame. She even remembered how the tassels from his helmet kept touching her ears and the itch that ensued kept making her giggle uncontrollably.

The temple fair was packed with people. She'd never seen anything like this, people singing and dancing, having a ball, dancing the dragon dance, carrying fancy parade floats, riding imaginary bamboo horses, walking on stilts, acrobatics, jubilantly making a racket.

She had a lot of fun, forgot all about the time, and around dusk she finally thought about heading home.

On the way home, they passed a small knoll, and he reined in his horse. She knew that small hill was not all that far from home.

He told her that they should go up the hill to rest for a moment.

In the meadow right in the middle of the woods, he removed his leather armor, and let her lie down on it. She was wound up, so giddy that she was dizzy, all she could see was the buntings and brightly colored flags of the temple fair, and all she could hear was the resounding beat of the drums and gongs. He removed his cotton robe, and covered her with it. She felt the body heat from his robe and could smell the musky scent of his perspiration.

The sun was slowly setting behind the mountains, with the fading light behind the woods growing dimmer and dimmer. Every once in a while there was the chirping of birds, echoing and resonating into the hills.

What followed next, regardless of how hard she tried, she could not remember for the life of her. Her memory was like a black hole, with all details sucked within, disappearing into the depths of her subconscious, and all that was left in her recollection was the dazzling bright emptiness and scattered stains and spots of sensation.

Occasionally she felt as though she was in a trance, like she was floating in a sea of giddiness. In the grasp of a warm embrace, she felt that she was still galloping on that horse, faster and faster, ascending upward, drifting toward the distant summit of that hill, becoming a cloud, slowly dispersing, dissipating ...

At times she suddenly became aware of him becoming wild, savage, holding her tightly, and pressing her to the ground. She struggled, resisting, kicking but powerless; there was no resisting this man, brutal and ferocious like a wild animal. She felt her undergarments being torn aside, her head covered by her skirt, with her body compressed under his hefty, rock-hard physique ...

And yet, it wasn't like that at all. She vaguely recalled him kneeling prostrate before her, clutching her arm, imploring, "Bear me a son!" He told her that his wife was neither able to bear him sons nor daughters, so he took a concubine who only bore him a single son, a cripple. He was over fifty and wanted a son, a healthy and strong son. He told her, "You can definitely give birth to a good baby." She was moved by his words and could care less about anything else. She also wasn't afraid of a thing.

Finally, at the moment the sun went down, she felt so much pain that she cried out.

She lay there, and slowly awakening from the chaos and confusion, felt great shame within. She had no idea what she had just done; all she felt was that she had just committed a great sin, and in the future she would never escape divine retribution.

Such divine retribution would come quickly.

Ten months later she went looking for him with her month-old son. By this time, she knew his surname was Kong, his given name was He, and he was also known as Shuliang, with most people referring to him as Shuliang He. He was a general of the armed forces that defended the city, braver and more heroic than most, immensely powerful. Once, while in a battle against another city, he was even able to batter down the hanging doors of the city using just his bare hands, allowing the troops and horses to drive straight in behind him This made him a hero within his prefecture.

While she was pregnant, she never went to see him, nor did she tell anyone whose child was in her belly. Hiding away at home, she had to endure her parents' constant complaints and scolding; when she went out, she was ridiculed by the townspeople. She didn't dare have the child at home; when it was nearly time to give birth, she hid in a cave at the foot of Mount Niqiu and had her child there.

Only after she had the child did she go looking for him. She wanted to let him know that she had given him a son.

But when she finally brought her child to him, what she saw was no longer the strapping, sturdy general who had come galloping up to her on his steed, but rather an ailing old man with white whiskers, so frail that he was incapable of standing up on his own. His pale, sickly appearance made it difficult to believe that it was even the same man. Those same burly arms with which he had broken down doors and embraced her tightly were now slim and slender, with muscles atrophied, black and festering.

Her mind went instantly black, like that evening, and she was filled with fear and horror. She knew that this was divine retribution, that there was no escaping it, that neither he nor she could ever escape it.

"Give the baby a name," she knelt in front of his bed, her two hands holding up the wailing child.

He opened his cloudy eyes and, leaning his head to the side, glimpsed at his own son. Immediately the infant boy stopped crying, and then opened his little eyes, staring curiously at his own father.

"Good, good. My son, my son," he spoke softly and appeared very happy, paused for a moment, and then asked, "What was the name of that mountain again?"

"Niqiu[1]."

"Niqiu? OK, then this boy's given name will be Qiu, and his nickname will be Ni. Since he is the second eldest, his

---

[1] Qiu means "mount" and "Ni" was the name for this particular hill.

name will be Zhong[1] Ni." He then started coughing and gasping, rested momentarily, and then resumed talking, "After he grows up, make sure that he takes care of his elder brother. Don't let people pick on him."

He was never again able to rise from his sickbed. In the middle of the night early that spring, after persistently coughing and gasping for many years, he coughed and gasped no more. His family members took one look, saw his arms and legs splayed open on the bed, not moving, and then placed a wisp of cotton under his nose and found that he was not breathing at all.

On the day that he died, she took her three year-old Zhongni, left her home in the Zouyi and returned to her old home in Changping. Shi-*shi*, the first wife of her husband, forbade her from attending the funeral held by the Kong family, and after that, no one told her where he had been buried. The Kong family was not willing to take them in, and of course they would never consider allowing her to be buried together with him.

By now both her parents had passed away and when she arrived she found that their bamboo-fenced yard was falling apart and their old thatch cottage was covered in dust. Unable to stay at the old shack in the countryside, she brought her three-year-old Zhongni back to the capital city of Qufu. In the southwest corner of the city she found a small house in a narrow alley that was tacked up against the city wall, and there orphan and widow took up residence and began what was to be a difficult, arduous life.

She made her living by sewing, taking great pains to bring up Zhongni, watching him grow every day. All she could think about was that inexorable divine retribution, wondering when it eventually would come upon her. She

---

[1] "Zhong" denotes second eldest at birth.

waited silently, all the while praying that heaven would spare Zhongni.

The jammed shuttle was freed and the loom resumed its clacking noise.

Over there, Zhongni placed a wood chip that had been shaved into a memorial tablet neatly upon the sacrificial altar, on it there were no characters, but she knew that this was a memorial tablet for his father.

She never again mentioned his father to her child. She only wanted to forget all about him, and yet somehow this child still remembered him.

A few years later she became suddenly ill, and, like a wilted flower, she began to whither away when it soon became apparent that she would not pull through.

Just before passing away, she beckoned Zhongni to her side, saying, "My son, your mother is not going to make it, so I won't be able to take care of you from now on." Tears flowed from her eyes, and she added, "Just remember, never do anything unethical or sacrilegious."

"Mother, you can't go." Zhongni gripped her collar tightly, as if that would keep her from going.

"One other thing, you have a brother, and his name is Mengpi, he is the only relative that you have in the whole world."

"Mom, you'll get better, you'll surely be fine." Zhongni wept.

"My son, your mother can't take it any longer. After I die, just bury me anywhere."

"No, I want to bury mommy and daddy together," Zhongni wailed, "Tell me, where is dad buried?"

Yan-*shi* helplessly shook her head, and, without a response, closed her eyes.

Chapter 3 Wei
(Spring and Autumn Period: 14th Year of Duke Ding of Lu's Reign, 496 BC)

His first talk with Duke Ling of Wei did not go agreeably. Confucius was rather disappointed. As soon as they met each other that day Duke Ling asked him about military strategies and the forming of battle arrays, particularly the double-circling array in the shape of the character 回 and triple-squared array in the shape of the character 品. Confucius was embarrassed by these perplexing questions. He knew the Song troops were in the array of a "goose," the Zheng troops in the array of "fish," the Chu troops in the array of "Chu's Formation," and the Wei troops in the array of "Dispersion." But he never heard of the double-circling array in the shape of the character *hui* and triple-squared array in the shape of the character *pin*. He hesitated for a few moments before replying with carefully weighted words, "I've not studied military strategy. But if you're interested in the arrangement of utensils, personnel positions, and the procedure of rites at sacrificial ceremonies, I'm rather familiar."

Another grinding silence ensued. Finally he broke the still and said, "To reign depends on benevolence. Without benevolence the state's power can be obtained and lost as well. Benevolence always comes with rites and music. Without rites and music masses may abide by or violate laws. Cultivating sacrificial rituals involving various vessels and procedures propagates benevolence and boosts the rites and music. It has a

45

far-reaching influence ..." As he talked he noticed the duke turning to the window and looking outside. Confucius gradually stopped and followed his glances, only to find the duke's attention completely focused on a flock of wild geese flying over to the south in the range of the character 人. Duke Ling was aware of his misbehavior and quickly turned back. Recomposing himself and forcing a smile, he praised, "Well said, well said. It's the character 人. Oh, no, it is benevolence, benevolence ..." Confucius knew it was time that he should leave.

Among the dukes of all the states, Duke Ling of Wei was the oldest both in age and governing experience. Over seventy years old, though his head was a little muddled, he was still physically vigorous. In his forty years of tenure, Wei was not run very efficiently, but he was rich with wisdom of political affairs. He did not deliberately embarrass Confucius when inquiring about battle formations. He targeted the wrong person with his questions. It turned out that he was scheduled to meet with certain other guests that day, a court minister from Qi and two surrendered military commanders from Jin. He confused the two parties. At that time, Qi and Wei were allied to fight the Jin, and battles were being fought in the town of Handan. So, both sides were gambling for victory by making hard guesses regarding their enemy's battle arrays.

Earlier, when setting off from Lu, Confucius and a few dozen of his disciples traveled west toward the state of Wei. Among Lu's neighboring states, Qi was an enemy and therefore was not on the list of possible destinations. Those states, Ju, Teng, Cao and Song, were too small to be able to accommodate a party as large as theirs; Chu, Qin, Jin and Yan were fairly distant and might not be easily reached given their travel provisions; Wu and Yue, two states in recent years engaged in endless wars and distant in the south, were not good options either, since chances were that when they arrived in the war zone, they themselves would become refugees. After repeated deliberations, the decision was made to head to Wei.

Their first sight of Diqiu, capital town of Wei, felt surreptitious.

Duke Ling of the state was advanced in years, and behind his back sinister plots brewed surrounding who would become his successor. In the state court, two factions were taking shape, as incompatible as water and fire. The prince, Kuai Kui, for years had been tapped as heir to the throne, and, with deep political roots, he had built up a full-fledged cabinet of assistants, known as the prince's clique. He was young and held high rank. And with high rank he was more conscientious than sensible of the feelings of others, tolerating no bit of grit in the eye, let alone annoying people. Given this disposition, he had offended many senior officials.

The duke's wife, Nanzi, was from Song and was a stunning beauty. She was also the stepmother of the prince. She was not only good looking but also fairly intelligent, a rarity that blended her nature with nurture. It was not long since she was married to Wei, but her influence on the aging duke was growing with each passing day, due to her flirtatious grumbling, cursing wisecracks, teasing and amorous smile whenever in front of the duke, as well as her ear-to-ear and temple-to-temple fooling around with him, and her nighttime pillow-talk. In addition, she had a patient, sensitive ear to others and responded to every plea. Those officials nursing grievances against the prince and those coming from afar to seek employment in the government flocked to her and vied to become one of her followers. They constituted the madam's gang. Gradually the affairs of Wei were all arranged behind her bed curtains.

Since Confucius left Lu in a hurry and did not contact his connections in Wei, he did not have a place to stay when he arrived in Wei's capital town. Therefore he went to see Yan Zhuozou, brother-in-law of Zilu, and first settled in there for the time being. Yan Zhuozou was a pork butcher and slaughtered swine each day to sell in the market. An experienced trader, he was an influential businessman and was often responsible for assigning spaces for vendors in the market as well as mediating quarrels and disputes. Periodically, he received small fees for his service.

A lively natured man of a vigorous disposition, he relished partying and dining with his friends. But the rare, fine part of his character lay in his instinctive reverence for scholars. That day when Zilu brought the learned and knowledgeable Confucius to his home, followed by a large number of literary men, Yan Zhuozou was overjoyed. That evening he himself slaughtered a pig and prepared an ample amount of food for the visitors. In particular he opened a new jar of meat paste, saying it was Zilu's favorite food and that the guests should enjoy it as well.

That night the Yans cleared out the side yard and helped the men settle in. The yard was not big, and the rooms were small. But with the make-shift beds spread on the floor, the large group managed to lie down and rest. However, it was the chariots that were somewhat troublesome; the house had no stable, the horses had to be tethered to posts in the yard, and they defecated on the ground, stinking up the place. And since there was no carriage shed, the chariots had to be parked outside on the street. The chariots were exposed to constant sunshine and rain, causing the paint to peel and the wood to rot away mournfully.

Afterwards, Yan Zhuozou was influenced by the high culture of his visitors, even proposing that he become a formal disciple of Confucius. The master hesitated because he knew the butcher had a poor background and bravo practice of the wide world. But on second thought, how could he turn his host down after so many days of hospitality in his house, with the best food and drink? Besides, Confucius remembered his own firm belief in "teaching men of all kinds." It would not damage his group accept people from all walks of life. Then the master decided to satisfy Yan Zhuozou's request and took him in as a student. Years later, despite the absence of his name on the list of the seventy-two sages of Confucianism, Yan Zhuozou was formally included in master's three thousand disciples.

Yan Zhouzou learned *The Book of Songs* from Confucius. The first poem was "The Quacking Male and Female Waterfowl," which he quickly learned by heart.[1] But he always read the line, "A beautiful, pure and virtuous girl is a suitable match for our lord," incorrectly by saying, "A beautiful, pure and virtuous girl is a good ball for our lord." When someone pointed out his error, he wouldn't correct his interpretation, believing "a good ball for our lord[2]" was meaningful, while "a suitable match for our lord" simply did not make sense.

Before long, Duke Ling of Wei sent someone to ask Confucius about his official salary in Lu. Though it was one of the principles that Confucius painstakingly instilled in his disciples that a *junzi* sought the Great Way instead of the way of living, he knew very well that a *junzi* could not seek the Great Way without food to eat. He then reported his income as it was, sixty thousand *dan*[3] of millet. Duke Ling did not haggle over the number and swiftly granted him the same salary. In Lu, Confucius could easily feed his family of three with his sixty thousand *dan* of millet. But now, with a few dozen mouths depending on him, particularly those able-bodied men, this amount of food forced him to budget carefully.

His meeting with Duke Ling ended in a baffling conversation with no clear results, which drove Confucius to his wits' end. Among the court ministers of Wei, only Qu Boyu, an old acquaintance in the past, was a *junzi*, who was upright and well-behaved and appeared amiable but was insistent on important issues. He unfortunately died a couple of years earlier, a useful contact lost. Some of the disciples suggested calling upon prince Kuai Kui, and others thought about pulling strings through Madam Nanzi. But Confucius thought these choices somewhat backhanded and unethical, and so he firmly ruled them out. He deeply believed a man who wanted to engage in politics and hold a post in the government must be temperate, kind, courteous, restrained, and

---

[1] "The Quacking Male and Female Waterfowl," the first poem from "Zhou nan," Section "Airs of the States" of *The Book of Songs*.
[2] The original Chinese text has a pun on *qiu*, which can be either "逑match" or "毬ball."
[3] *Dan*, a unit of dry measure for grain equivalent to 1 hectoliter

magnanimous.

The best Confucius could expect was that the duke would come to recognize him as a talent and therefore ask him to work within his government. Confucius, on his part, should repeatedly decline the duke's offer before finally accepting, as if he were not capable of assuming a post of such significance. One of course had to be sharp and agile, otherwise the opportunity could easily slip through his fingers. Today it was rather popular to be frank and straightforward, introducing oneself at the first meeting and immediately asking for a position. But the request should be made directly to the duke instead of going behind his back. This was the elementary code of conduct for all *junzi*, well known to dukes and subjects, as well as the basic process for appointing officials, and thus was not easily altered or skirted. Furthermore, the court affair was rather intricate and involved complex human relations. Meeting with the prince would offend the madam and vice versa. The path ahead was clear and the gates wide open, but still one should hold back, weary of making a misstep.

Confucius was anxious and from time to time would pace up and down the yard, with long sighs and short breaths, mumbling repeatedly, "If I am appointed to a post, twelve months should be enough time to get started. Three years will be enough to make noticeable progress. Three years will be enough to make noticeable progress!" Twelve months meant one year. He often told his disciples that a *junzi* looked like a glittering jade in a casket, precious and available for purchase. The one who knew all about goods would sooner or later come out. One need not worry. However he himself was shelved now and still had not sold after a few months had passed. He became unsalable. Should he be the one to first wait three years?

There was an old elm in the yard, which used to be healthy with a tall trunk and lush foliage. But before anyone knew it, all the green leaves fell to the ground, the bare trunk pointing to the sky. The autumn wind was rising again.

He had already stayed in Wei for almost one year.

To pass the time while waiting, Confucius concentrated on reading *The Book of Changes* and talking to his disciples about learning and the Great Way. He felt that over these years he had studied and gotten a good grip on the truth of human society. The Great Way was simple, direct and self-evident. It was perplexing that the dukes of the many states couldn't be convinced. Why wouldn't they listen to his teachings? Was it true that the Great Way would be enforced by the will of heaven? To understand the will of heaven he started reading *The Book of Changes*. It was an abstruse book. At the age of fifty he began reading it and until now had not read it through even once. He was contemplating the meaning of "*yuan, heng, li and zhen*" on the masculine divinatory symbol.[1]

Originally there were three remarkable books on the study of the will of heaven. The first was *he tu* (River Sketch), a marvelous picture that was carried on the back of a dragon horse while leaping out of the Yellow River at the time of Fuxi.[2] When Fuxi saw it, instead of assisting his sister, Nü Wa, in her patching the holes in the skies with stone blocks, he went into the mountains.[3] He lived there for three years in seclusion, lying on his back and stomach, wracking his brains, and eventually painting the "Eight Trigrams."[4]

The second was *luo shu* (Book of Luo), written by Yu. One day, while working on his flood prevention project along the River Luo, Yu saw an immortal turtle rise from the river with several odd numbers engraved on its shell. Yu stopped fighting the flood and shut himself in his house for three years, inscribing characters on animal bones and tortoise shells,

---

[1] "*yuan, heng, li and zhen*," four characters of the masculine divinatory symbol: *yuan* meaning largeness, *heng* the tributes paid by the dukes of all states, *li* benefits, *zhen* practicing divination; the masculine divinatory symbol, one of the eight divinatory symbols in *The Book of Changes*.

[2] Fuxi, a legendary ruler in ancient China, the first of the Three August Ones, who invented hunting and fishing and domesticated animals

[3] Nü Wa, a legendary female creating goddess in ancient China, who patched with stone blocks the holes in the sky made by Gonggong, the legendary Spirit of Water, in a conflict with Zhuanxu, the Spirit of Fire.

[4] The Eight Trigrams, eight combinations of three lines used in divination.

drawing sketches and working out mathematic calculations, eventually producing the work known as the "Nine Models", a writing of nine methods of taming rivers. Unfortunately, both the "River Sketch" and the "Book of Luo" were long lost. Only *The Book of Changes* was handed down through history.

Legend had it that Emperor Wen of the Zhou dynasty had studied the River Sketch and the Book of Luo. He divided everything in two, combined the two into one, formed three components into one, and achieved mastery through a thorough analysis of the universal elements. He finally succeeded in writing *The Book of Changes*, thereby laying the groundwork for future generations to carry on the study of heaven. People in later times, if keen to understand the Great Way of heaven, had no choice but to study *The Book of Changes*.

Besides studying *The Book of Changes*, Confucius practiced striking the *qing*. The *qing* was a percussion instrument made of polished stones. It was hung on a rack with an arrangement of the stones according to a musical scale and was struck using the mallet. Its sound was clear and harmonious. In his earlier years he was taught to play the *qin*. He also dabbled in the *sheng* pipe[1] and drums. Now, he enjoyed playing the *qing* and started practicing after lunch each day, and the rattling sound went on endlessly as if a building were under construction.

After lunch that day, Confucius was striking the *qing*, playing an old, rather nostalgic tune entitled "A song of Mount Turtle." Before the end of the song, someone appeared outside the window. Confucius stopped and asked Zilu to go and take a look. Zilu returned and said it was a farmer carrying a basket on his back. He was passing, heard the sound of the *qing* and was interested and so stopped to stand outside and listen. Confucius asked whether the farmer had said anything after listening to the song. Zilu replied the farmer saw Zilu come out to him and then said

---

[1] The *sheng* pipe is a wind instrument.

the music was mellow but that the percussive strokes were a little stiff, as if something was troubling the mind of the player. He then wandered off without turning back.

Zilu's words puzzled Confucius, "This farmer is extraordinary!"

Zilu scratched his head, "Yes, he is. He has fine features and a fair complexion. He wore clean, neat cloth garments, and even his basket was brand new."

At that moment, Gongsun Yujia, a court minister close to Duke Ling of Wei, called upon Confucious from outside. He was sending greetings and inquired about the master's health and well-being. He also brought some soldiers along with him. After exchanging greetings he left but the soldiers remained, standing on guard outside the yard, saying they were tightening security. From then on the disciples all had to go through a round of interrogation before leaving or entering the abode.

Confucius' heart sank as he heard this. He knew this was called "living under watch." That man who just stopped by at the window might not have been a farmer. He was probably a plainclothes agent. Was Duke Ling of Wei suspicious of Confucius himself? Or did some one slander him in front of the duke? Or would the clan of Ji from Lu make attempt on his life, plotting to have him killed by Duke Ling's own hand? Confucius contemplated and realized Wei was not a safe place to linger and that he should leave as soon as possible. Any delay might bring serious trouble. But he was hard put to find a way to make his escape.

Accordingly, Confucius confined himself at home and closed the door to visitors. He even gave up playing the *qing* for fear that someone might eavesdrop on his conversations and activities. He sent away a few of his disciples to make a living on their own so as to reduce the number of disciples living with him and to avoid being accused of gathering a mob to make trouble. He felt safe with Zilu at his side because the disciple was good with his hands and could defend the master dauntlessly with his fists and legs if it came to that, even though he could hardly pit himself against ten enemies.

Zilu, surnamed Zhong and with the given name You, was first picked up as a vagrant boy on the street by Confucius years ago. At that time, the boy roamed the streets and found shelter in alleys at night. He was sallow, emaciated and ragged. He plucked fruit from trees and gathered rotten cabbage leaves from the food market to fill his stomach. Confucius saw this wretched homeless orphan and took him as his disciple. He fed the boy and taught him to read and write. A few years later, the little boy grew unexpectedly from a small, skinny nasty youngster living on husks and filthy vegetable leaves, into a sturdy, masculine man with broad shoulders, a fat waist, bulky arms and big, strong hands. He possessed tremendous strength and was brave beyond all others. From him one could apprehend that people cannot be judged just by their appearances, particularly little boys.

Years later Zilu grew up. He was chivalrous and filled with persistent sense of justice. The thing he enjoyed doing most in life was hanging around with friends, driving chariots, wearing a fur coat, and scarfing down large cups of wine and chunks of meat. When the carriage was broken, the fur coat worn out and no more coins left jingling in his pocket to spend on wine and meat, he simply shouted, "Absolutely content! Absolutely content!" He thought that was the state of Great Harmony that Confucius preached. He did not read and write attentively or think a lot. He did not improve his learning by absorbing new ideas and reach a higher level of understanding or follow recent developments in learning. It seemed that he was not eager to achieve a higher level of understanding. He felt it was more comfortable to listen to the master's lectures in the large main room with his fellow disciples than to learn through one-to-one tutoring. In the large room he could rub his fists and palms, stamp his foot and kick his leg. Seeing that he loved martial arts, Confucius kept him around as bodyguard and instilled in him the principle that "gentlemen speak rather than strike." Though only nine years the master's junior, Zilu looked on his teacher as his father and would surely risk his own life to protect the Master without hesitation. With Zilu constantly by his side, Confucius no longer heard rude, abusive words against him. In the past, when the master and disciples marched down the street in the town of Qufu in a three-step-forward-and-one-step-backward gait, wearing the high hat on his head and loose garments with broad collar and wide cuff, a throng of locals soon drew around them, hissing, booing, sneering and cursing. Someone even went out of his way to throw chunks of watermelon rind and pear cores at them. When that occurred again, Zilu would stare at them with his leopard-like eyes wide open and bear-like fists clenched. In most such cases the onlookers would suddenly become quiet out of fear and swallowed the abuse which they would have hurled at them.

That night, Confucius once again dreamed that he had returned to the Zhou dynasty, standing in the procession about to offer a sacrifice to ancestors. As he followed the heavily built, fine-featured head of sacrificial offering and walked slowly up to the hall of the high shrine, he suddenly felt someone pull at his sleeve, trying to take him out of the procession. He woke up immediately only to see Zilu in front of him. He was startled, thinking the troops of Wei were about to storm in and capture him. He rolled off the bed and groped for his shoes on the ground. Zilu propped him up and said in a low voice, "Master, a man is here from your home in Lu. He said your elder brother Mengpi died."

Chapter 4   The Brother
(The Chronicles: Confucius at the Age of 17)

Mengpi, leaning against the door, from a distance could see Zhongni slowly approaching. Seventeen year-old Zhongni, slender in frame, had not quite filled out in a way proportional to his height. He looked like a thin bamboo staff with a wide-sleeved ceremonial robe draped over it, swaying back and forth. It appeared more as if he was hiding in his clothes than wearing them. He also had on a high hat, which shook and quivered as he walked, making him appear even taller and longer, and so wherever he walked, he made a scene. He followed the base of the wall, shuffling along with small steps, straight as an arrow, as though he were walking a line, almost like pacing on a catwalk. Every three steps, he would pause, shift with small steps and then swiftly move forward, like a bird spreading its wings and gliding; at the same time, he would raise his arms with his fists clenched, making obeisance with hands clasped to both left and right. He then bended down and bowed low. Next, he proceeded three steps, advancing forward, again raising his fists and arms, greeting to the left and right, hands clasped, again bending down, even lower, bowing for an even longer time ... and like this, starting and stopping, bowing and then rising, he continued along the edge of the wall, taking forever to move in one direction, slowly but surely.

Mengpi felt anxious for him. He knew that Zhongni was following *The Book of Rites* guidelines for walking: "when setting out, follow the edge of the wall; walk on tiptoes; when walking forward, take short, fast steps, with both arms swinging backward and forward, and also holding one's breath, keeping a straight face, frequently raising one's belt, swinging one's lower hem of the gown; when making obeisance, both shoulders should be kept even, both arms stretched out, with a distant look in one's eyes, earnest; when bowing, first face upward and then bow, straightening and bending one's back and then hunching one's shoulders, with undulating delicacy and in a frightened manner."

Zhongni said the ancestors had practiced these rites and norms. His late grandfather Zhengkaofu once held a position in the Song government. One day Zhengkaofu was promoted by three ranks to that of prime minister. To express gratitude to the duke, he hastened up the stairs to the main room of the court and carried out the ritual three times, with one bow and bending at the waist three times, each one lower than the last, methodically and meticulously, until he hit the ground with his head, prostrate and unwilling to get up. His show of loyalty and dedication amazed those present and left behind a legendary saying "the first promotion is accepted with a bending of the back (or "half-bow"), the second with a bow (or "full-bow"), and the third with full-body prostration." Such official etiquette should be practiced often, otherwise when the time comes, one will find it hard to perform correctly.

Mengpi admired his brother but thought he was currently too young to practice such basic skills, and it was too early to tell whether or not he would become an official in the future. Mengpi himself also wanted to learn how to walk in a ritual manner but was unable to practice yet. He was lame. It was true he could walk with the rhythm of bending and raising the body, but the movements were not the least bit ritual. Because of his lameness he was called Mengbo. The character *"bo"*, meaning being "lame", was hard to pronounce and complicated in form and so he gradually came to be called Mengpi for unknown reasons, due possibily to mispronunciation or just the desire to simplifying matters. Since his parents died when he was young and the family fortune was lost, no one corrected the mistake for him, and so he eventually became Mengpi.

Since childhood, he had been alone and uncared for, and so he never knew he had a younger brother. Three months ago Zhongni stood in front of him. "Brother, I'm Zhongni." His brother stood there, tall and lean, all skin and bones. "I'm your younger brother."

Startled, Mengpi was at a loss for what to do. At that moment, he was in the middle of hacking at a tree stump, trying to craft a stool out of it. He was holding an ax high with his hand, one foot placed on the stump. Seeing the tall Zhongni, he attempted to let down his arm but was afraid of hitting his own foot; he would move his foot down from the stump but feared he might stand in an unsightly posture. For a while he was motionless, stuck in a wood-hacking position. After the family financial situation deteriorated, Mengpi dropped out of school and yet could not leave home to make a living due to physical constraints. He then studied carpentry. Luckily he could do his work at home regardless of the tasks he had to complete—sawing, cleaving, hacking and chopping—and so he was never hindered by his deformed foot.

"My mother died." Zhongni wore the white hemp garments of mourning, the borders of the cuff and lower hem of his gown unsewn and threadbare. "Before she died, mother asked me to tell you that I would be left with you as my sole family member."

"I heard of this, and of you," said Mengpi.

For a while, people from the town of Zouyi all talked about a filial son who had moved his mother's coffin out of the town and laid it on the corner of a broad road. It had been there for a dozen days. Every day, people passed by the place, seeing the filial man seated there from dawn to dusk, living on thin porridge and sleeping with his head on mud bricks, to keep vigil beside the bier. Some of them sighed while others, deeply moved, shed tears. However, as the scene dragged on more days, the coffin still left on the street, people in the neighborhood started to gossip, saying that since the woman was dead, the family should bury the remains as soon as possible. But the filial son would never let his mother's remains be buried. The locals gradually grew furious with the man's behavior. They felt that they had never seen such a filial son, concerned only with expressing his filial affection and wholly neglecting his mother's feelings after death.

Mengpi had not dreamed that this filial son could be his long lost younger brother, Zhongni.

"Bury your mother as soon as possible!" Mengpi said, bringing his foot down from the tree stump. Standing in front of his tall brother, Mengpi immediately noticed that he was a great deal shorter than his brother. "Or would you like me to make a better coffin for your mother?"

"No. I would like to bury Mother and Father together."

Looking at Zhongni, Mengpi didn't know what to say.

When Mengpi was five, his father died first and then his mother soon after. The family's forture began to decline; the young servants all left the family, and only one old nanny stayed on to care for him in the ancient, run-down residence. Mengpi's memories of his childhood, fragmented and faint, blurred in his mind just like the color paintings that hung on the walls of the house.

"Zhongni, I have no idea where our father is buried," Mengpi said. Fearing Zhongni would not believe him, he continued, "If I knew, I would tell you."

"Brother, you should tell me what you know."

"I honestly do not know." Mengpi was anxious and said, "If I knew I would take you there right now."

Zhongni's eyes were flooded with tears as he stood there, motionless.

"Brother, I have a favor to ask of you. If I cannot find Father's grave, I cannot bury Mother. I promised Mother when she was alive." Zhongni said, "If Mother could not be buried with Father, which family would she belong to?"

Mengpi was silent, thinking Zhongni was right.

"For Mother not to be buried with Father, this, to me, is unfilial." Hanging his head, Zhongni said painfully, "One lives for filial duty. When one's parents are living, he should treat them according to the rites. After their death, he should bury them with proper rituals. Father died when I was very small. When he was living I was unable to perform my filial duties with the rites. After he died, I did not know where he was buried. Zhongni is unable to fulfill his filial responsibilities. Now Mother is gone. If she cannot be buried with Father, it will be yet another unfilial misdeed I've done. If one is not filial, how can he live to be a man?"

Mengpi listened to his brother and thought his words reasonable. But hearing this all at once left the elder brother feeling a little dizzy, overwhelmed by such principles. He could not make much sense of the idea that one should base one's life on filiality. But he felt he should not prevent Zhongni from becoming a man.

"People say one shows filial respect to his parents when he returns home and shows love and respect to his elder brother when away from home." Zhongni went on, "Brother, you are my blood brother and the only family member I have now. If you refuse to help me, who can I turn to?"

Somewhat touched, Mengpi said, "Zhongni, it isn't true

that I wanted to lie to you. I really don't know. When Father died I was too young to know anything. Then my mother died. After that, no one was in charge of our family. I don't know where our mothers are buried, let alone Father's burial place." As he spoke, Mengpi started to cry.

Seeing this, Zhongni heaved a sigh as tears welled up in his eyes as well.

"I have already been unfilial. I wouldn't do anything to disrespect my brother. Brother, I won't push you and make you feel embarrassed. I'll go back and keep vigil at Mother's coffin. Sooner or later someone in the neighborhood will tell me where Father was buried."

Zhongni made a measured bow, turned around and strolled off. When he walked to the door, Mengpi called to him, "Zhongni, do you want to go find the wet nurse who cared for me when I was young? She was there when Father died. She might know where he was buried."

A couple days later, Zhongni came back. He had been to a place a few dozen *li* away in the mountains. His face was covered with dust, body full of dirt, and his white pure hemp garments of mourning turned grey. He found the wet nurse of Mengpi. The old lady was over eighty, half deaf and blind. But she could clearly remember Mengpi's father being buried by a river in the area of Fangshan, thirty *li* east of the town.

Three days later, Zhongni found his father's grave and buried his mother there.

At that point, Zhongni was drawing near. Strolling slowly toward Mengpi, he started to bow while still at a distance. Thanks to the burial of Zhongni's mother, the two brothers had grown much closer. Nevertheless, Zhongni still performed the perfunctory round of greeting etiquette.

Mengpi saw that today his brother was immaculately dressed. Surprised, he asked, "Zhongni, why are you so dressed up?"

Zhongni replied, "Brother, I have just gone through the 'hat placing rite'[1] and become a grown-up. How could I overlook my behavior and dress? The rites require one to keep a pleasant appearance, assuming a demure expression, using appropriate language and wearing a complete set of garments and adornments. When a pleasant appearance is kept, a demure expression assumed, appropriate language used and a complete set of garments and adornments worn, the rites are established."

Mengpi knew his brother was very knowledgeable and feared he would never stop when he opened his mouth. So Mengpi headed off his brother's speech by asking, "Where are you going in such a hurry?"

"To a feast."

"At whose home?"

"At the Ji Mansion."

Mengpi was practically scared out of his wits. The Ji Mansion was the home of a minister of the state of Lu, and its head, Ji Wuzi, was in power in the state. How could anyone be casually invited to his family dinner?

"Would they allow you into their house?" Mengpi asked anxiously.

"The court minister is inviting learned men to attend this dinner. I am learned. Of course I am among those invited." Zhongni said confidently, stroking his waist. "See. I am carrying all of them on me. Probably they will be put to use."

Hung around Zhongni's waist like a belt, there were many objects, one after another strung together like fish scales and oyster shells. Mengpi noticed that, as he walked, the objects kept slipping down. Every few steps he had to pull them up along with his pants.

"What are they?" Mengpi asked curiously. He reached

---

[1] The "hat placing rite" is a coming-of-age ritual performed in ancient China. When a young man turns twenty, a hat is placed on his head to signify adulthood.

over to touch them and found they were bamboo slips.

"Works by sages and worthy men." Zhongni answered. So saying, he carefully pulled up the objects hung around his waist.

Mengpi drew back his hand in awe. He was illerate, and so thought the curved strokes of the characters carved on the slips were far harder to understand than the circular lines on logs. His brother was literate and that made Mengpi proud. Zhongni had read so many books and his head was filled with so many strange ideas incomprehensible to Mengpi.

"Zhongni, as your brother, I want to give you some advice," Mengpi said seriously. "We ordinary people had better not play up to the rich. They look down on us."

Smiling, Zhongni said, "Brother, how could they? They would not look down on us. I looked up in the archives and found that the Kong family is old and great and has held ranking positions for generations. One of our forefathers used to serve Fufuhe, the brother of Duke Li of Song, as a court minister. So in fact, we are descendants of the minister."

"That was then," Mengpi said, "Our family was fairly affluent in the past."

"Brother, I am not envying them for their rank and wealth, nor am I drooling over the chicken, duck, fish and meat they eat. If a man has learned to read and write and become an intellectual, he is a *junzi*. A *junzi* should have the country's interest at heart. He should not be concerned only with himself. I am going to the feast in hopes of meeting with the head of the house, Ji Wuzi, and celebrities from all over the land and discuss with them important issues regarding state governance and the people welfare and security."

Mengpi had only a vague understanding of these ideas. He remembered his earlier talk with Zhongni, discussing one's filial duty as the fundamental principle of living; otherwise one could not become a man. Now Zhongni was a man, but he still wanted to become a *junzi*. He aspired to something higher. Mengpi found Zhongni's desire hard to emulate.

"In my mind, it's more practical to learn a craft," Mengpi said. He had been trying to persuade Zhongni to learn to drive a chariot, believing that was solid craftsmanship. If he learned the skill well, he probably would have the opportunity to drive a chariot for the Jisun clan or others in the future.

"Brother, a *junzi* is a pillar of the state who seeks service rather than living. A pillar of the state, brother, you know this. You are a carpenter."

Mengpi did not understand what a pillar of the state was. He took a look at a tree stump and thought he only knew what material could be used to make a wooden bench.

The two brothers continued to talk to each other for a little while before Zhongni took his leave in a hurry. Excited, he shuffled away along the base of the wall to attend the great feast at the Ji Mansion.

Chapter 5 Kuang
(Spring and Autumn Period: 14th Year of Duke Ding of Lu's Reign, 496 BC)

The town of Kuang was nearby now, up ahead the low city walls now visible. Its wall had a hole in the southeast corner. The invading troops of Lu wrecked the wall years ago, causing the damage. Due to lack of funds, the wall was never repaired. The wall now remained as a relic, and with the passage of time, weeds and wild plants fostered along it. Small trees, vital and exuberant, dominated the area in an unbridled fashion.

Confucius, upon seeing the hole, felt a sense of uneasiness gradually seizing him. Throughout his life, he was guided by order and completeness. Fragmentary objects befuddled him.

The town of Kuang belonged to the State of Wei and was less than ten *li* in circumference with a population of ten thousand. Small though it was, it contained all the infrastructures for a self-sufficient town. Four administrative teams worked in their respective positions. The inhabitants ate, drank, defecated and urinated all within the confines of the town wall. The town people adhered to their isolation, relished their rejection of the outside world, and refused to search for opportunities and prosperity elsewhere. Accordingly, locals were particularly cautious about travelers passing by, suspecting that all strangers intended to cause harm.

From the State of Wei to the State of Chen, one must pass through the town of Kuang.

Two days earlier, when darkness fell and during the changing of the guards, Confucius led Yan Yuan and others out the back entrance. One after another, they jumped onto the horse carriage waiting outside and left the capital of Wei. Zilu stayed behind, on his teacher's request, to report to Duke Ling of Wei the next morning that his teacher's brother had passed away and that the urgent call at night to attend the funeral did not allow him time to bid farewell. By then, the master and his entourage would be beyond Wei's borders.

The carriage rolled along the rugged dirt road, up and down, jolts and jars, whipping up clouds of dust. The Master stood in his usual stance, hands grasping the horizontal bar of the carriage. He tried to hold his posture upright and steady against the sway and rocking of the carriage, eyes focused straight ahead, retaining the composure of a *junzi*.

As the horses galloped onward, he reminisced about past times with his brother, Mengpi. Though not born to the same mother, the two brothers grew up closer than blood. Bearing different interests, they had deep affection for one another. Mengpi was physically disabled and not ambitious. He earned a peaceful living to support his family by chopping wood, all within the limits of his capabilities. Humans are like plants and trees, growing in cycles from spring to autumn, blossoming then withering. Mengpi was fortunate to have lived a life free of mishaps. Unlike Confucius himself who took on the world as his responsibility, and until the age when most retire, he was still rushing off to places, making requests, having no place of his own in which to settle. To those who did not know him, they would think that all these years he only had focused on the pursuit of power, wealth and fame.

As he reflected on the reality—that he had weathered extreme hardship and setback all for the sake of bringing the Great Way to the world—a sense of deep sadness overwhelmed him.

He now was on his way to the State of Chen. Its new ruler, Duke

Min, who recently ascended the throne, was a youngster. The Duke was curious by nature and had an affinity for new things. Perhaps he would be receptive to new ideas. Admittedly, the State of Chen was small in size, but as long as the new ruler would employ him, he believed that three years would be enough to see the results of his reforms.

The carriage driver was named Yan Ke, one of Confucius' lively and cheerful disciples. He was young, not yet twenty years old, and had become a disciple just over a year ago. After years of being cooped up in the cramped yard of the House of Yan in the capital of Wei, now having the opportunity to venture out, the young man was naturally excited. He cracked the whip repeatedly, forcing the horses to hasten their gait, leaving the carriage carrying Yan Yuan and others far behind, hardly visible in the distance. After crossing the border into the town of Kuang, instead of entering through the town gate, Yan Ke whizzed pass the gate, lashed the horses and dashed toward the opening in the wall. He even pointed his whip at the hole, saying to the Master, "years ago, it was through this hole that we charged into town."

He had barely finished his sentence when the horse let out a loud whinny, rose on its hind legs, kicked his hooves into the air, and fell onto the ground in a loud thump, its four legs lying bent. In the same movement, the carriage was hurled up and down, swung violently back and forth, and finally screeched to a halt with the shafts and yoke shattered on the ground, the seat broken and scattered all over the place. The left wheel was ripped from the hub and the right wheel was knocked off with broken spokes. The carriage itself was thrown to one side of the road and the canopy was tattered and torn like a shredded banner fluttering in the wind. Yan Ke flew out of the carriage and landed in a puddle of mud, face covered with dirt, grime and mud. In the carriage, the Master fared differently as he was tossed forward and backward. He desperately held steadfast onto the bar to prevent from being thrown out of the carriage. In the end, he managed to regain his composure, standing upright on top of the wreckage, his body tilted slightly.

As they struggled to pull themselves together, there was suddenly loud shouting in every direction.

"We've caught them! We've caught them!"

Squinting, Confucius looked around. Crowds of Kuang locals stood around the area, brandishing swords and cudgels. They surrounded the carriage to prevent its advance or retreat. The Kuang men had set up ropes to snare the horses, causing them fall into the traps, landing flat on their faces.

Confucius had been through myriad experiences, but nothing of this sort. He felt uneasy and regretted leaving Zilu behind in Wei, who would have provided him with extra protection.

"You old silly criminal, you didn't think you would ever end up like this, huh?" said one of the wall guards, who seemed to be in charge. Dressed in armor and pointing his long spear at Confucius' chest, he said, "Should we settle an old score years ago?"

Flabbergasted, the Master immediately stood up, bowed his head with hands clasped saying, "I am an ordinary court minister of Lu and I come to your town for the first time. I wonder what crime have I committed to offend you so?"

"We are capturing Lu criminals of precisely your kind," shouted the commander, "You wonder what wrong you did? Years ago, your troops invaded our town, burned our houses, killed our men, raped our women, and looted our grain. How dare you to pretend not to remember those things?"

Even more perplexed, Confucius replied, "To say you know when you know and to say you do not know when you do not. I am humbly telling you the truth, commander; I do not know what you are referring to."

The commander let out a laugh, thrusting his long spear at Yan Ke, saying "Were you not the one, along with this rascal, who came through this hole to invade us? In two days, you both will be beheaded and we will hang your heads on this town wall. By then, you will gradually regain your memory," so saying, he shouted, "Take them!"

Before Confucius could reply, a few soldiers darted up, dragged him off the carriage, and bound and tied him together with the mud-covered Yan Ke. The two captives, one following the other, were hauled off to the town jail. They were paraded down the street jammed with crowds of spectators roaring and cheering. At this turbulent moment, Confucius remained composed with a stern face. He stumbled and tripped but continued to walk with a measured gait, rhythmically stopping and pausing, proceeding quickly and slowly. As his hands were tied, he could not greet the crowds with his customary gestures, so he nodded his head instead.

They were locked up in a dark cell.

Once inside the jail cell, the Master now had a moment to reflect on the event, which puzzled to him. He felt he had been wronged. He never offended anyone in Kuang but yet was bearing the blame for someone else. He felt anxious that he was not given the opportunity to defend himself nor an opportunity to escape. He did not fear death, but to die in vain, with a bad name and his arguments misunderstood, was unacceptable to him. At this moment, he became aware that Yan Yuan and the others were missing, their whereabouts and wellbeing unknown to him. This event certainly was an ill omen, and he felt uncharacteristically worried.

They were detained for five days straight without anyone showing up to interrogate them or making an inquiry about them. It seemed they were on death row.

At twilight on the fifth day, the guards brought soup with a few pieces of fatty pork floating on top. Seeing this, Confucius realized he would be executed the next morning. For the last few days he had only eaten cone-shaped steamed rolls made of corn and bran, without any soup or vegetables, let alone meat. Now in his final hours, the food improved. The previous days left his appetite unsatisfied, and so there was little time to think of tomorrow or beyond. The Master picked up the bowl, relishing the taste of the meat soup. He sighed with appreciation, "At least the Kuang men are conscious of the Rites. They know to care for the dying."

In the midst of his dinner, a man with hands bound behind his back was suddenly thrown into his cell. A closer look revealed it was none other than Yan Yuan.

"I thought you were dead. But look, you're still alive!" The Master was stunned and happy.

"You, the Master, are still living, how would I dare die first," Yan Yuan said genuinely. It turned out Yan Yuan had been in the carriage directly behind Confucious when the Master's carriage flipped and had been seized by the Kuang men. Seeing the predicament, he immediately turned around and rushed back to find help. Galloping day and night, he returned to the capital of Wei capital, found Zilu and the others. He urged them to come up with a plan, and to seek assistance from inside the Court to rescue the Master. Unable to quell his anxiety, he galloped for another day and night, all the way back to Kuang. There he turned himself in, requesting he be jailed together with his Master.

"Tomorrow is the day I am to be executed. What is the point of coming here to court death?" asked his teacher.

"If I'm to die, I prefer to die with you," his disciple replied.

Hearing these words, Confucius' eyes moistened as he looked up into the heavens, letting out a long sigh, "If there is a will of the heaven, then I shall not die like this. Just as when King Wen of Zhou was captured in Youli and escaped death, thereby allowing the Great Way to survive and be manifested on earth, so it is today with me. Am I not the only one who currently grasps the Great Way? If I die, the world would be deprived of the Great Way. And so, if the world desires to keep the

Great Way, then I will not die. The mandate of the heaven won't allow the Kuang people to dictate my fate."

Yan Yuan listened to his Master, and realizing their great importance, , he wanted to record them by carving them onto bamboo strips, which would later become the analects of the Master. Unfortunately, the knife and bamboo strips he carried with him on his journey had been confiscated long ago by the Kuang soldiers. Jail cells, of course, are not stocked with any sort of writing implement. He anxiously repeated the words to himself a few times, committing them to memory.

"Come, Yan Yuan. You are just in time for dinner. Let's eat together," Confucius said as he poured Yan Yuan half of his meat soup and broke off over half the steamed bun for Yan Yuan. "After having eaten a few days worth of meals in jail, I now can appreciate your life years ago, living every day in that poor region, surviving only on a bowl of rice and a ladle of water. Those days must have been truly hard for you."

Yan Yuan smiled, "I've indeed gone through hardship. My life improved only after I followed the Master. Even in jail with the Master, I feel contented."

The Master's eyes moisted again as he listened, and his heart swelled with warmth.

Yan Yuan was born a Confucian. His father, Yan Wuyao, was Confucius' colleague in the Ji Mansion when he was young. When the Master established his school and began teaching, Yan Wuyao was one of his first pupils. Yan Wuyao often brought his infant son Yan Yuan to class, saying a baby nurtured early in an academic environment would later naturally become a *junzi*. As it happened, the son grew up according to his father's expectations. He was talented and different from ordinary boys. Born into a poor family and growing up in a run-down neighborhood, his life was full of hardship. More often than not, he did not have enough food to eat. With little rice today and a meager ladle of soup for tomorrow, he was malnourished, unhealthy and pale. This stunted the development of his right brain, leaving him slow in response and sluggish in action.

However, he had extraordinarily intelligence, able to infer myriad lessons from a single story. His memory was impeccable. Even more amazing, he was naturally inclined towards benevolent behavior, without almost any need to cultivate it. As an infant, whenever he heard the word 'benevolence' he would show delight and move his hands and feet as though he were dancing. When he was growing up, his father followed the common wisdom of the time and put his son on a strict food regime, feeding him nut kernels such as almonds and peaches. At the age of fifteen, Yan Yuan formally became the Master's disciple. Once admitted into the school, Yan Yuan studied tirelessly. He often stayed up late, sitting in the yard reading alone. Holding the bamboo slips under the dim lights of the nighttime lamps, he would read until dawn.

Even more notable was his style of learning. First, he studied with complete absorption—listening to all the instructions without any questions and taking down every detail without any word going unnoticed. He accepted everything taught by the Teacher as truth. Second, he studied with unshakable determination—closely following the Master every step, evenly paced, holding a steadfast distance from the Master, not too far ahead or behind, not too far to the left or the right. In this fashion, he quickly rose to the head of the class.

That night, the Teacher and the disciple lay down to sleep next to each other. The cramped jail cell was so small they had to lie on their sides with their bodies bent. Yan Yuan even resisted stretching out his legs for fear of disturbing his teacher's sleep. He was young and suffered from insomnia. But today, he felt honored to accompany his teacher, and, without any more regret in his life, he found himself fast asleep as soon as he closed his eyes. In contrast, while Confucius concerned himself daily with the welfare of all people, he still slept peacefully each night. However, tonight was different. His mind raced with many random thoughts, and he realized that he only has yesterdays and no more tomorrows. The grim thought made him profoundly depressed. He had strived for greatness his entire life, but now it was all ending without any purpose. This was unacceptable to him. In retrospect, he had never thought about death. In the past, Yan Yuan had raised the issue of mortality, but he skirted the topic by remarking, "If one does not know how to live, how can he possibly know how to die?" But now that his death was imminent, he regretted he had not thought more deeply about this issue. If he had, he would have been more mentally prepared to deal with his current situation.

Confucius had no sleep all night, and around dawn he started to feel slightly fatiqued. In a drowsy state, he heard a hubbub of voices in the distance, growing louder and louder. He thought the time for his execution had come and that men were coming to take him away. It then dawned on him that since being executed would be the final event in his life, he should not take it lightly. He needed to wash his face, brush his teeth and dress properly in order set an example for generations to come. He nudged Yan Yuan, still sleeping soundly beside him, and urged him to wake.

At that moment, a voice bellowed,

"Master, where are you?"

Then came a bang as the door flew open. Amidst the sunlight beaming through the door, a sturdy, muscular man stood tall with a long sword in his hand.

The Master was frightened, but the man continued to shout,

"Master, Zilu is here!"

Confucius took a closer look and saw that the man was in fact Zilu, and behind him stood Zigong along with a group of other disciples.

"Zilu, is it really you?" the Master was shocked and overjoyed. His emotions swung back and forth between elated joy and gloomy sadness. "If you had been a bit later, Yan Yuan and I would have been executed."

The master calmed down and asked, "How did you manage to rescue me?"

Zilu said, "It wasn't us. Here is the man who rescued you."

At that moment, a man wearing an official peacock feathered mandarin hat and courtly brocade robe, stepped out from the group and bowed to the master, his hands clasped. Murmuring softly, he said, "To your Excellency, I am Yong Qu sent here on orders from Madam Nanzi. You are cordially invited to return to Wei."

Confucius paused for a moment, trying to grasp the situation.

Zigong took a step forward and tried to explain to his teacher what had happened.

"When Madam Nanzi learned that Master's life was in danger in Kuang, she immediately sent the palace chief Yong Qu to help with the rescue plan."

Zilu, standing aside, snorted in disgust.

As it turned out, on the day when Yan Yuan returned to Wei to to spread the news of the Master's imprisonment and imminent execution, as soon as Zilu heard the news, he jumped onto his horse, drew his sword, and called for an immediate rescue plan. But Zigong, being more level-headed, knew that the situation required the help of the court. As he was native of Wei and had a large number of acquaintances in the city of Diqiu, he first made a call on Mi Zixia, a favored court officer. Mi Zixia, though only a court bodyguard, was a lover of Madam Nanzi. If he committed to help, Madam Nanzi would help as well. The noble lady of Wei was long ago apprised of Confucius' reputation , his erudition and wisdom, as well as his lofty stature. She had longed to make his acquaintance. And so she sent her palace chief Yong Qu, along with Zigong and the others, to Kuang to carry out the rescue mission. Zilu was not pleased that Zigong had called on Madam Nanzi for assistance. But though he disapproved, he recognized it was all in order to rescue his teacher, and so he managed to hide his discontent and went along.

Arriving in the town of Kuang, they found that the Kuang men had in fact simply captured the wrong man, meaning it was all a mere misunderstanding.

"Who did they intend to capture, then?" Confucius asked.

"Yang Hu from the Ji Mansion in the State of Lu," replied Zigong. "Two years ago, he led the Lu troops in an attack on the town of Kuang. They burned, killed, raped, looted and committed atrocious acts of every kind. People in Kuang despised him. The locals had this time mistaken the Master as him, saying the two men looked exactly alike."

Confucius listened quietly, without saying a word. Yan Yuan, after being jailed along with his Master for the whole night, was enraged, "Nonsense! Yang Hu, what a villain! How could he look like the Master? A sage and a villain can't possibly look alike!"

After a long silence, Confucius sighed and said, "A man's facial features are predetermined by fate. A man can be moral or immoral, but can facial features be moral or immoral? I could be born to look like anyone, but how could I look like him of all people?"

Chapter 6 The Minister
(The Chronicles: Confucius at the Age of 17)

Meng Xizi, a court minister, along with his two sons arrived late at the Ji Mansion, just north of the city. The two boys, aged seven and eight, were dressed in identical silk garments. The elder one had a precious stone hanging on his chest, rimmed with silver and gold, while the object adorning the younger boy was made of pure, transparent white jade.

As he entered the house, Meng Xizi saw that the residence was decorated with lanterns and streamers, bands of red and green silk draped over the furniture and hanging from the ceiling. Serving boys scampered around on errands, and the female servants repeatedly got in each other's way. The mansion bustled with the jubilant air of a festival. Musicians plucked *qins* and other stringed instruments, sending mellifluous notes into the air from the front of the main room into the yard, while the brass band and wind instruments blared out joyful melodies, which blended with men's shouts and dogs' barking. The musicians played a tune of welcome called "Guests at the First Banquet." Dancers sang and moved in formation, eight rows of eight dancers each, waving long red bands of silk.

Meng Xizi frowned slightly in reaction to the festivities and walked up a flight of stairs, making his way into the main hall.

Today the Ji Mansion was holding a large family banquet. Though called a 'family banquet', it was actually conducted in accordance with the formal "Yan's Rites." A banquet using the "Yan's Rites" was the norm among dukes, and was not a tradition that men of lower status could perform. The duke of a state typically performed this rite in honor of a high-ranking official who had been in the military service for the ruler of the Zhou dynasty. The banquet also served as a farewell party for some one who had recently been appointed to a higher post at court in the capital. The duke also welcomed foreign dignitaries with a similar ceremony, and sometimes they hosted a banquet simply for personal entertainment, as an extravagant cure for boredom. The Jisun clan, nevertheless, held a rank of officialdom and was not qualified to hold a banquet of "Yan's Rites." However, he currently held power in the state of Lu. Who had the nerve to turn up his nose at that?

The clan of Jisun was the most influential family in Lu. Though the king of the Zhou dynasty granted the duke of Lu power over the land of Lu, the day-to-day governance of the state were performed by the Jisun clan. There were three major clans in the country: the Jisun, Mengsun, and Shusun. Meng Xizi was a descendant of the Mengsun clan. The three clans were all affliated with Duke Huan of Lu and were dubbed the "Three Huans (Pillars)." For a few hundred years, Lu's affairs were administered in turns by the three clans on behalf of the duke. However, twenty years ago, without seeking the consent of the duke, the three clans decided to divide the military and taxes into three equal portions, each clan taking a part. Duke Xiang of Lu groaned to himself but dared not voice his frustration, since the daily expenses of the Lu court relied on the tribute paid by the three clans. Three years ago, when Duke Zhao of Lu came to power, the three clans conspired together and once again divided the military and taxes, this time into four portions, with the extra part going to the Jisun clan. Young Duke Zhao was outraged by this but was unable to come up with any adequate reponse. He pounded the walls with his fists and struck the poles in his room, swearing to avenge this wrongdoing within the next twenty years. The mastermind behind both of the clans' plots to embezzle the wealth of Lu was Ji Wuzi, who was now over seventy year old and had held power for forty years. As astute and sly as he was in managing public affairs and as experienced and far-seeing in calculating the development of his career, it was difficult to know whether or not he would live for another twenty years.

On this day, the thousand guests invited to the grand feast at the Ji's home were court ministers and celebrities from near and far.

During the Zhou dynasty, people were classified into four classes. Dukes of a given state fell into the first class, such as the Duke of Lu. Court ministers made up the second class, such as Lu's Jisun, Mengshun and Shusun clans. The third class consisted of scholars, distant blood relatives of the Duke who still retained farmland of their own and earned an official salary. Common people belonged to the lowest class, having no special social status or income. They worked in the fields, labored in workshops and ran businesses. Below the common people were various servants. Though human, they were treated differently and thus were not worth categorizing.

A few years earlier, when the three dominant families of Lu divided the state for the second time, they originally planned to carve up the country into three parts, each family to receive an equal share. Due to the persistence of certain court ministers and celebrities who proposed to divide the country into four portions instead of three, the Jisun clan reaped a small fortune by taking home two shares as opposed to his two counterparts who had to be satisfied with just one each. This was what led him to hold the opulent return banquet.

On the menu today, the host of Ji prepared "Eight Treasures", which were typically served for the king of the Zhou dynasty. There were eight dishes—ground pork in brown paste served with rice, oil-coated meat and sorghum, a roast suckling pig, stewed lamb, wine-preserved beef, slow-cooked chicken breasts, flat-pot simmered meat with three seafood delicacies, and a combo of sheet fat and beef liver. Originally these were specialties prepared exclusively for the Zhou emperor. Only later on did they make their way outside the imperial court, and Dukes from all over got ahold of the recipes and clandestinely started to enjoy the dishes cooked for themselves. The Jisun clan uncaringly followed suit, not concerned by breaking imperial law. The banquet tables were loaded down with "Eight Treasures", and the host family ate them with relish, also offering its guests a rare taste of court cuisine.

The banquet was held in a hall of the residence in which one hundred tables and a thousand chairs had been set up. There were ten major tables, each holding an ox head. Sheep heads were placed on the rest of the tables. To convey respect for elders, a jug of wine was placed in front of each ninety-year-old man, five *jue* of wine in front of each eighty-year-old man, four *gu* of wine in front of each seventy-year-old man, and three *zun* of wine in front of each sixty-year-old man.[1] Everything was set up. The tables groaned with glittering goblets containing mellow wines and silver plates of delicacies, all awaiting the guests to take a seat and pick up

---

[1] *Jue*, an ancient wine container with three legs and a loop handle, popular in the Shang and Western Zhou dynasties; *gu*, an ancient bronze wine container with a tall slender body and bell-shaped mouth, also popular in the same time period; *zun*, an ancient bronze wine goblet.

their chopsticks.

To prepare for this grand feast, the Ji family worked over half a month, slaughtering ten cows, twenty pigs, fifty sheep and countless chicken and ducks. For four straight days, more than twenty chefs were up to their neck in stewing, boiling, stir-frying and deep-frying, filling the entire abode with steam and smoke. Hovering overhead, the fragrance of food could be smelled in the streets and alleys ten *li* away.

Meng Xizi and his two young sons came to the door of the main room. Yang Huo, chief steward of the house, rushed out to meet the visitors on behalf of the host. With a large head and long face, Yang Huo was tall and stout, with wide eyes and a broad mouth, a character not to be disregarded by any means. Even his clothes—a navy-blue satin robe with an embroidery tiger and panther—left a deep impression. Upong seeing Meng Xizi, he immediately smiled and bowed in greeting. Meng Xizi bent slightly in reply, and both men clasped their hands in front of their chest in repeated salutations.

Meng Xizi knew the Ji family was the most powerful in the state of Lu and that Yang Huo was the most influential member of the household. Yang was intelligent and capable and had won the trust and confidence of Ji Wuzi. And, since he daily followed his master closely around the house, he had more opportunities than most to voice his thoughts into his master's ear. In charge of managing the entire household, Yang managed over ten courtyards, scores of rooms, almost a thousand people, and ten thousand cattle.

In terms of loyalty to the Jisun clan, Yang Huo was second to none. In Yang's mind, Lu had only one name deserving of his service and allegiance, and that was his master, Ji Wuzi. It was as if the Duke of the state did not exist. In fact, in his early years he was a servant of the Mengsun clan. But later, when the Ji family rose to power and prominence in Lu,

Yang thought the Meng family, in comparison, as light as a feather. Thus he deserted his master while still quite young and went on to adopt a new name, throwing his lot with the Ji family.

At birth, his name was Yang Hu (虎, meaning "tiger"). Ji Wuzi thought his subject's name sounded wild, and though he was confident in the servant's loyalty, Yang's alien status was always a source of anxiety, often depriving him of sleep at night, thinking that in the future there might be a revolt against him. With this thought, Ji Wuzi gave him the name, "Huo," replacing "Hu (货, meaning "goods")," with meaning 'useful' instead of 'harmful'. Yang was saddened by his name change but, afraid to raise his objection, he resolved to be "Huo" for the time being.

The moment Meng Xizi and Yang Huo exchanged greetings, large bronze bells rang loudly in the main hall, and drums and chime stones were struck, the music of the "Bell Tune" was played. In the past, this melody was played exclusively for the emperor of the Zhou dynasty. Now it came into the repertoire of the Duke's family. The start of music signalled that it was time for Ji Wuzi to come out and meet the guests.

As Meng and Yang turned to enter the main hall, a tall, skinny youth appeared from behind the corner of the building, walking in small steps towards them along the wall of the yard. The young man was clad in a loose fitting, broad-sleeved official's robe with a tall hat on his head. He looked a little funny. His easy gait suggested a relaxed temperament, and he slowly made his way to the foot of the stairs. He lifted up his garment and walked up the stairs. He climbed the stairs tranquilly, each of his steps complete and each movement immaculate.

He walked in such a striking manner that Meng Xizi and Yang Huo paused, turning around to watch him.

When the young man moved closer, Meng Xizi scrutinized him and felt his heart stir: the young man had a long face, broad forehead, long eyebrows, wide eyes, hooked nose and large mouth. To Meng, the youth's features somewhat resembled those of Yang Huo. The two were the same height, though the youth had a much more slender physique.

Meng thought to himself: was this young man the second son of the Kong family that people had talked about so much? He had heard the first son of the family was crippled. The second son was healthy but a little bit crazy, often walking back and forth in the streets, practicing the steps of the rites. The style of walking was unique in the town, nobody was able to emulate it. As it was, the Kong family was actually descended from aristocracy, its ancestors having been blood relations of the Duke of Song. After the country fell into turmoil, the family fled to Lu where its fortune turned foul. When it came to the young man's father, the family was reduced to such poverty that their only recourse was to earn a living as guards of the town of Zouyi.

At the same time Yang Huo was wondering what had brought the boy here.

"Stop!" Yang Huo shouted, "What are you doing around here?"

Zhongni, having spotted Yang Huo, who he knew was the chief steward, stopped immediately. He straightened his clothing, brushed the dust off his sleeves, raised his hands high in clasped gesture, and then bowed deeply in a polite salute, replying, "I am humble Kong Qiu and have come to attend the banquet."

Finding the answer somewhat odd, Yang Huo gazed at him, "Did someone invite you?"

Making a second deep bow, Zhongni said, "His Excellency, the court minister Jisun is well known for his hospitability toward scholars. All the guests coming to the feast today are men of lofty ideals and learning." He babbled on excitedly while continuing to bow a total of eight times. An eight-bow salute was the highest form of greeting made by a junior to honor a senior. Ordinary occasions only called for a salute consisted of three bows. With bright, lucid eyes, he looked steadily into the eyes of Yang Huo, "Though I'm not gifted, I started reading poetry at age five and the classics at age seven and declared learning as my lifelong career at fifteen. I'm intent on bringing peace and stability to the land under heaven and building prosperous countries. I'm both educated and ambitious. I should have been invited on this occasion."

Yang Huo laughed, "Our master Ji only invited those full-belly scholar. Do you know what a full-belly scholar is? It means you first eat your fill and then discuss scholarship. Your belly must be empty I'm guessing?"

As he said this, Yang Huo grinned, stroking his round belly. A crowd of onlookers chuckled as they walked up.

Zhongni, though slightly embarrassed, held strong, saying, 'I learned the rites and forms of etiquette in childhood. I read books and recited poems. I don't boast that I'm well-trained in the classics, but I'm knowledgeable and behave in accordance with the rules of conduct. I can take a test on those things. I can recite from books and poetry. If you don't believe me, feel free to test me randomly."

A dark expression leapt onto Yang Huo's face as he said, "Who are you to claim a seat at this banquet? Today we have court ministers and descendants of noble clans among our guests. How could I allow you to sneak in here and steal our food?"

Zhongni's face reddened, but he refused to be silenced, saying, "My father died when I was very small and our family fortune vanished. However, our ancestors were blood relations of the Duke of Song."

"Whose reign and what era are you talking about?" Yang

Huo snapped at him and then broke into laughter. "Besides, who knows whether you're one of the Kong family?"

The crowd exploded into another bout of laughter.

Zhongni blushed, forgetting to let down his hands which were still clasped up in the air. He shivered, "You shouldn't make such flippant remarks. I can forget about attending the feast, but a scholar can't tolerate humiliation."

Meng Xizi, standing to one side, saw that things were starting to get out of hand. He started to say something but, glancing at Yang Huo, stopped, shaking his head and pulling his sons to his side.

In the meantime, the hall of the residence rumbled once again with the sound of drums and bells. The second playing of the "Bell Tune" marked the time for the guests to take theirs seats and for the host, Ji Wuzi, to make a toast. To comply with the "Yan Rites", the host was compelled to make nine rounds of toasts with wine during the banquet. At its onset, the host raised the bronze goblet and sipped the wine. He then presented the goblet to the guests, who took sips in turn. The goblet was then returned to the host who filled it with wine, drank again, and then presented it to the guests for the second time, now asking them to drink as they wish. This completed just one round of toasts . At the same time, music was played, usually beginning with the "Deer Cries", which would stimulate guests' appetite, and then moving on to the "Fresh Fish in the South" and "Sheep" during the main courses of meal. Finally, they would wind up the meal with a song called "Echoes Through the Trip", which would aid digestion.

Annoyed, Yang Huo waved his hand, shouting, "Get out of here! Go home and eat your steamed rolls."

"I'll take my leave," said Zhongni, raising his arms with hands clasped. But he stood there without moving, "The meal, I'm not going to eat. But I have something on my mind that I must say."

Yang Huo was about to go in. Hearing these words, he turned around. Eyes opened wide, he was surprised, "Why... you're not done with your rubbish?"

Ignoring his anger, Zhongni continued, "When I entered your residence, I noticed the dancers in the yard performing the Formation of Eight. A moment ago, I heard the "Bell Tune" melody being played in the hall."

"So?"

"From ancient times, the Formation of Eight Rows of dancers has been reserved for the emperor, the Formation of Six Rows for Dukes, and the Formation of Four Rows for court ministers. The emperor uses the bell striking melody, the duke uses the *sheng* pipe wind instrument, and the court minister uses a stringed instrument. And yet the Ji family now has the Formation of Eight and uses melody of bells. Is that not a violation of the rites?"

Yang Huo suddenly became furious and shouted abusively, "Quiet! What's it to you?!"

Again Confucius bowed deeply and earnestly performed the eight-bow salute, hands clasped and held high and body bent low. His motions were impeccable.

This done, he adjusted his hat and clothes, stood up, and descended the stairs, walking off in measured steps.

Yang Huo was left there motionless, confused and tongue-tied. It was true that the Ji family had used this set of imperial rituals for a long time, hosting stately parties, enjoying lavish meals and playing the finest music, and yet they had never felt uneasy about it. However, a violation of the rites would surely lead to the execution of the whole family.

By this time, Zhongni was not far away as he walked down the long flight of stairs. He returned to the corner by the wall and tiptoed in ritual steps, holding his cuff.

The poor treatment he had just received and the failure

to attend the feast did not in the least disturb the tranquility in his heart. His gait remained measured and placid. In his stride, he would display to Yang Huo and his men just how a *junzi* cannot be affected by insults nor harmed by starvation.

Zhongni's walk annoyed Yang Huo, whose eyes were still riveted on this young man out of the Kong family, when a heinous thought flashed through his mind. He waved to the houseboys nearby and then made a hand gesture toward Zhongni's.

Zhongni was concentrating on his posture, feeling dignified. Suddenly a gust of wind zipped up from behind. Someone was chasing him. When he turned around, he spotted not a human but a big brown dog running up to him, mouth open. He was terrified. He tried to maintain his stance but could not and his steps became uneven. Finally, he gave up his ritual walk and started running, leaving behind the gatekeeper's cries, "The guest is slipping away ..."

Many years later, Meng Xizi rode down the street in a carriage with his two boys. He saw a funeral procession coming toward him, blowing trumpets and beating drums, with white banners and streamers fluttering in the wind. It was long, winding through the avenue with horses and donkeys pulling the funeral cart in the front and a herd of cattle and sheep dragged behind as sacrifice. Through the window of his carriage Meng Xizi saw a tall, thin young man walking at the head of the procession and blowing the trumpet. The young man, a white turban wound around his head and dressed in a white hemp gown of mourning, was blowing the horn, his cheeks pouted as his feet moved back and forth, stopping momentarily in an assured, variable rhythm. His face seemed familiar to Meng Xizi. A closer look convinced him that the lad was the Kong youth that had been driven off by Yang Huo at the Ji Mansion many years earlier. It was a pathetic scene. He lowered the carriage's curtain and became lost in thought. It took only a couple of generations for the family fortune of a high-ranking official to decline to such a low status that the descendents were forced to eke out a living leading funeral processions, serving as a horn blower, mourning for others, joining the flock of horses and donkeys, and herding cattle and sheep. It was too pitiful. He took a look at his boys sitting beside him and sighed quietly.

Chapter 7 Pu
(Spring and Autumn Period: 14th Year of Duke Ding of Lu's Reign, 496 BC)

The group set out from the town of Kuang, whipping horses and driving the carriages at a doubly rapid pace. Leading the procession, Confucius's carriage was driven by his disciple Gongliang Ru, who was sitting in for Yan Ke who was injured. Gongliang Ru was also a young man, sturdy, muscular and vigorous, who became a student of the master only recently. Upon hearing of the teacher's plight, he immediately took five of his own carriages and rushed to the rescue from the capital of Wei. The master's carriage had been wrecked, and so it was the right time for the student to give the teacher one of his tall carriages, pulled by a team of four horses. Gongliang Ru was anxious and wished that the legs of his horses could carry the carriage forward more quickly. He whipped the horses constantly and the four animals galloped at an amazing rate, as if they were pulling an empty cart. The dirt road was full of bumps and depressions, making the carriage bump along. It rose up and dropped down as if it were bouncing on a trampoline. Tossed back and forth, Confucius held the horizontal bar in the carriage to keep his body erect and steady. Nevertheless, he continued to swing from side to side, as his body denied his attempt and flung him into a run of physical movement like calisthenics. Yan Yuan and Zilu were following closely behind in their own carriages, wobbling like drunkards. They raced ten whole *li* in one go before slowing down. Approaching a big tree, they decided to stop to catch their breath, believing the Kuang men would not be able to catch them even if they decided to go back on their word. Then they were amused with the thought that if the Kuang men went back on their word they had the palace chief Yong Qu with them, who was left there in town drinking wine. They could make him a dish to go with their wine. By this time the travelers were exhausted, their breathing heavy. Though it was already the beginning of winter, they all still sweated profusely.

By the side of the road stood a rough stone marker with the two characters 蒲界 (Pu Jie "The Territory of Pu") engraved on it. Confucius knew he had entered the region of Pu. In the distance, the skyline of a town was now visible. He thought to himself that must be the town of Pu.

Like Kuang, the land of Pu was also under the jurisdiction of the Wei state. Though part of Wei, it was autonomous, having its own government, military, border patrol and sovereignty. Such a small stretch of soil was sacred and inviolable.

Beyond the town of Pu, there were two roads ahead of the travelers, one leading north to Wei and one leading south to Chen.

"Going to Wei or to Chen?" Confucius pondered. Zigong, riding with the master, raised the same tricky question, "Master, in a while we'll be out of Pu. Should we head north or south?"

Standing on the right of the carriage, Zigong wiped away the sweat from his forehead with a silk handkerchief. He wore brand new, embroidered satin garments, embellished with gold and jade ornaments and trinkets that glistened in the sunshine. His apparel contrasted sharply with the dark-colored cotton attire of Confucius, who was lost in thought, gazing intently ahead. He had worn the same clothes for days in prison, and they now were stained by dirt, oil and soup grease, overall a slovenly appearance.

Zigong had a fondness for clothing and decor. He always dressed neatly whenever away from home. At the start of his studies, Confucius disliked his trendy behavior and likened him to a "vessel." The master often said "a *junzi* frowns on vessels." Likening Zigong to a vessel means that he was not a *junzi*. Fortunately, Zigong took his Master's comment without any hard feelings. Instead, he was actually pleased, believing his teacher saw in him true potential for "becoming a great vessel." He even asked his master about what kind of vessel he should become. After thinking for a moment, the master answered, "The coral vessel, let's say." The 'coral vessel' was a famous imperial container. The master used the metaphor to scorn Zigong for having only flashy external appearances without substance. To Zigong, however, it seemed nothing less than a great compliment. He therefore continued to dress in style. Zigong's family name was Duanmu and his given name Ci. He began his career as a merchant in Wei, engaged in the business of selling goods between Wei and Lu. It had been only a little over a year since he became a student of the master. Younger than Zilu and less educated than Yan Yuan, Zigong was vain, thinking he was both more knowledgeable than Zilu and more capable of completing tasks than Yan Yuan. Even compared to the master, he thought himself on par in terms of political wisdom despite lacking the skill to write good articles on moral issues. By all accounts, though still young, he had already accumulated a fortune of one thousand taels of gold. Conceited as he was, his massive wealth was truly an impressive feat that nobody could deny. Otherwise, why would the master compare him with a coral vessel, such a marvelous, valuable imperial container?

Confucius was put on the spot. He did not look over at Zigong though the student shot searching glances in his direction. He did not answer the student's question directly. Instead, he murmured something under his breath, "A *junzi* should think thrice before he leaps ..."

On the day he left Wei, the master decided to go south to Chen and never turn back. Duke Ling of Wei disappointed him. He met the ruler only once, and the conversation between them was not encouraging. Nothing came of the meeting, and there was no follow-up on the content of their talk. He stayed in Wei, in the town of Diqiu, for close to a year, but his lodging was constanly guarded by soldiers. There was no opportunity to speak with the Duke. If he could not talk to the one in charge, what was the point of going on this political tour? If things continued in this fashion, it would be impossible for him to achieve his goals in three years, let alone one month. Since time was running out, he resolved to leave Wei behind and proceed to Chen.

Confucius believed that as long as the Great Way did not completely disappear, it could not be impossible to find an open-minded leader of a state. If he had not been stranded in Kuang, he would have already been in the capital of Chen, Wanqiu, for some time. He might have stridden confidently up to the Duke, greeted his officials with clasped hands, and fell in beside the ruler before they started to converse on state affairs.

But now, all of sudden, he began to doubt his decision to go to Chen.

His doubt stemmed from Madam Nanzi's invitation.

The lady had assisted in his rescue from Kuang, dispatching the rescue team with Zigong and Zilu, which put Confucius in her debt. She had also passed on the invitation to return to Wei.

This was not the first time that Nanzi passed a message on to him.

Madam Nanzi was an important personage in the Wei palace. As the Duke's wife, Madam Nanzi called herself a minor ruler, second only to her husband who was addressed as the major ruler. She personally looked into all court affairs, both those as significant as official appointments and those as trivial as the placing of a chamber pot in the room. It was said that anyone who tried to go behind her back to request an offical appointment would inevitably fail. When Confucius first arrived in Wei, Nanzi notified him that all gentlemen, regardless of origin, should pay a call to the minor ruler(Nanzi) first if they intended to meet the major ruler(Duke). If Confucius wished to pay a call, she would be willing to schedule him in. At that time, Zigong advised his master to acquiesce to her request in order to pave the way for future engagements with the Duke.

Born in the capital of Wei, Zigong grew up in Diqiu. Even as a child, he learned about the political state and functions of Wei's government. He could handle himself in any situation, using a torrent of innuendo, gossip, lies and half-truths, and he knew instinctively where the treacherous waters were located and which had to be navigated carefully. His background as a merchant complemented his political knowledge, and he knew how to act in accordance with the harsh realities of commerce and selfish economic gain. In performing the dance of commercial transactions, he was far from being a novice, and he reacted intuitively to others' expressions, ordered food based on his guest's identity, toasted to his client's health while completing the deal under the table, waving a friend goodbye with a smile but weeping while bribing the man he sought in need. In short, he was a shrewd businessman. Doing all of this was a piece of cake to him. Aware that the Duke was deaf and had poor eye-sight, he was positive that any suggestions and advice raised in front of the ruler would have no effect on matters such as benevolence, filial duty, loyalty, faith, propriety, righteousness, honesty and a sense of shame. However, if Madam Nanzi gently and softly spoke into her husband's ear, the Duke's mind would be bound to give an appointment of at least a third-rank position. Unfortunately Confucius refused to listen, sticking with his plan to gain an appointment by virtue of his uprightness and learning as opposed to pulling strings. At the same time, he taught Zigong a lesson, telling him they had come to Wei to foster the Great Way under heaven, not just to seek an official post. To achieve this goal, the only way was to focus on upright conduct. Zigong felt ashamed and retracted his proposal.

In fact, there was another reason the master did not wish to meet Nanzi. This second but main reason was his concern over one element of the lady's reputation. Possessing stunning beauty, she was noted for her charming facial features, seductive form, flirtatious personality, and enticing manner. There was rarely a man not enamored at first sight. In reality, only a few men had the opportunity to see her, and she also had only met a small number of men.

Like many attractive women, Nanzi grew up within a cloud of scandalous gossip. She was born in the state of Song. While still young, she fell deeply in love with the Duke's son, who left her pregnant. Taking the immortal herb of crimson pearl, she succeeded in having an abortion and remaining a virgin. At sixteen, she married Duke Ling of Wei. As soon as she entered the Duke's palace, the then sixty-year-old ruler became immediately bewitched by her, his bones weak and numb, and his body soft and docile. He was out of his senses, feeling that his past thirty years of life as Duke had been a waste. Her vigor and liveliness in bed stuck out among the many mistresses and concubines who lived within the walls of the palace. Even by day, her mellow, enchanting moan often found its way out of her bedroom, through the thick palace walls to the outside, hovering over the court and disturbing the officials as they conducted routine imperial business. She had numerous, brawny male guards by her side, and many fair-complexioned young males shuttled in and out of her living quarters. Of all these men, Mi Zixia stood out from the rest. Originally serving as a court guard of the Duke, Mi Zixia was red-lipped and white-toothed with delicate features. It was said that he had been intimate with the Duke. He soon became the madam's star companion in bed, becoming a bisexual. People close to the head of state were sympathetic: the duke was not young any more and, physically, "you could only cut your coat according to your cloth." Therefore, it was acceptable that the ruler's subject should bear a portion of his ruler's burden. Straddling two boats, Mi Zixia wore many hats in an attempt to fulfill his responsibilities as a subordinate. Hearsay of this kind circulated and was hardly tied to reality. But people chatted and gossiped about it, enriching the story as its account became gradually more developed in plot and description. Fortunately, Duke Ling himself was not particularly concerned with the stories and so no restrictions were placed on the gossip, which in effect fueled the general desire to further flesh out of the narrative as it became the town's primary entertainment.

As a *junzi*, Confucius often kept a "*dis*respectful" distance from women. Over fifty, he himself was free of scandalous liaisons. How could he frivolously let the moral code that he had upheld for years be broken in an affair with Nanzi?

As a result, he opted to not visit the lady. Instead, he called on Duke Ling directly. During the meeting, the Duke cast amorous glances around the room and generally had an air of restlessness. This confirmed Zigong's previous advice.

In this matter, the person most let down was not Confucius but Zigong. He had joined Confucius to pursue a successful career, holding his master in high esteem and taking advantage of his fame. As a merchant, he knew all too well that his professional pursuit would lead, at most, to financial success and would not get him far along the path of becoming a respected man, unless he sought higher learning or pursued government positions as a military general or minister. In following Confucius, he could either move ahead and realize his scholarly goals, or he could turn back and fulfill his goal of becoming financially prosperous. It was indeed his niche at times of risk and need. With this in mind, he had gone to great lengths to direct his master to Nanzi's residence. He even prepared a gift for her, a pair of gold-plated jade bracelets. It was said they were part of the collection of Zhuang Jiang, the beautiful wife of Duke Zhuang of Wei, who had ruled many years ago. They were a rare and suitable gift for Nanzi. Coming from the merchant classes, Zigong was rather pragmatic. He knew that to accomplish a mission, a man needs more than just ideals. He needs to be realistic. To his astonishment, the master acted out of bookish learning; he was ambitious, but over-cautious and indecisive; he taught students passionately, but was tongue-tied when talking to strangers. In the past, he thought his master was competent, but later on he found Confucius was not good at making money, nor was he capable of dealing with ordinary people. He could claim credit in few areas except for his scholarly accomplishments. For all of these reasons, Zigong started to suspect he had made the wrong decision when he chose to study with Confucius.

After a brief period of rest, the master and his followers hit the road again, heading northeast. Confucius rose up, his hand on the horizontal bar in his customary riding posture. He was riding with Zigong. Ahead of him, Zilu rode in his carriage and behind them Yan Yuan follow along with the others.

The territory of Pu was just around the corner. When its wall gate was in sight, the master said to Zigong, "After we pass the town of Pu, we'll go north to return to Wei."

Hearing this, Zigong beamed. He kept his joy to himself, but knew the master had finally seen the light. He was sure that if they were back in Wei the master would be certain to call on Nanzi. If he met her, things would undoubtedly start to improve in the country. At last, they would not have to roam about the wilderness with no prospect of settling down, no clue where to put up for the night.

Indeed, an awful truth had begun to dawn upon Confucius. He should meet Madam Nanzi. For one, the lady had rescued him, and so he was indebted to her. That a kindness must be repaid was of an axiom of the rites. Besides, he could hardly turn down a second hospitable invitation, and to refuse such an invitation would also be in violation of the rites.

Overall, he was not afraid of seeing Nanzi. It was well known that she was stunning and extraordinary, like a fox. Her beauty bewitched men, leaving them lustful and perplexed. Nevertheless, he was curious and wished to meet her. When in his entire life had he been infatuated by an attractive woman? At eighteen he had stood against such temptation. How could he fall at fifty-eight?

A deeper level of considerations, he kept wholly to himself. He did not want to lose this opportunity. If Duke Ling granted him a position, he could help put the country on the right track within a month and in full accordance with the rites within three years. By then, the Dukes of all states would all follow suit, and the Great Way would once again prevail in all the lands under heaven. At almost sixty, he feared he would not have many more opportunities such as this in the future.

The carriage suddenly stopped just a stone's throw from the gate. The carriages in the front came to a standstill. Several men on horseback blocked the way, holding lances in their hands and brandishing swords.

Zilu jumped off the carriage and dashed up to report the situation to his master. Confucius asked if they were highwaymen, since they were in the territory of Henan, which was periodically plagued by road robberies and hijacks. Zilu told him they were a garrison of troops and that they had closed the city gates since the city was under martial law. The master asked whether they could bypass the city and continue on their way. Zilu replied that the soldiers ordered them to return where they came from.

Confucius looked ahead and saw the troops were dressed in the same uniform despite the fact that some had incomplete suits of armor. They were ordinary troops. They held up a large yellow flag with the characters "Gongshu-*shi*" embroidered on it. Looking up, he noticed that the flags of Wei atop the city wall had been replaced with the flags of "Gongshu-shi", which now fluttered in the wind.

It was obvious that some significant event had taken place in Pu. A couple of days ago, rumor had it that Gongshu Xu had been driven out of the capital city by Duke Ling and banished to this area. Did Gongshu Xu rise in rebellion and capture the town of Pu?

Meanwhile, Gongliang Ru, who had driven the carriage, became enraged. A young man, he was tall and strong, and at times his temper easily got the better of him. He was ready to stand up for anyone if the cause was just and dive head-first into a fist fight or scuffle. Later he turned to the master, determined to start anew. He gradually became temperate, kind, courteous and restrained. But the wildness and ferocity of his youth did not entirely leave him. During the last few days, he was barely able to curb his temper during the predicaments in Kuang and Pu. Now his pent-up rage exploded. Throwing the reins to Zigong, he leapt off the carriage, picked up a long sword and shouted to Zilu, "Come on. Let's fight together and see if we can force a way out. The master has run into so many adversities in the journey. If we fail to crack this nut, none of us will end up in a good place. We will have to fight at the risk of life. If we die, so be it!"

As he said this they charged forward. What followed were murderous shouts, mingled with the sound of metal weapons being struck against each other repeatedly. After a while, the two were beaten back. Zilu was injured, having sustained a few sword wounds to the body and Gongliang Ru was worse, with bleeding cuts and a battered head. On the other side, the troops had been taught a lesson. After the troops being pushed back a few dozen *zhang*[1], they then ran into the town.

---

[1] *Zhang* is a unit of length equal to approximately 3.3 meters.

They shut the gate and held it tightly, disregarding the aggressive taunting from the men outside.

The two sides confronted for a while.

Confucius was anxious that if they stayed here at the town of Pu, they would neither proceed up north to return to Wei nor travel down to Chen. They were then left with only one road to take: to Kuang. He quickly brushed aside that last choice, momentarily reliving the recent memories of tough life behind bars.

With no way out, Confucius told the troops that he would like to enter the town in person and visit Gongshu Xu to ask him for a way out. A long while passed, before the troops passed on the message that Gongshu Xu had invited Confucius for a meeting, but that he was not allowed to carry any weapons into the town.

Seeing Zilu was badly wounded and Gongliang Ru's head was bandaged with rags, the master had no choice but to leave them outside the gates, ignoring concerns about his personal safety, and take Yan Yuan and Zigong with him into the town. The three of them unfastened their swords, left them behind, and walked into the town, a white towel wound around their head and hands held high, posturing an unflinching stare in face of death.

When they were at Gongshu Xu's palace, Confucius found that his face was quite familiar. At first, he could not recall when he had met him, but all of a sudden a memory flashed through his mind. It was Gongshu Xu who had led him to the court on the day he made a call on Duke Ling many years ago. At that time, Gongshu Xu was a favorite of the Duke. For one reason or another he offended the old ruler and had been sent here in exile. The host also recognized his guest, who was, by all means, prominent, with a well-known face.

Since they knew each other, conversation flowed easily. Gongshu Xu treated the three visitors to dinner. After three drinks of wine, formal etiquette relaxed to a point where they began speaking about business. Confucius explained to his host that he was traveling from state to state to restore the Great Way in all the lands under heaven. He was stuck here on his journey and hoped Gongshu Xu could lend him a hand. He added he would be willing to give some money, if necessary, as a toll for passing through. Gongshu Xu waved his hand as he heard his guest's request and said he could not care less about the Great Way or Small Way. Using the road through his town was definitely out of the question. To Gongshu Xu, the Duke of Wei was an old dunce who had exiled him from Diqiu to this wilderness. There was no way for him to contain his anger. He was preparing for a rebellion and intended to declare independence. For the last few days, his troops had sealed off the city, allowing no one to enter or leave the town, for fear that someone might make it to the Wei capital and give word of his plans. Therefore, he requested that Confucius stay in Pu until the rebellion started. The master replied that he only needed to pass through the town and had no intention to reveal Gongshu's secret. Gongshu Xu nevertheless still doubted his guest. Confucius assured his host that a man who failed to keep his word was not a *junzi*. The master's words had little effect on his host, who shook his head and asked the master why a *junzi*'s word had to be credible. Gongshu Xu then said he did not mean to anger Confucius' and that he would be willing to let him pass. But Confucius had to exit from the eastern city gate and swear not to return north to Wei. Hearing this surprising turn of events, Confucius sat in silence for a moment before vowing to leave the town and take any road but the one to Wei. Sitting beside him, Zigong winked at his master, anxiously warning the master not to speak too candidly in order to leave leeway if anything went wrong in the future. The master seemed to have missed Zigong's hint and had one more drink with Gongshu Xu. The deal was finished.

At twilight, Confucius and his students exited from the eastern gate of the town and finally left Pu behind. Before they departed,

Gongshu Xu offered the guests dinner and lodging for the night as a gesture of goodwill. Fearing that any delay could lead to trouble, Confucius thanked his host and bid him farewell, saying that as Gongshu Xu was busy preparing for the rebellion, Confucius would leave him alone and be on their way as soon as possible. To himself, Confucius thought that any perceived involvement in this insurgence could ruin his reputation forever.

As Confucius and his followers departed from the town's eastern gate, they proceeded on their journey at a fast pace, quickly leaving behind the tall flags and banners that hung upon the town walls, which receded in distance, becoming shrouded in darkness.

This time, Confucius' carriage led the way, and he drove the carriage himself, grasping the reins and holding the whip. Zigong rode with him. In the second carriage, resting with Yan Ke, Gongliang Ru lay with his injured head wound tight with a white rag. Zigong was unable to drive a carriage, since he came from the merchant class and always had a carriage driver. He was a good rider but lacked experience as a driver. After becoming Confucius' disciple, he began to study the art of carriage driving, which was one of the six skills required of a *junzi*. He was happy to learn but had not yet perfected the skill, and so now he stood on the right, keeping an eye on the directions.

Before long, they reached a fork in the road, at which one route led to the south, leading to the state of Chen, and the other leading north, back to the capital of Wei.

Holding the reins, Confucius whipped the horses a few times, attempting to direct the carriage towards the southern route. But the horses stubbornly refused to turn south and instead headed north, ignoring Confucius' command.

With a sigh, Confucius said, "An old horse knows the way. Why should a *junzi* forget about the Way?" With this, he shook the reins, as the horses leapt forward, and gently whipped them. The horses were immediately roused into a frenzy, turning onto the road north, then settling into a joyful canter.

In the carriage, Zigong had been unsettled by the master's resolution never to return to Wei. Now he was stunned by the direction they were heading. He asked, "Master, where are we going? Are we not supposed to head south?"

"North, back to Wei."

"Go back to Wei?" Zigong stared at him, not believing his own ears. "Was it not the master's intention not to return to Wei? Can a *junzi* break a promise?"

Confucius fell silent as he drove and after a while remarked, "A *junzi* behaves to all people under heaven. There is nothing that he has to stick to, and there is nothing that is the only way of acting. What he should keep in mind is righteousness. If this is so that the Great Way can prevail in all lands under heaven, why should I care about going back on my word?" He smiled as he spoke. "In addition it should be understandable that one is coerced to say something untrue. I believe that behavior is pardonable by gods."

Zigong refrained from questioning further, and he stood in the dark mulling over the master's words. He had assumed the master would be bookishly rigid. It turned out that the teacher had a good grip on affairs of the mundane world. His breach of the promise was solemn and stirring. To go and see Nanzi would be an act regardless of his own safety. One could never fully know how much the master had grieved and sacrificed through these occurrences. At this thought, Zigong was overwhelmed by a feeling of profound respect. Even the horses galloping in front knew which road the master wished to take. He, however, was utterly ignorant of what was on the master's mind. Though how one came to live in accordance with the Way varied from person to person, he was certainly behind even the horses in this matter. He felt ashamed.

The carriage raced north on the road. Confucius raised the whip over his head and spun it in the air with a clear crack. The horses were startled into a vigorous gallop, heads held high. He gently urged them on with the whip, making the horses maintain a steady pace while keeping the rein taut to avoid any mishaps. The carriage shot straight ahead into the distance and sailed along the road as steadily as a boat. For years, Confucius had not laid his hands on the reins of a carriage, and his driving skills were by now somewhat rusty. In his early years he apprenticed with the teacher Wan Fu. The teacher's tips and advice now came back to him, and he took the chance to practice the skill.

When he was young, his biggest dream was to become a carriage driver.

Chapter 8 The Rustic
(The Chronicles: Confucius at the Age of 18)

At midnight, Wan Fu heard the neighing of horses. Out in the stable, the neighs were long and low, wavering, and sometimes one after another, in a spell of noise and commotion. He had driven chariots his entire life, and such an uproar in the stable was not unheard of. But a nightly disturbance hit a nerve. He could not let it go, and so he rolled out of bed, and got dressed in the dark, wondering what was happening. Walking to the stable, he felt suspicious about the strange sounds, some intermittently long and loud, in a way resembling those of horses and donkeys, but there were others that seemed nothing like the sounds of any animal.

As he approached the stable, though he had prepared himself for something unpredictable, he nevertheless was alarmed by the sight before him. He saw Zhongni standing upright among the horses, one head above them in height, with a candle in one hand and a book in the other, and reading poems loud, his chin up and voice full of emotion. The horses were agitated and neighed constantly as if joining in the reading.

"In the wilds a dead deer with white rushes well bound"[1]

That was a human voice.

"Puff, puff ..."

That was the neigh.

"Heigh, not so hasty, not so rough!"[2]

"Puff, puff ..."

"Heigh, do not touch my handkerchief. Take care, or the dog will bark."[3]

"Puff! Puff!"

Wan Fu felt like laughing but could not. He was annoyed but had to repress his anger. He said, in a bad temper, "Watch out for fire."

"Where's the fire?" Zhongni was surprised, asking anxiously, "Has any one been hurt?"

"I said you should watch out for the fire. I did not say there was a fire. You're reading in the stable at nighttime. You woke the horses and may carelessly ignite something,"

---

[1] From the first stanza of the three-stanza poem "A Dead Doe in the Wilds," Section Shannan, The Book of Songs, a collection of 305 ancient Chinese poems from the Zhou dynasty. The poem describes then scene when a young hunter meets a beautiful girl in the woods and presents the game he hunted, a dead doe, to her as a gift, and they fall in love with each other. The translation is taken from The Book of Songs: the Ancient Chinese Classic of Poetry, translated by Arthur Waley, New York: Grove Wiedenfeld, 1987. See the complete translation below.

In the wilds there is a dead doe;
With white rushes we cover her.
There was a lady longing for the spring;
A fair knight seduced her.

In the wood there is a clump of oaks,
And in the wilds a dead deer
With white rushes well bound;
There was a lady fair as jade.

'Heigh, not so hasty, not so rough;
Heigh, do not touch my handkerchief.
Take care, or the dog will bark.'

There is a girdle in the east;
No one dares point at it.
A girl has run away,
Far from father and mother, far from
Brothers young and old.

There is dawnlight mounting in the west;
The rain will last till noon.
A girl has run away,
Far from brothers young and old, far
from mother and from father.

Such a one as he
Is bent on high connections;
Never will he do what he has promised,
Never will he accept his lot.

[2] See note 1.

[3] See note 1.

Wan Fu said.

Zhongni was a little embarrassed, "I did not want to disturb people. I therefore roused the horses, and they disturbed people."

"Why, in the dead of night, are you reading poetry out here in the stable?" Wan Fu asked.

"These days I've been busy learning how to drive a chariot. I was afraid that I would neglect my reading and writing. And since I couldn't fall into sleep tonight, I came here to recite a few poems."

"Horses don't understand poems," Wan Fu said. "Otherwise this would be a way to nurture them."

Zhongni smiled, "You're right. But a *junzi* isn't a horse. He should learn something about poetry and prose. Otherwise he would be just like a horse eating fodder all day until he was full."

Hearing this Wan Fu sighed, waving his head. He knew another outburst of stubbornness had seized Zhongni. In contrast with scholars, he was illiterate and knew nothing of poetry and prose. Was he just another horse eating fodder until he felt full? Fortunately, he was familiar enough with Zhongni's character to know that the learned man sometimes dropped into self-absorbed moods and made disrespectful remarks. But Wan Fu was not bothered.

To Wan Fu, a learned man was harder to comprehend than the horse. When the horse neighed or whinnied, he could tell whether it was happy or hungry. But a learned man was full of peculiar ideas that constantly left him perplexed. The reason was self-evident. He had driven chariots for the Jisun clan for over ten years and had spent more time dealing with horses than men.

He simply could not grasp why Zhongni did not work whole-heartedly as a chariot driver. To be a driver for the Jisun clan was such a good job, with free food and clothing and even rewards from time to time! It certainly was not easy to find such a job these days.

Wan Fu's mother was the woman who had breast-fed Mengpi many years ago. She once had said that Mengpi had a brother, named Zhongni. Though an orphan, Zhongni had always been a filial child. To find his father's grave he went alone into the mountains to see her. Later Zhongni wanted to learn to drive a chariot and sent someone to Wan Fu. Due to their families' close ties, Wan Fu accepted Zhongni as an apprentice.

At that time, Zhongni also learned to play the trumpet and drums as part of the funeral and burial procession. Wearing a hemp gown of mourning along with a white turban wrapped around his head, he blew the trumpet and beat a small drum while walking up and down the street. On one day, the ritual would take him to one house to mourn and the next day he would grieve at another residence, hardly giving him the chance to put on a pleasant face.

Wan Fu often ran into him on the street. He noticed the young man marching in the procession with solid footwork, his feet moving back and forth, pausing and starting again as if in a dance. He knew the tempo and had a natural sense of rhythm, so he would make a good chariot driver. Yang Huo, the chief steward of the Ji Mansion, had once talked to him about hiring this young fellow for the position. Wan Fu was flustered, not wanting to be accused of favoritism for having recommended Zhongni for the job.

It turned out that Zhongni did indeed make a fine chariot driver. The art of driving consists of four major techniques, "starting, riding, turning and stopping." He quickly mastered each with minimum instruction. "Starting" involved setting the chariot into motion gently and efficiently; "riding" involved moving forward quickly and steadily; "turning" meant directing the chariot in different directions smoothly and steadily; "stopping" entailed bringing the chariot to a gentle and complete halt. Zhongni was tall and sturdy, with powerful arms. When driving a four-horse chariot he was able to brandish a whip in either arm, propelling the chariot forward as swiftly as lightning. When he wished to halt the horses, he could accomplish the task with a mere cry, holding the two straps in one hand and reining in the heads of the four horses, allowing the chariot to suspend in the air.

Equally impressive was Zhongni's general attitude and ettiquette when driving a chariot, which were reflected in his cultivated politeness and refinement. Even when calling to the horses, his voice was mild and manner polite and meticulous. When mounting the chariot, he would climb the steps as if entering the Duke's court. He would adjust his garments, tidy his hair, stand erect, look ahead, and be silent. Every movement and posture was carried out in accordance with the rules.

Equally admirable, he possessed an impeccable theoretical understanding of the art he was studying. He quickly absorbed new lessons and derived generalizations on his own, which he found easy to pass onto his fellow servants. Among those young men were Yan Lu, who drove a chariot with him, Zeng Dian who cooked meals for the host, Min Sun who kept the doors, Ran Geng who swept the floors, and Qin Zhang who managed the storehouse. They all performed various odd jobs around the Ji Mansion.

Zhongni first taught them the significance of chariot driving and told them the work occupied a higher status than cooking, watching the doors, sweeping floors and managing the storehouse. This was because "charioteering" was considered one of the "six classical arts." This made his young colleagues so envious that almost all of them began considering a career switch. His instruction did not fall flat on Wan Fu, either, who now felt he had moved up a rung on the social ladder.

Zhongni then explained how one could develop as a charioteer, and he told them that though performing the job well could make one prosperous, it could not lead to officialdom. To Wan Fu, Zhongni was correct. From Wan Fu's own experience, no cattle caretaker from the Ji Mansion had ever won the host's praise and been promoted to managing humans. Regardless, a competent charioteer could be guaranteed adequate food and clothing.

From his early career as a charioteer, Zhongni also gained quite a few insights about life, the most noteable being: "more haste, less speed." He found that the more one rushed towards a destination, the less likely you were to reach it. This was also true of life. Therefore, just as when driving a chariot, one should wait and yield to others, so in life one should put others' interests before one's own. Hearing this, Wan Fu kept patting his forehead, filled with admiration that through all his years as a charioteer he had not come to this realization.

A scholar was indeed different from ordinary men. Such a big fish in a small pond, it was inevitable that Zhongni would leave his job at the stable sooner or later.

At this time, Zhongni blew out the candle and walked out of the stable, his head hanging low. Bits of the horse's feed were scattered over his head, caused by the horses puffing and heavy breathing, and he smelled strongly of horse dung, an odor Wan Fu knew too well and enjoyed the smell of.

Wiping the top of his head and face, Zhongni dusted off his clothes. Carefully rolling up the bamboo slip from which he read, he said, "Learning shouldn't be ignored. Without reading poetry, could one really say something that makes sense? I haven't read for only a couple of days, but now I can't even articulate myself."

Wan Fu said, "Horses can only hear cries and obey orders. If you know how to yell order to the horses effectively, you can take good care of them. How does this have anything to do with reading?"

Confucius did not reply. A moment later he sighed and said, "I was born into an unprivileged family. Though one of my distant ancestors was a court minister, the country was in turmoil and the family lost its fortune in following generations. The official's income was all spent, and my parents died when I was young. I had no one to turn to for help, though fortunately I'm taller and stronger than others. But if I do not study more poetry and prose, who will treat me with respect in the future? Who will find me useful?"

Wan Fu said, "But you're still the descendent of an aristocratic family. You were born into the circle of officials and will receive an official salary your whole life. My family is completely different. For eight generations, my ancestors have been commoners, living by the sweat of their brows. If you were to drive a chariot your entire life and yell at horses and donkeys all day long, that certainly would be an insult to your talent."

Confucius said, "That's not necessarily true. Charioteering is one the 'six classical arts' that a *junzi* must master. I have you as my brother to teach me charioteering. I see this as a stroke of good fortune. I thus need to learn the six classical arts—rites, music, archery, charioteering, writing, and arithmetic. I cannot skip a single one; I need them all."

At first, Wan Fu thought Confucius was learning charioteering in order to make a living. He now realized the young man had far more lofty ideals. Wan Fu sighed with emotion, "To be a *junzi* is not easy!"

Confucius said, "No, it's not easy. My family was poor. I had to educate myself. Though my education was fragmented, I did my best to make my studies well-rounded. While still very small, I started learning the rites. Later, I read poetry. In this way, I grounded myself in a basic knowledge of literature and the rites. Later on, I learned archery and how to blow a trumpet. And so I'm not a complete layman when it comes to archery and music. Now I've started to master charioteering. But it's a shame that I'm still utterly ignorant of arithmetic and unable to make complex calculations. A *junzi* should have a strong sense of numbers. But I can't count even a small number of items. How will I become a *junzi* in the future? It's too bad that so far I've had no opportunities to study this subject."

With this, he looked up to the sky as if to let out a sigh or count the stars.

Wan Fu knew he felt tormented and refrained from touching upon any other distressing topics. There were not many horses in the stable, only a small number, and so only the most basic knowledge of arithmetic was adequate for his trade. But Zhongni's grand goals were inspiring and Wan Fu, eager to help, kept the matter in mind.

Before long, such an opportunity arose. Toward the end of that year, old Ji Wuzi passed away, and his grandson Ji Yiru inherited the family fortune, becoming Ji Pingzi. Immediately Ji Pingze made a thorough inventory of the property, rummaging through chests and cupboards in an effort to see how much treasure had been hoarded in the house. It was found that there was a shortage of staff in the storehouse, particularly accountants. Wan Fu thought of Zhongni and mentioned his name to the current chief manager of the Ji Mansion, Qiguan Ren, who, as Wan Fu knew, was a native of the state of Song, and, along with his recommendation, mentioned that Zhongni's ancestors also had come from Song. Meeting Zhongni, Qiguan Ren was impressed by the young man's stature and fine features and took a fancy to him.

Qiguan Ren arranged to transfer Zhongni, assigning him to the position of storehouse manager by day and bookkeeper by night. Later on, he saw that Zhongni was a competent and meticulous worker and did not commit any errors. His young colleague was also single and had no parents. All this made Qiguan Ren think of his young daughter who currently was looking for a man to marry. It turned out that his idea came true and the young man's marriage with his daughter originated an endless family line of the sage.

Chapter 9 Cao
(Spring and Autumn Period: 15th Year of Duke Ding of Lu's Reign, 495 BC)

It was early spring when Confucius and his students set out on the road again. This time, they departed from the capital of Wei for the state of Chen in the south.

On this trip, there were fewer followers with him, totaling only twenty odd people, young and old. The traveling procession was short, with just six chariots rolling one after another. Confucius rode in one chariot, and the rest took turns riding. The shortage of chariots left limited space for luggage and other odds and ends. Some disciples had to walk, carrying bags on their shoulders.

Zilu, Yan Yuan and Zigong each took turns marching beside the master's chariot, shouldering backpacks and carrying cloth bundles in their hands. Following them was Gongye Chang, who was son-in-law of the master and, older than the others, set an example for the younger members of the group. He carried the master's clothing on his back, one bundle stacked on top of another, and he balanced pots, bowls, ladles and spoons in his hands, which jingled incessantly. There were several large baskets of bamboo slips, a heavy load that Zizhang, Zixia and Ziyou shared on the journey. Those three were the finest of the master's young students, and each excelled at learning. Since they read the most books, their current duties mostly involved dealing with books.

Bringing up the rear was Zeng Shen, who, not yet fifteen years old, was the master's youngest disciple. Worried about his young age and fragile physique, his fellow students let him take care of the rice, flour, and vegetables. However, even the foodstuffs were beyond his strength as he tottered along and muttered under his breath, "I now understand why the master taught us "a *junzi* has a heavy burden to carry and a long road to travel."

The party first moved southeast, making a short detour to Cao, Song and then to Chen, for they feared the route leading directly south to the regions of Pu and Kuang. After more than ten days of traveling, they finally left Wei and crossed the border of Cao with its capital city Taoqiu just a short distance ahead.

They scaled the hills, hiked through villages and small towns, trekked across jungles and streams, took their meals outside and camped in dew-covered fields. It was a blessing that it was already early spring, the mountains and fields were turning green, temperatures were rising, and so they did not suffer frostbite or the harsh cold. Adding to the pleasure of traveling, delightful scenery kept coming into view in the distance. Tall trees, bamboo hedges, daffodils, idyllic rural landscapes lined both sides of the road. In the balmy days of spring, lands were a blaze of color. All looked fresh and gay. The picture of thriving nature fostered a sense of optimism, the blind belief in a bright future and that days of bounty were in store the following year. Though the travelers were exhausted, their shoulders hurt and their feet swollen, they nonetheless were in high spirits, singing and laughing happily along the way.

On the road, only Confucius remained silent, distraught by some upsetting point.

His students were aware of the teacher's state of mind and dared not open their mouths.

The cause of Confucius' low mood was Nanzi. Indeed, other than a woman, what else in the world could make a man feel so gloomy?

He had returned to and now was departing from Wei all for this woman.

A year earlier, when Confucius had returned to Diqiu, the capital of Wei, Duke Ling had thrown a grand welcoming ceremony for him on the outskirts of the city. Outside the eastern gate it was splendid and warm, with colorful flags flapping in the wind, the sounds of drums and music, young girls dancing and then warriors putting on a show of martial arts. Over eighty years old, the Duke of Wei showed up in person. He usually disregarded protocol, showing up whenever he pleased. Defining his behavior as treating worthy men with courtesy was not as accurate as taking it as being an old dunderhead. However, his presence, in one way or another, nonetheless warmed Confucius' heart, making him feel very flattered.

Duke Ling met Confucius and at once asked with concern, "I heard you were detained in Pu?"

Confucius gave a quick reply, "No, no. I was just stuck there. "

The Duke said, "The rebels were in revolt over there. I wanted to put down the insurrection, but the officials opposed the move, saying it would be impossible to take the town of Pu."

Confucius said, "Why is it impossible to defeat the rebels? The local people of Pu, the men and women, are all loyal to the Duke and are determined to defend the state. The rebels are only a handful of people."

The Duke said, "As I expected. How about you assume command and lead the troops in the attack on Pu? Get rid of the rebel leader, Gong-shu Xu, for me."

Hearing this, Confucius quickly declined, "My knowledge is of the rituals and offering sacrifices. I have never studied military strategy…"

Hesitating for a moment, the Duke broke down in laughter, "I've forgotten. You're interested in virtue and morality … Blame it on my poor memory."

Apparently, Duke Ling's memory was failing in his old age, and he often forgot what he said earlier that day. He never carried out the invasion of Pu and he never again requested Confucius to take command of his troops.

Once in the capital of Wei, the most pressing business was to call on Nanzi. That day, Confucius entered the Duke's palace for the visit. Nanzi opted not to meet him in the main, official room, nor in the wing reserved for guests. Instead, she scheduled the appointment in her bedroom. Early on, the palace chief, Yong Qu, went to wait outside the entrance of the palace. Yong Qu had departed the town of Kuang one day later and only by chance had escaped the Pu mishap. He took a devious route and got back to Diqiu. With Yong Qu leading the way, Confucius followed and with a few eunuchs and maids trailing behind. They passed the entrance and the courtyards, walking through alleys and gardens in a winding labyrinth of passages and chambers until they reached an embroidery-decorated tower in front of a pond. The tour was dazzling with the residence's magnificent colors of green and gold. When they finally stopped at the door of the palace, Confucius' head was swimming. Yong Qu entered first. He came out again to summon Confucius and then remained outside.

Confucius walked inside. He saw a room elegantly furnished, covered in a shroud of mist and dimmed light. But there no one was in sight. The only thing he could see were heavy, white bed curtains draped high and low, swaying in the breeze. A faint yet tantalizing aroma wafted out from inside. As if in a trance, he felt like he was entering the abode of an immortal.

Confucius assumed Madam Nanzi would be sitting behind the curtains, and so he dropped to his knees and bowed in a formal show of respect, hands clasped in salutation. Before he finished, he heard the clinking of jade bracelets and pendants as if the lady was raising herself slightly to return his greeting. The sound of jewels striking one another continued for a moment before he heard a snort of laughter.

Confucius felt strange. He looked up and watched as the curtains were pushed aside one after another, and, slowly, a lithe beauty emerged.

Seeing Nanzi, Confucius felt dizzy and blood rushed to his head. He felt on the verge of losing his mind. In his imagination, Nanzi was elegant and well-composed, with an affected unconventional streak in her ravishment. Completely unexpected, however, was this lovely young lady before his eye. She had a fair complexion, charming features, and appeared pure and innocent. Even one touch of her shining black hair could subdue one with excitement. The roll of her shining pupils radiated tenderness and love. And her cherry-like lips, when pursed in a smile, relayed an amorous shaft. Her blushing cheeks did not disguise a bashful disposition; when she smiled her ingenuous nature was unmistakable.

"I only knew you were a scholar, I did not expect you to be so tall and strong," Nanzi said, covering her mouth with a hand to repress the laughter. In fact, her praise was sincere.

Confucius felt her remarks were somewhat inappropriate, but he could not come up with a timely response. He said, "A *junzi* is righteous and behaves well and so naturally grows tall and strong." As he spoke, he realized that his words were inappropriate as well.

Nanzi invited Confucius to take a seat, and Confucius made polite remarks before sitting down cautiously. The lady then asked him to move closer to her. He had no choice but to do as she said. As he moved closer to her, a faint scent of perfume greeted him as the lady scrutinized him from head to toe. Not daring to raise his head, he noticed his female host was clad in a white robe embroidered with a golden phoenix and many elegant floral designs. The robe was not an official garment but carefully tailored to her slender and graceful build.

Confucius originally had planned out many things to say on the topic of state politics. But he now found himself at a complete loss for where to begin. Still worse was that he had glimpsed her waving hair, red cherry-like lips and her pale, tender neck, which quickly and inadvertently directed his attention to the rising and falling of her breasts. A surge of energy the likes of which he had not felt in a long time rose up in him.

Confucius knew his behavior was improper, and so he recited to himself, "Do not see what is improper fo seeing; do not listen to what is improper for listening; do not speak what is improper for speaking; do not do what is improper for doing." After slightly reciting these words to himself a few times, he calmed down. He then assumed his standard sitting posture, head lowered and eyes down, trying to focus on his feet and not on the woman. He spoke loudly, as if he was offering advice on at the imperial court, expressing his gratitude to Nanzi for rescuing him. Then he bid the lady farewell and made a quick exit.

Other than chuckling every so often, Nanzi said nothing. That day she did not press Confucius to stay longer. After the meeting she accepted him as a friend and periodically summoned him to the palace to help entertain guests, talking and laughing at the dinner table with wine and games. Sometimes she invited him to dances and vaudeville shows. Confucius found it difficult to turn down her invitations and, at the same time, he hoped that at these events he might find opportunities to educate her about his ideas of governance and virtue. And so he always accepted her invitations.

Sometimes, after three rounds of drinks or during the intermission of a performance, he would recite philosophical phrases to Nanzi, such as "First behave with virtue and then the country can be ruled by virtue; if one fails to behave with virtue, how will one be able to rule people with virtue?" However, each time he brought up this subject Nanzi would put her hand on her forehead and say, "I'm a girl. Do you really think your philosophy makes any sense to me? How about you read my palm and tell me my fortune!" With this, she would stretch out her soft hands toward him, cutting off his teachings.

Duke Ling, knowing Confucius amused Nanzi, was content. He knew long ago that Confucius was a gifted man but had not been able to find a way to use him. Now, he saw his talent being fully applied and felt satisfied that he had given Confucius an opportunity to exercise his talents.

In this way, Confucius grew infatuated with Nanzi and gradually became more relaxed in his daily routines. During the day he sat alone, stupefied, and while lecturing, his general distracted air spread to his students. His rehashed idea "In one year a minor goal can be fulfilled, and in three years a major goal can be reached" was no longer on his lips. Another year went by as he made no progress. He then changed his mind, deciding to stay here. He even thought of purchasing a piece of land and settling down for good.

Seeing Confucius frequent Nanzi's place, Zigong was excited at first, thinking his teacher's social contact with the lady would translate into tangible success in politics. But later on, he watched Confucius visit the palace daily, wholly engrossed in private affairs, and yet had obtained no position at all, let alone influencing the political leadership of the country. He was puzzled. In comparison, Zilu was even more annoyed with the recent chain of events. He tried to subdue his anger, finding it was hard to accept that the master was hanging around with someone like Nanzi. Confucius being summoned at will like a clown was all the more infuriating to Zilu, who was not the type to keep discontent to himself. His true feelings always were written on the face.

One day, Nanzi once again summoned Confucius to the palace. The Spring Festival had just finished and the Lantern Festival was just a few days away. Nanzi feared that since the time between the two holidays was so long, the festival would lose momentum. She thus chose to throw a dinner party on a random evening. A few drinks of wine left her feeling slightly drunk.

It then struck her that she should take a chariot into town and ride around the streets. Duke Ling, acquiescing to his wife's every request, at once ordered that an open chariot be made ready. Nanzi wanted Confucius to accompany her, and though the master thought it inappropriate, refusing repeatedly, the lady insisted, finally resorting to feminine pleading, pulling on the sleeves of the master and saying flirtatiously, "I really want you to go with me! I really want you to go with me!" Confucius simply could not handle this type of behavior. Besides, a *junzi* should never act against the rites, and so he joined them, accordingly.

The Duke and Nanzi rode in the first chariot. Nanzi wore a large, red silk shawl draped over her shoulders, decorated with phoenixes embroidered in golden thread. As the chariot zipped through the streets, those phoenixes stretched their wings and flew in a red blaze. Closely behind them, Confucius and Yong Qiu rode in the second chariot, one in court dress and the other in the palace apparel. The duke's chariot and its entourage left the palace and paraded through the town, sounding the whip all the way.

By that time the afternoon fair was not yet finished. Word got around that the Duke and his wife were making a plain-clothing tour of downtown, and the streets quickly became thronged with people vying with each other for a view. Though they all said they wanted to catch a glimpse of the Duke, they really wanted to see Nanzi. Following behind, Confucius was not recognized by the commoners, who thought he and Yong Qiu were either just two eunuchs or a new boyfriend that Nanzi had found to replace her old lover, Mi Zixia. They all felt the new pick was a little too old. The townsfolk's gossiping went on for quite a while in the alleys and doorways.

The rumors on the street found their way to Zilu's ear. He was filled with anxiety.

That same day, he went to see Confucius and asked abruptly, "Master, is the way of a *junzi* to seek virtue or women?"

Confucius replied, "A *junzi* should seek virtue."

Zilu said, "I've never seen someone both fond of women and morally upright."

Sensing his student's anger, Confucius said, "Cultivating virtue is like being fond of women. One is genuine in his cultivation as he abhors evil. His genuineness is like one's indulgence in lust. What is wrong with that?"

Zilu said, "So is the Master's meeting with Nanzi as morally genuine as it is lustful?"

Confucius was dumbfounded and blushed deeply, "I visit with Nanzi in order to help the Great Way prevail over all the lands under heaven."

Zilu said, "I doubt that during your meetings with Nanzi you were able to uphold your moral character and resist her beauty."

These words incensed the master. Pointing his index finger to the sky he said, "If I met with Nanzi for any other purpose, may heaven strike me down! May heaven strike me down!"

Witnessing his teacher's fury, Zilu bit his lip, holding back the flood of words. At this point, Yan Yuan was standing aside, listening to the argument, but did not interfere. He was busy carving their words into a wooden board. It was not clear whether he carved Zilu's words, "I've not seen one both fond of women and morally upright," deliberately or inadvertently as the quotations of the master. Later, when *The Analects of Confucius* were compiled, the error was not corrected, which indicated the master, though amorous of Nanzi's beauty, remained clearheaded and morally strong.

That night, a shocking event took place in the palace. An assassin leapt onto the roof, climbed the pillars, jumped over the gates, scaled the palace walls and sneaked into Nanzi's bedroom. However, no sooner had his feet touched the ground than he was caught, and all his training as a professional assassin came to nothing. Kuai Kui, the son of the

Duke, upon learning of the news, took flight by night. His hasty flight proved without a doubt that he had masterminded behind the plot.

To complicate the matter, after the initial commotion, the people in the palace found that the man who caught the assassin was not only empty-handed but also naked. What baffled them even more was that he was muscular and strong but was not one of the palace guards. How could such a beast pop up in the bedroom of the Duke's wife in the middle of the night? Someone identified the man as Song Chao, the Prince of Song.

Song Chao was Nanzi's ex-lover, who had been invited by the Duke to the palace a while ago and who often entered the palace by its side doors, causing little stir in the court. It was just that he was barely recognizable in his naked appearance. Reports were sent to Duke Ling, who was outraged. His hands shaking and beard quivering, he called the prince an "unfilial son" and his wife an "adultress". He was so upset that his body started to fail, and he had a stroke.

The court of Wei was in turmoil and the daily routines of government were in disarray. The duke remained bedridden, unable to lead. His son was gone, and no one knew his whereabouts; his wife Nanzi led a reclusive life and refused to meet anyone. Word circulated that she feared being assassinated.

Hearing this, Confucius was depressed for a while and he said, "Lu and Wei are politically wrecked like the suffering twins. Neither of them is able to get out of this hopelessness."

Thus, on a gloomy morning, Confucius bade Duke Ling farewell and left Wei once again.

The capital of Wei faded in the distance, as memories of Nanzi sank steadily deep into his brain. Occasionally memories of her shining eyes, beaming smiles, graceful steps, and waving hair, as well as the faint perfume, surfaced in his mind, nibbling at his heart.

The travelers pressed ahead in their journey and made no stop at

Taoqiu, capital of Cao, simply bypassing it on the road to the south. At dusk, they arrived at a small village as the sun was setting, shrouding the tile-roofed clay houses, dirt walls, and wood hedges all in an evening glow. Confucius called on everyone to stop. Raising his hand over his forehead, he looked at the village, and his eyes narrowed. It seemed familiar to him, and he tried to recall an early visit from the dim, distant past. He made an inquiry, which informed him that it was the village of Qiguan, a place within the territory of Song.

The name of "Qiguan" was somewhat disturbing to Confucius, filling him with the sense that he was traveling back in time. This was the place where he had married his wife Qiguan-*shi*, who was a native of this village.

In a moment of nostaligia, the past welled up inside him.

He recalled his wife and son Boyu. Since he had left Lu, he rarely had heard of them.

Chapter 10   The Couple
(The Chronicles: Confucius at the Age of 19)

The Qiguan girl lay in the new bed with her clothing on. Bashfully she pretended to sleep as she waited for her bridegroom to come over, who was reading a book under the light by the window.

This was her bridal chamber on her wedding night. The party had ended and the guests were gone, taking away with them the merriment and uproar, and a hush gradually descended, broken only by the periodic sputtering of a few tall candles. She wondered whether her new husband would be sleeping with her under the same quilt. Should she undress herself or wait for him to undress her? When she was finally undressed, what would he do to her? Such thoughts made her blush, and she was gripped in anticipation and bewilderment.

The chariot, in which the bridegroom had ridden to her home to escort her back to his home for the wedding, arrived in the village at twilight. The setting sun cast its glory over the distant mountains and made the windows of the chariot glow red. As the chariot, decorated in red silk cloth and colorful festoons, entered the village, it quickly became surrounded by a large crowd of children. It circled the yard of the bride's home three times before stopping in front of the entrance. Through the window she caught a glimpse of the bridegroom standing on the chariot. He was tall and thin, driving the chariot himself, holding the reins and whip in his hands, each movement of his body indicative of his expert driving skill.

Earlier, she had been in the rear east wing of her home, tying her hair into a bun, applying rouge and powder, and finally coloring her lips red. When she had gone to don new garments to look her best, she wept continuously in front of her mother, not wanting to leave home, but at the same time praying for the arrival of her future husband who would take her away.

Now the bridegroom alighted, walked into the yard, holding the edge of his gown, and in quick, short steps marched up to his father-in-law who was waiting in front of the house. Though it was only a short distance, he chose to walk along the walls of the yard, raising his arms in a repeated, formal salute. The throngs of villagers watched and giggled at him. The next moment he led the bride out of her room and lifted her onto the chariot. She had barely gained her footing on the chariot when he started bowing to the crowds, which caused the horses to a move forward, almost throwing the bride from the chariot. Another uproar broke out among the locals.

Nevertheless, she was pleased, since she felt he was not an ordinary man. A bibliophile, he was well-read and had acquired knowledge of the rites and etiquette, far different from those rustic halfwits who lived in her village.

The wedding drew to a close as the visitors all left, leaving the two of them alone in her bridal chamber. She was so embarassed that she kept her chin to her chest, unsure whether to sit or lie down. He said solemnly that marriage was a blessed unity of a man and a woman; it was both a tribute to the ancestral shrine and an obligation to continue the family line. It was a fundamental part of the rites. Therefore, it should not be treated lightly. He asked his bride to sleep first while he consulted *The Book of Rites* again to see whether there were passages about the wedding night. At that moment her admiration for him reached new heights. Why didn't he come over and sleep with her? Lying in bed, she was a little uneasy and embarrassed.

Her marriage had been arranged, which she took as her parents' mandate as well as her obligation. But it ended up being a delightful one. Her bridegroom's family name was Kong, his given name Qiu, and his courtesy name Zhongni. He had served in the Ji Mansion, was culturally literate and muscular, and though not perfect in every way, he was at least accomplished in letters and martial arts. What was left to be desired was his taciturn appearance at first sight. Would he look like that all the time? If he were so reserved and withdrawn in the morning, at noon and during the night, life would be so dull! Since she was only sixteen, she obviously enjoyed having fun, laughing and joking around with friends.

Why didn't he come over to me? What kind of book could be so riveting?

These thoughts lingered in her mind as she fell asleep. The next time she opened her eyes it was broad daylight outside. She knew she had made it through the night with her clothes on. Half awake, she saw her man still sitting at the table by the window, though his wedding dress was off and he had changed into a long, white robe. With a book in hands he read,

Peach trees are exuberant; it is in the bloom.

This girl is marrying and, with her man, will live in love.[1]

Then he murmured to himself, "The girl of Zhou is lovely!" She

---

[1] From *The Book of Songs*, Section 1 "An Exuberant Peach Tree."

heard her husband's emotional sigh. She thought he had another girl in mind, one from Zhou. A slightly jealous feeling arose in her. So that was why he would not drop his book! In a fit of annoyance she turned over in bed and fell asleep again. When she woke up again the sun hung high over the eaves, flooding the room with light and warmth.

One year later their son was born.

The day of his birth fell on the tenth anniversary of the reign of the Duke of Lu. The three clans, the Jisun, the Mengsun and the Shusun, each presented their gifts to the Duke in congratulations. The Duke sent his gifts to each of them in reply. Most of the Duke's gifts were food, including chicken and fish, which Ji Pingzi frowned upon and distributed among his subordinates. The Ji Mansion employed a large number of servants. There were only small amounts of chicken and fish, and the chickens varied in shape, lean or fat, while the fish were all different sizes. Commoners were unhappy about the unequal portions of the goods they received and ignored the meager amounts given to them. Then lots were drawn. That day, Zhongni was lucky and won a carp. He carried the fish back home, mumbling his indebtedness to the ruler. Entering the yard, he heard the cries of the newborn and was touched. He therefore named his son "Li"(鲤, meaning "carp") and styled him Boyu (*bo*伯, meaning "eldest of brothers"; *yu*鱼, meaning "fish") as a token of gratitude to the Duke.

On another day, the husband came back home with a joyful expression on his face and told her that there was a job opening, a low ranking position in charge of cattle breeding, and he got an offer. The Qiguan girl was happy too, knowing that he was leaving the storehouse and going back to the stable. Earlier, he was only a charioteer, but now he was promoted to tend the cattle and swine. But she was worried that he knew nothing of animal breeding. Her husband disagreed, "I don't see why the job would be hard for me? Only just in heat. That doesn't call for the rituals."

Before they knew it, eight years had past. Each day the husband meticulously carried out his domestic duties in the Ji Mansion. He made no errors driving the chariot. Having been put in charge of the storehouse, he kept the accounts clear and well-organized. As chief of the cattle, he worked hard to keep the herd healthy and breeding. Later, when he was promoted to take charge of construction projects, the works were always completed without any delays and carried out with no financial losses. As a result of these accomplishments, he came to be considered a model worker. Not only did the chief steward Yang Huo know about his deeds, but even Ji Pingzi heard about them as well.

Now the Qiguan girl had grown into a woman. She was busy everyday with household chores, cooking and caring for the little boy. Unwashed and unkempt, she gradually lost the look of a maiden, and became, from head to toe, a plump middle-aged housewife.

Through the years, she had been more and more content with her husband, though she began to realize that the more extraordinary a husband became, the greater the burden a wife had to bear.

Her husband was learned and held himself to a high standard. In the same way, he also had high expectations for women as well. On their wedding night, when she had fallen asleep early and woken up late the next day, her husband considered this a breach of "feminine morals." She felt this was unfair. After getting married, a wife should get up early in the morning, sweep the rooms, water over the garden, wash herself, change her clothes, and greet the parents of the bridegroom. But since her husband was an orphan, she did not have parents-in-law. So what was so wrong with oversleeping a little in the morning? Even in this, she had her own reasons.

127

Another case occurred a few days later when relatives visited to offer their congratulations and to eat a meal cooked by the bride. She prepared the meal and cooked a dish called "Wine Stewed Chicken" for the guests. When her husband saw it he shook his head, explaining that according to custom, the bride should prepare a roast pig, not chicken, for visitors. But how could she have known about such customs?

After dinner she wrapped up the leftover salty fish and gave it to the relatives as they were leaving. Once again her husband shook his head, saying that according to formal etiquette, she should give them dried meat to show that she had meat for dinner and therefore was well-treated in her new home. Salty fish, on the other hand, implied that since she had come to her husband's home, she was like a fish, unable to flip its body over to obtain freedom. Fortunately, her relatives did not mind and were delighted to accept whatever food was given to them.

His strict code of feminine morality was even more rigorously reflected in his demands in the kitchen. He was not only fastidious about the flavor of dishes but also very concerned with the act of cutting and slicing while preparing the food. In addition, the food selection was specified and scrutinized on the basis of his rituals. Any fish slightly off or meat somewhat discolored was sure to be thrown away. When eating meat he never failed to ask, "How did this pig die?" If it had not been slaughtered in accordance with the formal conventions of slaughtering, he would refuse to eat the meat. If the rice was burnt, the gruel overboiled, a dish stir-fried without spiced ginger, or green onions failed to be served with salted, fermented soybean paste, he would never touch them.

His demands about cooking was only one part of the problem, and she found the family dinner particularly dispiriting. It should be a pleasure to sit around the dinner table surrounded by the chatter and laughter of family members. But he sat erect, with his clothes neat and in order, and remained silent as if attending a state banquet. If she started to chatter, he would look over at her, gesturing his disapproval for speaking at dinner, a motion which often made her choke on her food.

That day, Qiguan-*shi* was busy fixing dinner in the kitchen when her husband returned from the Ji Mansion. He went to his room and started reciting poems from *The Book of Songs*. They were not new, but instead were ones he had uttered many times before. The sound passed through the wall and drifted over sentence by sentence,

Peach trees are exuberant; it is in bloom.
This girl is marrying and, with her man, will live in love.

The words sounded familiar and made her recall her wedding night years before. She felt uneasy and so deliberately neglected to flip the fish, which continued to fry on its side in the wok until it spit and burned.

At that moment, her son Li ran through the front yard. He enjoyed running back and forth, darting out the front entrance and racing back in the backdoor, never stopping for an instant. Seeing his father there, he wanted to steal off but was stopped by his call. Li was eight years old, already learning to read and write characters as well as to recite poems. Confucius asked him, "Have you read your poetry today?" Without waiting for a reply, he recited the beginning of a poem, "A big mouse, a big mouse," and asked the boy to finish it. The boy could not complete it. Confucius scolded him, saying, "Without studying poetry, how can you speak?" He then asked another question, "Have you reviewed the rites?" Li said nothing, his head hanging low. The father was incensed, "Without learning *The Book of Rites*, how can you take a stand?" Frightened by these words, the boy burst out crying, all the while casting sideways glances at the kitchen.

His mother came out and said Zhongni should not take his frustration out on the child. She then called for dinner. Zhongni was still frustrated when he saw that the sitting mat had not yet been spread out on the floor. He could not help but complain, "If the mats were not set out properly, the ancients did not sit. There's no mat here. How can I sit?"

She grew angry. She hurled the cooking ladle onto the ground, untied the apron around her waist and stopped cooking, saying, "I knew you were tired of me and my son. Why don't you just get rid of us." So saying, she started sobbing in grief.

Still annoyed, Zhongni shook his head, saying, "Okay, forget it. So it's true that only small men and women are hard to deal with!"

Hearing his abusive language towards women and children, she exploded with pent-up anger that she had held in for years, "I knew you only had that girl of Zhou in mind. Let her come here and take care of you!"

"What Zhou girl?" Zhongni was baffled.

"Are you denying it? You've been mumbling about her and saying how lovely she is! Do you think I'm blind?"

Zhongni quickly realized that his wife had mistaken the girl from Zhou in the poem that he often recited for a young lady of the Zhou family living the next door. He knew it would be difficult to clear up the confusion, and this added more to his depression. He was annoyed that, despite the "six classical arts" in which he had become well versed and the many books he had read, he still was not even able to make himself understood in his own family. How could he expect to restore order to the lands under heaven? He then considered his achievements. At thirty, he still had not completed in any praise-worthy deeds, nor had he obtained fame. The odd jobs in the Ji Mansion, which he detested, were obviously not a suitable career for a *junzi*. As he mulled this over, he could not help but heave a long sigh.

At that moment, two young masters suddenly walked into the yard, both of them wearing tall hats and carrying jade articles and swords. Coming to the center of the yard they asked in a high voice, "Is Mr. Kong Qiu in?"

Zhongni hurried out to meet them. With a salute he asked, "I am humble Kong Qiu. May I inquire who you two young masters are...?"

The young men immediately bowed, returning the greeting, while looking at Zhongni and smiling. One of them said, "You probably have forgotten us. We're from the Mengsun clan. I'm Zhongsun Yue. This is my elder brother Zhongsun Heji. We once met each other in front of the Ji Mansion."

The man's words brought a faint blush to Zhongni's cheeks, as he remembered being barred from the party at the Ji Mansion years ago. In the dim and distant past, he remembered his encounter with an old man with his two young sons outside the residence of Ji.

The young man went on to say, "When my father was still alive, he said you were a descendant of a royal family, well versed in books and the rites, and would undoubtedly become a success. He asked us to take lessons from you on *The Book of Rites*. The Duke of Lu sent us on a journey to the capital city Luoyi of Zhou to observe and study the rites of Zhou. Now we're taking the liberty of calling upon you without invitation and wondering whether you would like to go with us brothers?"

Zhongni was delighted by the news and said, "Did you say you're going to the capital of the Eastern Zhou dynasty?"

Chapter 11 Song
(Spring and Autumn Period: 2nd Year of Duke Ai of Lu's Reign, 493 BC)

Confucius did not hear of the news of the death of Duke Ding of Lu until he had reached the capital of Song, Shangqiu. Ran Qiu brought him the news. The student made a trip back to Lu to meet his aging mother. He was back from Lu now, telling many stories about the state, occurrences both past and present. He recounted the grand ceremony of the new Duke ascending the throne. In contrast, the funeral for Duke Ding was disrupted by a downpour, scattering the participants and cutting the formal ritual short.

When he heard this, Confucius felt depressed. In lingering despondency, he remembered the first time he answered the call of Duke Ding of Lu years ago. That was one night in midwinter when snowflakes fell thick and quickly, the streets and alleyways carpeted in white. The summons from the palace came after the third watch, around midnight.[1] He jumped to his feet from the bed, hastily slipped into his garments and put on his hat, checking that nothing was out of place. He would not wait for his chariot to be made ready, worried that he would be late, and instead opted to go by foot. He waded through the heavy snow and made his way to the palace a moment earlier than his chariot.

---

[1] In ancient China, nights were divided into five two-hour periods. The third of these periods was called 'third watch', *sanjing* in Chinese, and fell on midnight.

The Duke was waiting in his bedroom, which, lit dimly with candles, felt warm. The Duke, hair in disarray and beard untidy, was wearing a large, loose sleeping robe on his tall, thin body. He was pacing back and forth at the foot of his bed, apparently up late considering matters of state and caring for his people.

When Confucius entered the room, the Duke first stared at him for a moment and then asked abruptly, "Is there a single sentence that sums up the steps to make a country prosperous?" His words and manner clearly revealed his eagerness. Confucius was touched by the ruler's sincerity, but before replying, he sneezed three times, spraying his face with mucus. Having walked in the snowy streets, his hands and feet were freezing, and his head and shoulders were covered with snow. Even his eyebrows were frozen with small pieces of ice. Upon entering the warm, cozy room, his body was barely able to adjust itself to the warmth and ended up producing the symptoms of a cold. Certainly one, ignorant of his state, would think he was moved to tears.

Then again, in retrospect, he seemed to be moving closer to the truth. A ruler and his subject were in a close relationship. Without a wise ruler, the subject could not expect to be successful in his position. He might not even have the chance to become an official in the first place. The Duke of Lu was not really a wise ruler by any normal standard, but he at least cared about his mission. He often looked into the court affairs, and took seriously the governance of the state. It was a shame that such a promising and capable ruler indulged in the pleasures of the girls of Qi and afterwards ignored the affairs of the state. It seems that beautiful women, if not a source of ill fortune, are able to bring the downfall of a country. When a ruler became infatuated with beautiful women, his sense of judgment was drawn away from what is most important. That year, instead of going to the outskirts of the town on the marked day to make sacrifices to heaven and the ancestors, Duke of Lu traveled out of town to watch erotic dances...

Those memories dismayed Confucius, and he sighed repeatedly. For no reason at all, all of a sudden he was struck by memories of Nanzi. He could not help breaking a smile. Years ago, when Ji Huanzi said he did not understand the attraction of women, perhaps he was right. After Confucius met Nanzi in Wei, he forgave Duke Ding in one way or another. In the past, Confucius often said to his students that a young man was full of vigor and vitality and should control his own lust. Now the truth was manifested that even if one was advanced in years and his vigor and vitality on the wane, the commandment remained on lust.

The next day, Confucius let his disciples set up a sacrificial table on the outskirts, just south of town. First, he intended to mourn over the death of Duke Ding, to show his respect, and second, he wanted to practice the ritual, with such a virtual scene, due to the long lack of drilling on the rites resulting in students' rustiness. In the vicinity, an old cypress tree stood towering and upright, appearing unshakable. Confucius saw it and was delighted, thinking it bore some resemblance to a *junzi*, and so he had the table of sacrifice placed under it.

It was not far to the capital of Shangqiu, about 10 *li*. As he traveled through Song this time, Confucius chose the route that passed through villages and bypassed cities. To avoid entering Shangqiu he also made a detour and put up for the night outside of town.

In Song he avoided a foe of his, General Huan Tui, the Minister of War. Though he had never met him, there had been a long-term feud between Confucius and Huan Tui.

Like court minister Jisun in Lu, Huan Tui was a powerful man in Song. As the state minister of war, he had influence in all affairs, military and political. He was also a bully, far more influential than the duke of Song. He indulged in luxuries and trivialities. Not only did he give himself up to sensual pleasures, he was also deeply interested in the afterlife. To this end, he had marble transported from the wilderness of southwestern China to be carved into an outer stone coffin for himself. The marble casing weighed a thousand *jin*[1], and was square in shape, fine-grained and as white as jade. It was thought that an outer stone coffin crafted from it could preserve a dead body for a thousand years without decomposing and ten thousand years without rotting. The dead man could thus remain alive forever.

He hired two hundred craftsmen to work day and night, carving birds, engraving beasts, chiseling plants, and printing landscapes on the sides of the coffin. After three years the project was still not finished, revealing his desire to make it an artifact that could be excavated a thousand years later and shock the world with its exquisite craftsmanship.

Huan Tui's wild ambition got around among the states and became an object of ridicule. When word reached Confucius' ear, the sage was very angry. In his lectures to students, he often used it as a fine example of a "violation of benevolence". He even said, "For such a degraded man, given to extravagance and wastefulness, it would be better for his body to rot after death." However, his words somehow found their way to the ear of Huan Tui, who clenched his fists in rage, saying, "Kong Qiu, you wish my body would soon rot, then I will make sure that you suffer a violent death! You better not let me capture you in the future."

Now that Confucius had arrived in Song, he was determined not to get captured by Huan Tui.

To return to the story, Confucius and his students donned garments and hats of mourning and started to rehearse the offering sacrifices. Following the instructions of the rites, his disciples stood in a row, came forward in file and performed a whole round of movements. Sitting on the side on a tall stool, Confucius occasionally pointed out their mistakes and scored each of them as if a judge of the competition.

Suddenly they saw a man racing toward them from the direction of

---

[1] A *jin* is a Chinese unit of weight equal to 0.5 kg.

town, and cried, "Master, something has gone wrong. Some one is coming to kill you!"

As the man came closer they saw it was Sima Niu, a disciple of Confucius. He was a native of Song and a half-brother of Huan Tui. He had gone into town the night before to visit his mother.

The students were in the middle of kowtowing, making a bow and setting sacrifices on the table. Suddenly they learned that someone was coming to kill the master. Frightened, they stopped, some prostrating themselves on the ground, others bending over at the waist, and still others standing, holding the plates of fruit in a daze.

Zilu drew his sword from its sheath, scowling and preparing to protect his teacher. Yan Yuan quickly gathered the sacrifices and utensils for fear of forgetting things in a rushed departure. Zigong walked to Confucius' side and said in a low voice, "Master, would you like to go somewhere and hide yourself for the time being?"

Undisturbed and waiting until Sima Niu came closer to him, Confucius asked him quietly, "Who wants to kill me?"

"Huan Tui."

"How did he know I was here?"

The master's fixed, firm look at Sima Niu revealed his suspicion: did any of his disciples divulge his whereabouts?

The master's gaze fretted Sima Niu and he lowered his eyes, replying nervously, "I have no idea. I just saw troops leaving the town ..." A thought grabbed his mind: did the master suspect that he had leaked something about him? The student was Huan Tui's half brother and that was enough to make him a target of suspicion.

Confucius said calmly, "I'm not afraid of Huan Tui. Morality and justice are on my side. Is he really trying to kill me?"

Zigong saw the master relapse into rigidity and become laughable, worried that his teacher would suffer in a penny wise and pound foolish position. He stepped forward and said to Confucius, "Huan Tui doesn't care if you have morality and justice. When the troops are here with their swords and lances, none of us could survive. We would be martyred for our faith. You'd better get out of harm's way."

Still Confucius would not budge, "Heaven bestowed morality on me and has decreed my fate. What can Huan Tui do to me?"

Zilu and Yan Yuan, both getting anxious, persuaded him to leave immediately, saying that morality could be preserved only if he was alive. Without life, how could morality exist? Besides, there was no reasoning with villains.

Showing no sign of changing his mind, Confucius sat motionless on a tall stool and repeated, "Heaven decreed my fate. What can Huan Tui do to me? What can Huan Tui do to me?"

Meanwhile, a cloud of dust billowed up in the direction of the town's gate, and through it a group of soldiers galloped ahead on their horses, their sabers, spears, swords and halberds glistening in the sunshine.

Seeing that the situation was critical, Zilu shouted frantically, "Master, time is up! Don't say another word. Let's leave at once!" So saying, he darted up and, ignoring the master's protests, removed the master's ceremonial dress and helped him slip into a brown garment. Then he pushed him up onto the chariot and whipping the horses before the chariot sped south. The rest of the disciples quickly changed their clothes and scattered in every directions. In an instant, the sacred spot was deserted. When Huan Tui and his troops arrived at the place, what they saw was a pile of sacrifices on the ground, cooking vessels and wine goblets all over the places. Only the sheaves of joss sticks and candles were burning quietly on the table of sacrifice, curls of smoke rising into the air.

At seeing this, Huan Tui kicked his stirrups wildly with rage. Looking up he saw that old cypress, magnificently tall and straight, which appeared offensive to the eye from all angles. He immediately ordered his soldiers to cut it down. The men were at first dumbstruck and then understood their superior's command. They rushed up and knocked the gigantic tree down by hacking, chopping, cutting and stabbing with their sabers, swords, spears and halberds. Though an easier job than stabbing a man to death, it took them quite a while to finish the job.

Huan Tui felt more at ease after venting his anger.

Failing to capture Confucius, Huan Tui order the gates of the capital and all towns along the route to the border to be shut and tight security, with interrogation and examination of all travelers, to be enforced to ensure that Confucius and his men, the group of fugitives, were arrested.

After a desperate race Confucius got separated from his traveling party and got lost. He saw the wanted sign, posted on the wall of each town gate, with a sketch of him. The painting was clumsily drawn, not quite resembling him. But there were three crimes listed under the sketch: first, gathering crowds to disseminate heresies; second, building a sacrificial altar to worship a pagan duke; third, wearing strange clothes and damaging the appearance of the town. Each of them was punishable by death. He feared traveling on major roads, and so he deserted his chariot, donned plain clothing, and trekked stealthily on paths that crisscrossed in the fields and trails in the wild. He ran east and headed west. He staggered and stumbled on the rough trail, with only one thought in mind, getting out of Song immediately.

As he pressed ahead, he found his route more and more perplexing until he suddenly realized he was lost, standing alone in the wild. Looking around, he could not identify which direction he was facing.

In a split second, the skies darkened as fog closed in around him, cloaking heaven and earth in darkness.

Confucius became frightened. At that moment he had a feeling of loss, isolation and helplessness, something he had never felt before. For many years in the past, he held the conviction that heaven had conferred on him the mission of transforming the land under heaven. He had met one duke after another and was never intimidated or filled with dread.

He remembered his meeting with Laozi at Luoyi, the capital of the

Zhou dynasty, in which Laozi had told him that the kings and dukes were more powerful because they each had their own state, and throne, kept the troops and weapons, and upheld the laws and prisons all on their own. Confucius was not convinced, believing he himself was more powerful since he stood for morality and justice, which are invincible in the world. Now he realized that Laozi was correct. Despite the morality and justice he had embodied in the past, he was now the target of a statewide manhunt, a runaway to be chased down and killed.

Was he coming to the end of his life? He raised his head and asked heaven. If he died here it was a revelation about his life that he had no mission bestowed by heaven on him after all. If heaven had not granted him a mission, what was the significance of his life?

There were no stars and moon in the sky, not even a small shaft of light. Everywhere a hush reigned. The world seemed to return to the primeval ages, in which the conflicts and disputes, the hatred and love of mortals were treated with timeless apathy.

He had dedicated his life to advising dukes on the correct way to govern. But now he was unable to find his own way out of the wilderness.

Chapter 12　A Wise Man
(The Chronicles: Confucius at the Age of 28)

The archives of the king of Zhou was tranquil, where the bookshelves stood languidly, loaded with thick bundles of bamboo slips, quiet and motionless. The afternoon sunshine shown inside the room and cast a motley array of tree shadows on the ground, which were inching unwittingly and stealthily in their steps.

Laozi[1] sat behind the rows of tall bookshelves, reading with rapt attention some inscriptions on a tortoise shell of the Shang dynasty (1600 BC – 1046 BC). Due to his poor eyesight, he craned forward so much that his face almost touched the shell.

He had sat like that, motionless, for sixty years. He was only known as a historiographer[2], and no one knew his original name, nor did any one know when he had arrived there. In respect to the elderly and for convenience, people called him 'Laozi' and knew he would live there until his last day.

Laozi had dishelleved hair and an untidy beard like an uncivilized native. But he often bathed, the only refined habit that he had cultivated.

He had just finished his bath and donned the clean gar-

---

[1] Laozi, 老子, also translated as Lao-tzu, literally means Old Master, a reverent term of address for Li Er, the founder of Taoism.
[2] A "historiographer" was an official historian in ancient China.

ments for his guests.

Each day Laozi was confined to his room, which was filled with bundles of bamboo slips, long and short, and flame-smoked-and-blackened tortoise shells. He mulled over abstruse, unpractical issues. Other than his assistant Geng Sangchu, he did not see a soul, let alone a guest.

Today he would make an exception.

The visitors were two sons of Meng Xizi, a court minister of Lu. They were sent here by the duke of Lu to investigate the rites at Luoyi, the capital of the Zhou dynasty. All mortals loved the formality of etiquette and hollow rituals. Dukes indulged in these practices. Laozi felt helpless. But Meng Xizi was an old friend and had corresponded with him often in the past. Now when his sons, or nephews as Laozi looked on them, called upon him, it was hard to turn down the meeting. He also learned that their party included another man, a young man named Kong Qiu.

Outside of the archives room the thumping of steps was heard. Laozi smelled the dust in the room. His room had not been cleaned for years, sticking to his philosophy of reigning with no effort, as dust gathered everywhere naturally and evenly. Ordinarily there were no visitors to cause a stir. Now clouds of dust were sent up as the men entered the room.

His assistant Geng Sangchu led the visitors to greet him. Laozi wanted to stand, but his legs were weak and he could not. He had been sitting for years reading, and by now his leg muscles were useless, unable to support his heavy body and large head. He extended his greetings with a slightly raised body and then started to size up the three young men: two of them were dressed in gorgeous silken robes. They were the two sons of the court minister Meng Xizi, fine-featured and intelligent, with the look of a respectable family. The third one was tall and clad in the cloth garments, with a tall hat on his head and broad cuffs, having an old-fashioned, peculiar appearance. This was Kong Qiu.

Laozi cast a further glance at him, as the youth stood there, reserved but radiating through his body the slight, purple-colored aura of ambition. It was little wonder that that morning Laozi felt assailed by a purple breeze. He thought, by that time, it was due to the increase in ultraviolet rays of sunlight after the Spring Equinox.

"A *junzi* rides in the chariot when flushed with success but goes alone into the wilderness when thwarted in his career. You three young masters ride in ornamented chariots and appear high-spirited and vigorous. I believe you are all successful?" Laozi said in a loud voice, full of warmth and friendliness. He had a heavy Henan accent and, though with an indistinct pronunciation, uttered words with a rhythm of clear pause and transition.

The three young men all laughed, though a little shy.

The elder brother, Zhongsun Heji, spoke first, "We've been sent by the duke of Lu and come to the capital to observe the practice of the rites. It's our honor to meet with you, the great master, and to ask a few questions that we cannot solve."

Laozi said, "I'm not versed in the rites. I just read ancient books and have some knowledge. Since you young men have traveled thousands of *li*, I'd like to answer your questions."

Zhongsun Heji asked, "After the death of the emperor or the duke of a state, the successor should set up a place for the deceased in an ancestral shrine. After the funeral, at what time should the successor return to assume the throne?'

Laozi replied, "After he stops grieving."

The younger brother of the two then asked, "What should be done when people on the way of funeral see the solar eclipse?"

Laozi said, "Set the coffin on the right side of the road, stop weeping and wait for the sun to come through before continuing."

The elder brother raised another question, "Under what circumstances should the emperor not blame the dukes who fail to comply with the rites in meeting with the ruler?"

Laozi said, "There are four circumstances. First, if there is a fire at the shrine. Second, if there is a solar eclipse. Third, the death of one of the younger generation. And fourth, if their clothes are wet from rain.

...

The two brothers bombarded Laozi with one question after anther, who replied to them all, as Zhongni stood aside busy jotting down the answers.

The questioning ended and a solemn silence was restored in the room.

Suddenly Laozi said, "Why bother with the rites when there is the Great Way under heaven? The rites are the origin of chaos. When the Great Way is lost, morality comes into being. When morality is lost, benevolence rises. When benevolence is lost uprightness and the rites are born. At the moment the rites become a center of concern, the Great Way is lost and chaos is born."

These words shocked the three youths who, long saturated with the knowledge and profound scholarship of the rites of the Zhou dynasty, now gazed at each other, perplexed.

Having been silent the whole time, Zhongni jumped into the conversation, "May I ask what is the Great Way under heaven?"

"How could I, an old man, be qualified to talk about the Great Way? Probably only the learned men of today have the guts to talk about it. The Great Way can be elaborated, but at the same time it is not one in the conventional sense. It can be spoken but not understood in a traditional way. The Great Way is an element in existence but was born in a trance before the formation of heaven and earth. It is inexplicable. It is influential for its name but best manifests itself in letters ..."

As Laozi paused, Zhongni cut in, "The Great Way is abided by across the land under heaven. If it is not clearly defined, what is the right conduct of behavior?" Laozi smiled and said, "The Great Way produces one, one produces two, two produces three and three produces the ten thousand things of creation. The land will be united under heaven, giving rise to the Chu-Han War, Three Kingdoms ... Think and understand it. Think and understand it."[1]

The two young brothers were utterly lost at what Laozi was talking about. Zhongni too was baffled, grappling with the meaning, with knit brow, though he was challenged in understanding.

After mulling it over for a while Zhongni took another approach and set the ball rolling again, "The Great Way has been lost for a long time. Dukes are warring amongst themselves, states are in a shambles, rulers and officials are looking after their own interests, and the people's morale is sapped. What can be done to restore order to the land? I have read *The Book of Songs*, *The Book of History*, *The Book of Rites* and *The Book of Music*. But I have found no answer."

With a slight nod, Laozi spoke slowly, pointing to the shelves heavily loaded with bundles of bamboo slips, "What you said is truly bookish. Books offer accounts of the past and obsolete views. Words are spoken by people. If one is dead and his bones are rotten, his words are out of date. Footprints are left by shoes. If the soles are decayed, where can they make footprints? The concept specified in the book is only meaningful in the book. How could it be applicable in reality?"

"I would be greatly honored if you would enlighten me with your illuminating advice."

---

[1] The Chu-Han War, the Western Han dynasty (206 BC – 25 AD); Three Kingdoms (220 AD – 280 AD), Wei (220 AD – 265 AD), Shu Han (221 AD – 263 AD), and Wu (222 AD – 280 AD).

"The way of heaven is more deduction-oriented than production-oriented. In contrast, the way of humanity is more production-oriented than deduction-oriented. If the way of heaven prevails, order can be restored to the land under heaven."

"How can the dukes of states be convinced by these concepts?"

Smiling and opening his eyes slightly wider, Laozi looked at Zhongni with keen interest. He liked this young man standing in front of him, argumentative and stubborn, which was reminiscent of his own early character.

"Why do dukes want to listen to this kind of talk?"

"A man is reasonable. The duke is a man. Certainly he should listen to reason." Zhongni was intractable in response, "If an idea is correct, the duke should put it in application."

"The duke has his own ideas. He does not want to listen to you. He wants you to listen to him."

"Then that depends on who is correct!"

Laozi laughed, his shrunken mouth revealing no teeth inside, "The duke possesses the land, state power, military, weapons, laws, and prisons. He is more powerful than you, and so his words are more reasonable than yours. Besides, don't you all make a living by the state salary?"

Zhongni was dumbfounded for quite a while before responding, "It's just because of my salary that I'm responsible for expressing the way of heaven in front of the duke. Otherwise isn't the *junzi* failing in his duty to his country?"

Laozi shook his head and said, "I heard that a wealthy man gives his friends money and a wise man gives his friends words. I would like to give you some advice, though it may be presumptuous of me to take the honor of a wise man. Keep in mind: One who is intelligent but prone to gossip about others is not far from death; one who is eloquent but disparaging towards others is close to danger; one who is a son of someone

145

should not be concerned with his own interests; one who is an official of a duke should not have his own ideas."

At this time the sunlight disappeared and it became cloudy outside the windows. Laozi sat in darkness, his body clearly silhouetted with a dim outline of his face except for his eyes, which were glittering like the phosphorescent glowworms flying in the night.

"Should chaos be let to run its course like this under heaven?" Zhongni, still musing on the issue, murmured quietly as if he were at once questioning and talking to himself.

Obviously shifting his attention away, Laozi lowered his head and resumed his wading through the tortoise shell, completely covered with characters. It was too dark to read the text. However he never really depended on his eyesight in reading.

He mumbled, "Heaven takes a natural course and the Great Way originates in nature. It adheres to voidness and peace; it repeats itself and goes in circles. The Great Way specifies largeness; largeness goes to distance; distance returns to the origin …"

The visitors were leaving. Laozi wanted to rise but failed. He sat on a seat and slightly bent his back in salute. The three men stepped through the dust to the door. As they were about to exit, Laozi called for them to stop.

He looked at Zhongni and, opening his mouth and pointing to it, asked him, "Do I have teeth now?"

Zhongni shook his head.

Laozi pointed to his tongue and asked, "Do I have a tongue?"

"Yes, you have a tongue."

Laozi did not say any more. He raised his hands high and clasped them in the air as a farewell.

The youths were puzzled at Laozi's words, trying to figure out his riddle. They were at the door and thought it was improper to go back to inquire what he meant and then bade farewell with hands clasped.

Geng Sangchu sent them outside as Laozi, gazing at their receding figures, sighed, "What a respectable young man! His respectability stems from his simple-minded streak. The world needs a few simple-minded men and these people to do some deeds of simple-mindedness. Otherwise the world would be desolate and historical books would be empty of materials worth recording."

So saying, he was about to continue reading the tortoise shell. He found it very dark in the room and could not even see the shell. Outside it was completely dark. Before his assistant came back and lit the candles he could not do anything, and so he sat quietly in the darkness.

Chapter 13 Zheng
(Spring and Autumn Period: 2nd Year of Duke Ai of Lu's Reign, 493 BC)

Throughout the night, Confucius dashed through the wilderness, thinking all along that he was heading south. Initially he passed through a field of wheat, stumbling along, one leg up, one leg down, with mud on his feet. Next he passed through a field of sorghum, with each stalk whipping him in the face. During early autumn, the days were still warm but the nights were chilly, and his clothing, soaked through with dew, stuck to him, and each time the cool wind blew, it chilled him to the bone. He scrambled over gullies and ditches and after slipping into a small creek, sprained his ankle.

As dawn broke, finally Confucius could see a city beyond a moat in the distance. By now, he was thoroughly exhausted, thirsty, famished, and nearly unable to take another step. What he wanted more than anything was to go inside the city, find a place to rest, drink a bowl of hot water, and eat something. However, he had no idea where he was, what city, which moat, and was afraid that a warrant had been posted for his capture and arrest. So how would he ever dare enter the city gates? Alone, he paced back and forth just outside the city gate, griping and grumbling with hesitation.

Just as he was pacing back and forth, from behind him he heard someone shout: "Master, you're here! We've been looking everywhere for you!"

Startled, Confucius looked up only to be pleasantly surprised by the sight of none other than Zigong!

Standing in front of Zigong was Confucius, in the flesh, unscathed, safe and sound, leaving Zigong as relieved as he was surprised.

Originally what had happened was that when Confucius and his disciples fled in every which direction, it was every man for himself. Everyone fled south, leaving the state of Song behind. Later on Zigong, Zilu, and Yan Yuan all bumped into each other, and after taking a head-count and realizing that Confucius was gone, they panicked. At the time, Confucius rode on a carriage, and by all rights should have been at the front of the group, so how could he have disappeared? Had he been captured by Huan Tui? His disciples were worried and split up to look for him: Zilu went back the way from which they had come, and went up north; Yan Yuan headed east, Zigong went west, all vowing not to stop searching until they had located Confucius.

With his clothes and hat perfect as always, Zigong could barely stand the sight of Confucius, disheveled and unkempt, clothing in tatters, shoes torn apart, looking like a homeless vagrant, and said, "Hurry, let's enter the city."

Circumspect as ever, Confucius inquired, "Is it safe there?"

Zigong replied, "Definitely safe. This place is the capital of Zheng, Xin Zheng."

Confucius stood there, dumbfounded, as if in a trance, unable to make sense of it all, "I kept going south, and should have ended up in the state of Chen, so how on earth did I arrive in Zheng?"

Laughing, Zigong retorted, "It would appear that Master only knows the Great Way but doesn't know the smaller routes. After you walked and walked, maybe you ended up veering west, hard to say."

His disciples, scattered all over the place and searching for him, heard that he had safely turned up and they were all relieved and very happy, passed on the word, and immediately rushed to the capital of Zheng to be reunited with Confucius.

Everybody who saw Zigong asked him how he had managed to locate Confucius and he replied, "I asked everyone I saw along the way whether or not they had seen someone matching this description: A forehead like Yao, a neck like Shun[1]; shoulders even broader than Zichan[2], taller than Da Yu[3], with a waist and legs slightly short, as though they were missing three inches. But nobody said that they had seen anyone like this. Finally, when I had reached just outside the city walls of Zheng, I encountered a lumberjack that was just about to enter the city. He told me that he hadn't seen a great man matching this description but at the eastern gate there was a guy who kept pacing back and forth, with a look as if he had taken leave of his senses. He didn't look like a sage, but rather looked like a dog that had lost his home."

Confucius listened, but was not annoyed, rather he laughed. "Describing me as a sage, how did you ever expect to find me? Saying 'a dog who had lost his home' now that description is just accurate and vivid for me …" Sighing, he continued, "Even dogs love their homes, so how could people not love their country?" Confucius then thought of his homeland. If only Duke Ding of Lu hadn't been mesmerized by those dancing girls from Qi, how could he have ever bid farewell to the land of his parents? Moreover, there would be no need for him to flee alone through the wilds like a madman.

As everyone laughed, only one member of the group was cheerless, and looked deeply depressed. That person was Sima Niu. This time when Confucius was nearly killed in Song, the one who had tried to kill him was none other than Sima Niu's brother, Huan Tui, and as a result, he felt guilty, unable to face the others. Moreover, he had entered the city

---

[1] Yao and Shun are legendary model monarchs in ancient China.
[2] Zichan was a statesman of that time.
[3] Da Yu was founder of the Xia dynasty.

the previous day, and it was hard not to appear responsible for having leaked the details of Confucius' location.

Zixia, another disciple, noticed how dejected he was and asked him why.

Sima Niu stammered for a moment and said, "Everyone has brothers, and I'm the only one who doesn't."

Zixia knew that he was referring to Huan Tui and all he could say was:

"Across all four oceans, all men are brothers. How could *junzi* be without brothers?"

Sima Niu seemed inconsolable and angrily replied, "With brothers like this, I would have been better off being born an only child."

With this episode weighing heavily on him for a long time, Sima Niu soon took ill. First it was a persistent cough, then it was a high fever, and after three days, he was even throwing up and had diarrhea, and remained in a persistent vegetative state. His fellow disciples were concerned that he was contagious, and as a result, quarantined him in an adjoining chamber. Every day they took turns bringing him food. Actually, the first to be infected by this disease was Boniu, who died after only a few days of falling ill. Soon afterward a rumor spread that this disease was contagious, and now that Sima Niu was ill, the rumor was proven true and everyone was scared to death. Both Boniu and Sima Niu's name shared the character "*niu*" (cow) and so all the disciples secretly called this "Mad Cow Disease."

Confucius heard that Sima Niu was seriously ill and wanted to check up on him. His disciples cautioned him against it, afraid that he, too, would be infected. Adamant, Confucius wouldn't listen and insisted on going to visit him. After a lengthy debate, everyone reached the consensus that Confucius could only go as far as the window, but could not enter the room.

Confucius went to the west wing-room and even from far away he could smell a rotten odor. When he reached the wall and opened the window, he felt the heavy, fetid stench of sickness overwhelm him. The disciples who had accompanied him rushed to cover their mouths, but Confucius remained unruffled, not the least bit appearing nervous.

The room was dark, with Sima Niu covered with a cotton-padded quilt, laying on the *kang*[1] closest to the window. On the *kang* was an old mat with a bowl of porridge and clean water on one edge. Beside the *kang,* there was a bucket containing vomit and assorted excretions.

Sima Niu was sick and drawn out, both cheeks ruddy, almost to the extent that he no longer seemed human. From the depths of his coma, he somehow opened both his eyes and noticed that Confucius was standing outside of his window. At that sight, he became excited and struggled to sit up, but was too weak to do so. Reaching in through the window, Confucius took hold of his scalding hands.

Sima Niu spoke first, "Master, I'm about to die."

Confucius replied, "Life and death are a matter of destiny, stop thinking wild, senseless thoughts."

Sima Niu had a violent coughing fit and asked, "Master, are you afraid of dying?"

Confucius retorted, "A *junzi* neither worries nor fears."

Sima Niu asked again, "How is it possible to neither worry nor fear?"

Confucius answered, "If you don't feel ashamed or guilty when you are reflecting on yourself, and then you are able to neither worry nor fear."

Sima Niu closed his eyes and listened, his lips trembling, straining to speak several times before finally saying, "Master, even though Huan Tui is my brother, I really didn't say a thing about our whereabouts when I entered the city. Do you believe me?"

Confucius grasped Sima Niu's hands even tighter and said, "I believe you."

---

[1] *kang* are heated sleeping platforms used in northern China.

Hearing those words, Sima Niu burst into tears, with his face showing a sign of comfort, then after panting for a while, said, "Now I neither need to worry nor fear."

After the day of Confucius' visit, Sima Niu felt relieved and gradually recovered from his sickness, although now it was Confucius who felt sickness in his heart, as he tried to figure out who had betrayed him. If it wasn't Sima Niu who had leaked news of their whereabouts, then who had? The day that Huan Tui had pursued them, the only other two disciples who had entered the city were Gongbo Liao and Gao Chai, only them. Gongbo Liao was a skinny man with a long face and one eye that was slightly cross-eyed, someone whose true intentions were difficult to fathom, but Gongbo Liao was a compatriot from the state of Lu, also someone who had no real beef with Huan Tui and by all rights should have had no reason to sell him out. Gao Chai was unsightly, a severe looking man, short and squat with deep furrows on his face, and even though he had all the looks of a foe, was actually someone who always had the desire to reach a higher level of human morality, having lofty aspirations. So who had it been? At the moment, Confucius did not want to think about it too much, and for now, could only put it to the back of his mind.

Before long, Confucius also fell ill. After that night of running through the dew and catching cold, his resistance was low, and after having close contact with Sima Niu he, too, became infected. Even though he was every bit a *junzi*, prim and proper, righteous and upstanding, all that was not enough to keep him immune from illness, and soon he too was sick in bed, with a high fever and relentless cough, vomiting and diarrhea, even slipping into an intermittent coma, critically ill.

His disciples surrounded Confucius on his sick bed.

"Master, please pray, appeal to the gods and spirits to save you!" cried Zilu.

"Is that useful?" Confucius weakly replied. "You know me, all along I have advocated respecting spirits and gods but keeping distance from them."

"People believe in this, just as a saying in 'Words of Prayer': 'Pray to the gods and spirits in heaven and under the earth for help.' When you're this sick, that is all you can do," Zilu said.

Confucius replied, "As wealth and rank are decreed by heaven, so life and death are preordained by fate. All I believe in is heavenly fate, and I've prayed in my mind for a long, long time."

After he had uttered these syllables, he once again fell into a deep coma.

Around the clock, his disciples kept watch, eagerly taking turns feeding him soup and giving him medicine, with all wishing that there was more that they could do to help. However, before long, each and every one of them also fell ill with the same exact symptoms. In the end, since he had fully recovered and was immune to the disease, Sima Niu was the only one who was able to take care of everyone, cooking, cleaning, and emptying bedpans.

After being unconscious for ten days, Confucius finally awoke and opened his eyes. Neither Zilu, nor Yan Yuan and Zigong were standing before him and all around the room, there was not a single other disciple. Panting, Sima Niu ran into the room carrying a porcelain receptacle, thinking that Confucius had to throw up again. When he asked where everyone was, Confucius was told that all of the disciples had fallen ill, and he gloomily closed his eyes. When they had left Lu, there had been over a hundred disciples, and when they had left Wei, there were fifty left. Still others went their own way, and now that there only remained just over ten disciples, nearly all of them sick in bed. Thinking about that year in Qufu when they had built a pedestal for him to lecture on, there were throngs of disciples, and his courtyard resembled a bustling market—what a sight that had been! Now, all of a sudden, thirty years later, everyone was sick, dejected, and morale was low. When he considered their options, Confucius knew that there was only one: To remain in Zheng. For the time being, he knew that their trip to Chen would be far, far off in the dim and distant future.

Chapter 14 Disciples
(The Chronicles: Confucius at the Age of 30)

The young Zhongsun Yue rushed over to the Ginko Pedestal to hear Zhongni lecture, arriving late. The courtyard was packed with people, some sitting, some standing, some squatting, with others even perched atop the courtyard wall, with still others on top of the roof. Zhongsun Yue had a hard time squeezing past the throngs to get into the courtyard. He wore a silk brocade robe that soon was covered with dust, and even though he was unable to brush all of the dust away, his elegant outfit stood out amongst all of the crude, simple clothing of Zhongni's audience. At this time, sitting high upon the Apricot Altar was Zhongni, and he had already started his lecture.

This so-called "Apricot Altar" was a mound in Zhongni's own courtyard. Soil had been heaped into a mound and leveled off, and topped with a large, circular stone. Growing next to the mound was a recently planted ginko tree with long, young branches and sparse foliage, and the new growth was just turning green. Because the altar was located at the base of the ginko tree and ginko shares the same name of apricot in Chinese, so it was soon called the "Apricot Altar" instead of the "Ginko Pedestal."

Zhongni's erudition was known among stable hands, cooks, gatekeepers, storehouse guards of the Ji Mansion.

Originally his reputation arose by word-of-mouth accounts of his character. Everyone had heard that he was teaching classes in his courtyard and, thinking that it was a literacy class, teaching people to read, people rushed to register, afraid that they would miss out. The first group of students was comprised of acquaintances that Zhongni had met at his various odd jobs at the Ji Mansion; Yan Wuyao, a carriage driver, a cook named Zeng Dian, a door guard named Min Sun, a janitor named Ran Geng, a guy in charge of guarding the storehouse named Qin Zhang, and even a homeless, wild child that he took in off the streets named Zilu. All of these men took Zhongni to be their venerable teacher. Because all of these were his friends, Zhongni did not ask them to pay, but rather asked that they all contribute whatever they could, a bit of rice, noodles, and that was what constituted their tuition. By all rights, the proper tuition was what was known as "*shu xiu*" or a bona fide piece of dried meat or jerky.

Of those who came to attend class, the only one who came from an aristocratic background was Zhongsun Yue. After his father Meng Xizi passed away, his brother Zhongsun Heji seized the fiefdom, and he moved out, taking up residence in the Southern Palace, eventually taking "Southern Palace" to be his name, with everyone calling him "Uncle." As people thought that "Uncle" would not be deferential enough, the word "Venerable" was added. Then his name became "Venerable Uncle of the Southern Palace" (Nangong Jingshu) even though he was only just over 20 years old at the time.

That year, on their return from the Zhou capital of Luoyi where they went to inquire about the rites, he and his brother debated the last puzzle that Laozi said about the teeth and tongue.

Brother Zhongsun Heji reckoned that Laozi meant that once the lips were lost, the teeth would feel cold, and when the teeth fell out, the tongue would feel cold. With no lips, teeth get cold, and with no teeth, the tongue would be even colder.

He did not agree and said that the Great Teacher did not mention the lips at all.

His brother said, even though he did not mention the lips, you could deduce it; there is logic therein. If that was not the meaning, then what did he mean?

He said that it meant that "misfortune emanates from the mouth." Although the teeth are hard, they can not control the tongue; without teeth, the tongue would provoke calamity and invite disaster.

Zhongni remained transfixed, as though in a trance, speechless, at which point he subconsciously uttered a phrase, "If the teeth aren't effective, then one has to rely on the tongue."

"Are you referring to eating meat?" Both brothers asked simultaneously, not understanding what he was talking about.

Zhongni shook his head, saying, "No, I'm not talking about eating meat, I'm talking about the Great Way. The Way of heaven, although *junzi* believes, who else believes in it? If dukes and warlords are about to attack, they rely on soldiers and horses, and on knives and swords. A *junzi* follows the Way, and the Way is a battle of tongues, based on righteousness and virtue, on the three-inch long tongue. Teeth, these are the hardest things in the world; and tongues, they are the softest of things in the world. The Great Teacher's meaning was that the softest things in the world ultimately prevail over the hardest things in the world, when the teeth fall out and the tongue ..." As he kept speaking, Zhongni seemed to think of something, as if in a *satori*-like flash of enlightenment, exclaimed, "I got it! I got it!"

"What do you get?"

"The movement of the Great Way begins under one's

tongue!"[1] Zhongni proclaimed.

After returning to the capital town of Lu, Zhongni quit his job at the Ji Mansion and started offering altar lectures to students and teaching his disciples.

One day he taught in class the character "仁 benevolence."

Zhongni said that "仁 benevolence" meant two (二) persons (人), a relationship among people. For the parents, it meant filial piety; for the brother, it meant fraternal love and duty; for husband and wife, it meant love; for children, it meant kindness; for the monarch, it meant loyalty; for friends, it meant trust; for others, it meant honesty. In the final analysis the basic guideline of "benevolence" was composed of two characters, "loyalty" and "forgiveness." "Loyalty" stood for exerting oneself to the full and whole-heartedly; "forgiveness" pointed to the treatment of others, in which "one did not impose on others what one himself did not desire." How could one be able to achieve "benevolence?" Actually it was simple, that is, "restraining oneself and restoring the rites." Internally one restrained desire, and externally one behaved in compliance with the rites; in other words one did not do anything that violated the rites.

All the truth under heaven, synthesized by Zhongni, had become neatly organized, flawlessly relevant and meticulously spelled out. It suddenly dawned on the audiences that filled the courtyard to capacity, making them feel enlightened and immediately closer to becoming a *junzi*; even the chicken and ducks outside the courtyard kept nodding and became so tame that they did not utter cries any more. The ginko tree, before one knew it, started to germinate leaves and fruits all over its branches, flamboyant and exuberant in a blaze of color.

---

[1] Humorous allusion to Laozi's "The journey of ten thousand miles begins under one's feet."

Once started, Zhongni's lecture ran a few years on end. Since it covered a wide range of topics and captured the cream of truth over heaven and earth, crowds of listeners kept coming, filling the courtyard and spilling out of it onto the street and were eventually divided into major classes and minor ones. Audiences were all listening with rapt attention, intoxicated and stupefied as if possessed by evil spirits.

When the lecture was over Zhongni took his disciples to see the Imperial Ancestral Temple and taught them the knowledge of those sacrificial vessels such as the *ding, fu, gui, li, zu, dou, fu, zhong*, as well as large cauldrons, bowls, gourd ladles and basins.[1] At that time Yan Yuan was only five years old. When seeing a hollow vessel hanging in the air, he thought it was a toy and was glued to it. Zhongni quickly took advantage of this little student's interest and taught him according to his aptitude by saying, "This is a tilted vessel. When void it is inclined. When appropriately filled, it hangs straight. When brimming, it capsizes. It exactly embodies the truth of conducting oneself in society." Still young, Yan Yuan looked puzzled with this murky idea. However, many years later when he grew up, he maintained a deportment of modesty and prudence, probably partially because of this inculcation that he received in his early years.

Zhongni also hiked up to the top of Mount Tai with his disciples, taking a bird's eye view over the vast landscape and experiencing a feeling of great aspiration. One day on their way downhill from a mountaineering trip, they saw a woman weeping beside a grave and grief-stricken. Zilu went up and tried to console her. She told her story that her father-in-law, husband and son were all eaten by a tiger from the mountain and how she could restrain her grief. Zhongni heard her story

---

[1] *Ding*, a cooking vessel with two loop handles and three or four legs; *fu*, a square grain receptacle used at sacrificial ceremonies in ancient times. *gui*, a round-mouthed food vessel with two or four loop handles; *li*, a cooking tripod with hollow legs; *zu*, a sacrificial vessel; *dou*, a stemmed bowl; *fu*, a cauldron; *zhong*, a handless cup.

and asked her with concern why she did not leave and go down the mountain. Wiping her tears off, the woman said the mountain was free of tyranny! At her words, Zhongni heaved a long sigh and turned around, saying to his disciples, "Keep it in mind that tyranny is fiercer than a tiger." Immediately after saying this, he added another sentence, for fear of being misunderstood, "I meant the tiger, not Yang Hu."[1]

Zhongni continued to lecture. With the passing of time he became mature and experienced, putting on a complete look of teacher. His disciples started addressing him as "master" instead of calling him "Zhongni" disrespectfully.

One day Zhongni ambled to the south outskirts of the town and crossed the Yi River. Watching the raging torrent of water flowing east, he was suddenly seized by a shaft of sorrow, feeling that time flew like an arrow. He murmured, "Time passes quickly as the flow of water regardless of the day and night!" Thinking that the years had flashed by and he was more than thirty and had not been able to put his learning into use, he could not help but feel sorrowful and sentimental for himself.

That afternoon, after he finished the two lectures of moral integrity and political affairs, he was fatigued. Though he had been teaching with tireless zeal, he did not go on to lecture on spoken language and literature this time. Thus he dismissed the class instead.

At that instant Zhongsun Yue came in. He planned to take a leave of absence and go to Qi along with his brother, so he was here to ask the master for permission.

It was last spring, with a breeze and a few clouds drifting in a clear, balmy sky. The master was sitting on the Apricot Alter, chatting with a few disciples who stayed at home.

Zhongni said, "I'm a few years your senior and your

---

[1] The pronunciation of the two characters, "tiger" and "Hu," makes a pun in Chinese.

teacher as well. Now the class is over. Let's talk. Tell me your aspirations. Make yourself at home and feel free to talk about whatever in your mind. In the past you have often grumbled that you are not known to the world for your talents. It is true that a *junzi* should not be irritated if his talents are not acknowledged. But if one day a king or duke wanted to employ you at high levels, what would you like to achieve?"

Hearing the master's question, Zilu rushed to answer by saying, "If I were given a one-thousand-chariot state[1], even at a time of facing the threat of invasion from abroad and being wrecked by a starvation at home, it would take me three years to make every citizen a soldier and both intelligent and courageous."

With a smile Zhongni said, "You are only interested in brandishing arms and fighting." Then he turned around to Ran Qiu, asking, "Qiu, what would you do?"

Ran Qiu hesitated before replying sedately, "If I were given a region with a circumference of sixty to seventy *li*, it would take me three years to complete the task of making its people have enough food and clothing. With respect to restoring the rites and music, presumably that mission would not be able to be accomplished until a *junzi* arrives."

Zhongni nodded and said, "Qiu, it is a worthy aspiration. But it is a shame that it is not ambitious!" Then he asked Gongxi Hua sitting beside him, "What is your idea?"

Gongxi Hua was a boy from a wealthy family and it had not been long since he was admitted into the school as a disciple. He was a refined and cultivated person. Now confronted with the master's question, he blushed before uttering words. He reflected and then said modestly, "I'm not sure of what I will be able to do in the future. But my only goal is

---

[1] In ancient China the soldiers riding on one chariot are enlisted from eight hundred households; if one household has five family members on average, a one-thousand-chariot state is a large country with a population of 4 millions.

to learn as much as possible. If there were opportunities for attending a sacrificial ceremony at an ancestral shrine or a summit of state heads, I would don the dark regalia, wear the 'zhangpu' hat[1] and be able to work successfully as the master of the ceremony."

As the conversation went on, a tune drifted over. It turned out that Zeng Dian was playing a *se*.[2] He had cooked dinner in the kitchen year in and year out, wielding the cleaver and ladle, stir-frying food and cooking rice over a slow fire. Now putting his hands on the *se*, he also executed a rhythmic and sonorous tune at a distinct tempo as if he rained chops on the meat and breezed through cutting vegetables.

Over here Zhongni called out to him, "Dian, what is in your mind?"

Hearing he was called, Zeng Dian did not stop playing instantly. He continued to play until he finished the melody. As the music died away to the last clang, he said in a loud voice toward the master, "I may have a different idea from those of the three."

"It doesn't matter. Say whatever is in your mind. Come on," Zhongni urged.

Zeng Dian explained, "On a day of late spring like this I would put on the spring clothing and go out with five or six friends, bringing a group of six or seven boy servants along with us. We should go swimming in the River Yi, enjoy spring breezes on the Rain Altar and then sing songs on our way back home."

The listeners all fell in silence, and for a long while they were lost in that thought.

Finally, Zhongni slightly nodded and said with a long sigh, "I have the same desire as Dian!"

---

[1] The "zhangpu" hat, a hat worn on an official ceremony in ancient times.
[2] *se*, a zither-like twenty-five stringed plucked instrument.

162

Zhongsun Yue had been listening quietly on the side. By now the master's words stirred his thoughts and filled him with an imagination. He seemed as if he were watching the grandiose scene of King of Zhou and boundless atmosphere of Yao and Shun.[1] He felt like saying something before shouts of killing sprang up all of a sudden from the distance. The earth was quivering as if thousands of people were marching. They were all frightened. Zhongsun Yue was about to send someone out to take a look as he saw his brother, Zhongsun Heji, storm in from outside, hasty and agitated, along with a couple of family guards, long swords in hand. Once inside, Zhongsun Heji shouted, "Bad news. Duke Zhao of Lu has revolted. He is leading troops in besieging the Ji Mansion. Ji Pingzi has asked the clan Mengsun and clan Shusun to join forces with him and bring their household guards over in fighting against Duke Zhao. The outcome of the battle is unforeseeable. The state of Lu will be unmistakably turned into chaos. Go and find a place to hide yourself now, everyone!"

Zhongsun Yue asked worriedly, "What is happening? Haven't the duke and his subjects been on good terms?"

Stamping his foot, his brother Zhongsun Heji replied, "It is only due to some trifles of cock and dog. Ji Pingzi played cock-fighting with the court minister Hou Zhaobo. Ji Pingzi had his cock's claws wear the horny gold covers. Hou Zhaobo had his cock equipped with the iron wings. In the end Ji Pingzi's cock lost the game, and then he unleashed his dog and let it bite Hou Zhaobo's cock. When Hou Zhaobo's cock was craning its neck and crowing, Ji Pingzi's dog unexpectedly broke its neck with only one bite. Its head narrowly missed falling to the ground. A horrible sight to look at! Hou Zhaobo was a man of ill repute and certainly not one to be taken advantage of and bullied. He went to the Duke of

---

[1] Yao and Shun are two legendary sage monarchs in ancient China.

Lu and made a complaint that he was a subject of the duke and his cock was definitely a property of the duke too. Duke Zhao had been nursing anger and resentment and wanting in dreams to kill Ji Pingzi. Now in agitation he became so arrogant that he overrated himself and led his troops in laying siege to the Ji Mansion. But that's another story. Let's get out of here quickly!"

The crowds of people who had been loafing around the gate of the courtyard and sitting atop a wall, watching fun, heard these words and broke up at once in a hubbub. In a blink of eye they all disappeared. Zhongni had been sitting on the high Apricot Altar and could not descend it. He was flustered. Luckily, a few disciples had not fled and deserved their teacher. They held his arms and helped him get down.

Both the master and his disciples stood dumb, staring at each other and desperate for a step to take next. Evidently Zhongsun Yue was quick to remind everyone by saying, "Let's go into hiding too!" Hearing his words, the master and disciples dispersed for their own homes.

Unexpectedly the turmoil of Lu lasted for seven to eight years. Duke Zhao of Lu was routed and fled to the state of Qi. Away from his state, the duke was in name only. Unable to return home except going around in exile, he was now an expatriate. Duke Zhao lived in the region of Qianhou of Qi and stayed there for seven years on end. Until his last breath he could not stomach his resentment.

Later, fearing for the master's safety, Zhongsun Yue persuade him to leave Lu with him and take refuge in Qi.

Chapter 15 Jin
(Spring and Autumn Period: 3rd Year of Duke Ai of Lu's Reign, 492 BC)

Confucius and his men stayed in Xinzheng for a few months. It was autumn again before they recovered. Then word came that Duke Ling of Wei had just died. Confucius sighed repeatedly. He did not inquire of the situation in the city of Diqiu. He was busy getting ready to go south and continue on to the state of Chen. Then, with the sudden outbreak of another war among the dukes of the neighboring states, the road to Chen by Zheng was totally cut off.

Hostilities first started with civil strife in the state of Jin, when court ministers Fan and Zhonghang rose in rebellion in Handan and attacked Zhao Yang, the long-time prime minister of the state. Leaders in the states of Qi and Wei were glad of their chances to take advantage of the situation. They immediately joined forces, invaded Jin and, at the same time, dragged the state of Zheng into the war by requesting its troops as backup.

Soon large numbers lost their homes and became refugees wandering about the lands and pouring from the northwest to the southeast. The fleeing throngs crowded roads. People supported the old and led the young, carrying bedrolls on their backs and bags on shoulder poles. The wide road leading to Chen was packed like sardines at the exit of a railway station, shoulders rubbing shoulders and toes kicking heels, hopeless signs of moving a half step further. In Chen the border passes were shut and security was tightened as passage was absolutely forbidden in an attempt to prevent the war from spreading to the state.

Confucius was anxious. It was impossible to go to Chen, but he could not stay in Zheng nor could he return to Lu, or Wei. He did not want to travel through Cao and Song and was afraid of venturing into Kuang and Pu. He felt like he had reached a dead end.

His only way out was making a risky journey west to Jin and meeting with the prime minister Zhao Yang. By coincidence, a messenger sent by Zhao Yang arrived and invited Confucius to Jin and contribute to the reign of the duke.

This was heartening news to Confucius who saw his opportunity for going into politics rise once again. He urged his disciples to get ready for the journey and started studying the terrain, roads and traffic of Jin. This, in fact, was not the first time that he had the idea of going west to Jin. The year he stayed idly in Wei he considered meeting with Zhao Yang in Jin and even got as far as the bank of the Yellow River before turning back.

Zhao Yang, the long-time prime minister of Jin, was described as a one-word-weighing-nine-*ding* person.[1] A few years earlier, he even had a "*ding* of punishment" cast with his decrees and writings carved on it in the capital to enforce the implementation of his orders. The duke of Jin had no heir so power fell into the hands of the clans of Zhao, Zhonghang, Fan, Han, Wei and Zhi, the six influential court ministers who ruled the state by turns. When it was Zhao Yang's turn to rule, his family held the other clans in sway and took control of all state positions, the military, politics and even the sources of revenue. In response, the Zhonghang and Fan rose in rebellion, leading to warfare.

Confucius' intention to travel west to Jin dismayed Zilu. Zhao Yang

---

[1] "one-word-weighing-nine-*ding* person," the original Chinese text meaning "a weighty person"; a *ding* is an ancient bronze cooking vessel with two loop handles and three or four legs, in the original Chinese text.

was neither a sagacious ruler nor was he a virtuous official. To Zilu, it simply made no sense that Confucius wanted to go and join him.

In the past few months, Confucius' followers continued to serve him meals and medicines as well as study so that they would be prepared to graduate. They often sat together under the vegetable trellis in the yard and discussed the fundamental ideas of managing state affairs and cultivating one's character. Gourds hung overhead, while bush beans and other vegetables grew underfoot, attesting to Fan Chi's successful farming and gardening of what had been a wasteland.

In that period Fan Chi had once asked the master about growing crops. Confucius replied indifferently, contrary to his usual tireless responses as a teacher, "I'm not as good as the old farmer." Fan Chi, not noticing the master's apathy asked another question on growing vegetables. Again Confucius said, "I'm not as good as the old gardener" and then fell into silence. Fan Chi felt snubbed and walked off with his hoe on his shoulder.

After Fan Chi left, Confucius vented his discontent to other students, "This Fan Chi, how could he be satisfied with being a small man? A *junzi* espouses rites, righteousness and good faith. When rites, righteousness and good faith prevail, the land under heaven is affluent. How could a *junzi* need to grow vegetables on his own?" However, Fan Chi tended his vegetable garden carefully and applied manure on time, and when it was autumn the gourds were large, the bush beans were long and other vegetables were fresh and juicy. Each day he would pick ripe vegetables from his plot and add the new food to the menu. Everyone was delighted, and Confucius relished the meals too. This matter was dropped.

One day the disciples gathered under the wooden framework of gourds and conversed on their prospects for political careers. The issue was brought up by Zixia, Zizhang and Ziyou, three of the master's brightest students. Zixia excelled in literature, Zizhang had strong reasoning power and Ziyou was proud of his writing and rhetoric skills. All less than twenty years old, they never failed to plunge into heated debate whenever they met. The topic on which they argued that day was whether a *junzi* should engage in affairs of state.

To Zixia, a *junzi* should to go into politics. He questioned the use of learning if a talented student did not take office and hold government positions. This opinion stemmed from his being a straight A student. He studied hard and persisted when he did not understand something until he figured out the answer.

When he was reading *The Book of Songs* he encountered a line, "She has charming smiles showing her two dimples; she bestows two amorous glances on me; she looks with a lightly made-up face rather than wears the heavy cosmetics."[1] He understood "She smiles charmingly with two dimples; she bestows two amorous glances on me." Though he had never been in love, he saw and appreciated the beauty of a young lady. However, Zixia could not understand the rest of the line— "she looks with a lightly made-up face rather than wears the heavy cosmetics." Did it mean that a girl appeared young and attractive even though she wore no makeup?

Zixia asked Confucius even though the master had never been in love either. He distractedly looked at the line describing the noted beauty, Zhuang Jiang, of Wei years earlier and said with a sigh, "Apply it and then look straight!" These words confounded Zixia. He wracked his brains all day and night until the crack of the dawn and the crow of cocks.

What the master said was that a young lady needed a little of make-up, first brushing the face with face powder as background and then drawing the eyebrows. Only on delicate white skin could "charming smiles" and "amorous glances" be "painted." Zixia pondered this until he

---

[1] The line is taken from "A Beauty," the third poem of Odes of Wei, *The Book of Songs*, dedicated to Zhuang Jiang, daughter of Duke Zhuang of Qi and wife of Duke Zhuang of Wei.

recognized that one indeed cannot appear respectable without dressing up, just as one cannot lead a respectable life without learning the rites.

The following day the first sentence he uttered to the master was an impetuous, confusing question, "What else thereafter with the rites?" Surprised, the master gazed at his student in delight for quite a while before exclaiming in admiration, "My inspiration can only stem from Zixia!"

In comparison, Zizhang tended to take things to extremes. He was absolutely opposed to *junzi* taking office. In the past, he sold horses and knew how to judge a horse's value by looking at its appearance. Extending the meaning from horses to humans, he also understood the official conduct of currying favor with superiors.[1] To him a *junzi* should keep away from politics. Once he assumed a government position, he was like a horse entering a country fair of horses being led around. In his desire to be favored by his superior he tended to lose his moral character and failed to uphold virtue and good faith.

Ziyou had yet a different opinion. Younger and more arrogant, he believed it was incorrect to take a general perspective on the issue. Specific circumstances mattered. It was incorrect to conclude that no *junzi* should go into politics. It all depended on which *junzi* took a court position. For example, Zixia and Zizhang were not fit for government. Zixia was benevolent but incompetent, only suitable for tasks like serving wine and receiving guests. Zizhang was competent but lacked benevolence. He was unable to bring welfare to the masses of a country. Only he, Ziyou himself, was a gifted enough man to be an official. But it also mattered what kind of position he was to assume. He would not take any post lower than the three major ministers. He wanted the position of prime minister.

The three young men debated hotly on the issue with no consensus.

---

[1] A pun in Chinese, *ma*, with *xiangma*, knowing the horse, and *paima*, licking one's boots.

Then they went to Confucius for a ruling. The master listened and then said with a smile, "Zizhang is going too far. Zixia is not going far enough. Going too far is as bad as not going far enough. They are both disqualified for office."

Confucius meant that Zizhang was disposed to go to extremes, and Zixia was a bit slow and dull. Going to extremes and being slow and dull were the same in reality and not good qualities for a political career. He then turned to Ziyou and said, "You're quite appropriate for a state seat. But you're too talented to find a proper post. Why does one use an ox cleaver to kill a chicken?" His words made them all laugh.

The master continued, "Generally speaking a *junzi* should take office. A *junzi* who is educated but refuses to pursue his career in politics is just like this," pointing to the gourd hanging overhead. "It can only hang there for show. You can't pluck it and eat it. What a waste!" The disciples all nodded their agreement.

Zilu, standing by the side, could not help himself. He asked, "Should a *junzi* choose a place to go into politics? The master once said going to no state of chaos. Now the state of Jin is in civil strife. Why does the master want to travel west to Jin?" Confucius, aware of innuendos, answered, "I did say something like that. But masses are longing for the rule of benevolence. States hope for the rites and music. I have engaged in pressing on with the goal of making the Great Way prevail over the land under heaven and would go into the region and have a try even if it is treacherous."

Seizing the chance Zilu continued, "The master also said once that a *junzi* does not make friends with a depraved person. Zhao Yang of Jin monopolizes power, domineers over subjects, and bullies others. How could he embrace the government of benevolence and rule of morality, resurrect music and restore the rites? This kind of person like him, even if he did not inflict harm on the master, your reputation would still be tarnished."

Confucius said, "I'm a *junzi*. What fear do I have? A saying goes like this, 'The hard withstand wear without being damaged. The white defy dying without being blackened.' Besides, I have morality and justice on my side. What could Zhao Yang do to me? The Great Way is like the sun and moon in the sky and their light is visible to all. As long as I keep talking to him about ideas I will not be worried about his refusal to listen."

Zilu would not give up, but Yan Yuan, who had been taking notes, feared he would contradict the master so he stopped Zilu by plucking his sleeve.

Now Zigong opened his mouth and spoke slowly, "Master, we just can't go to Jin."

"Why?" Confucius asked.

Zigong said, "Master, do you still remember Dou Mingdu and Shun Hua?"

Dumbstruck, Confucius looked depressed and said, "Yes, certainly I do." Dou Mingdu and Shun Hua had been two well-known court ministers of Jin with integrity, and both were killed by Zhao Yang the year Confucius traveled west, with his disciples, to the Yellow River in hopes of going to Jin. Before crossing the river he learned of their execution and decided to turn back immediately. At that time, he even vowed at the river bank, "I'll never cross this river in my life!"

"Master, aren't you afraid Zhao Yang would do the same to you as he did with Dou Mingdu and Shun Hua?" Zigong repeated. Before he came to power Zhao Yang was assisted by Dou Mingdu and Shun Hua. After he succeeded in achieving his ambitions they were two of the first Zhao Yang had killed.

Confucius sighed and said, "Seeing the belly of a goat ripped open and the fetus taken away, the unicorn would flee the spot. Watching the pond being drained and the fish captured, the dragon would leave the water. Spotting the nest overturned and eggs broken, the phoenix would soar to the sky. If birds and beasts see dangers, they would try to go out of harm's way. So would humans. A *junzi* laments the death of those of his kind. How could I ignore that? However, I don't have many years to live that heaven has granted me. The gourd cannot just grow and hang without becoming the food to be eaten. A *junzi* cannot just read and learn without putting book learning into application. As long as some one would like to employ me and give me one year or at most three years, I will be able to run the state well, make the society prosperous and restore order on the land under heaven. Then I would ignore my personal safety and reputation."

Hearing this Zigong paused, at a loss of words, before saying, "You should not go to Jin anyway."

"Why, again?' Confucius asked.

Zigong said, "If you go to Jin and meet with Zhao Yang I'm afraid that you won't be able to return to Wei, nor to see Madam Nanzi again."

Confucius, astonished, asked, "What do you mean by this?"

Zigong said, "Wei is the primary source of Jin's civil strife. After Duke Ling of Wei died, Mme. Nanzi placed the duke's grandson Ji Zhe on the throne instead of Prince Kuai Kui who went to Jin. Now Kuai Kui is the leader of Jin's invasion forces. Having nursed his grievances in Jin, he wants to take back the throne with the assistance of Jin's Zhao Yang. Some time ago he tried to take advantage of the Wei's large-scale involvement in a state funeral by sending a group of Jin's soldiers disguised in mourning apparel to sneak into the country. They planned to kill Mme. Nanzi and oust the new duke ..."

"Was the madam all right?" Confucius asked anxiously.

"Yes, she was alright. Kuai Kui's plot was seen through and the disguised party was captured at Qiyi. But a long-term feud started between Wei and Jin."

Confucius was silent, lost in thought for a while, before saying, "The Great Way runs in the course designed by heaven. If it does not go to Qi, Lu, nor does it go to Wei, Cao, Song and Zheng, how could one know it does not go to Jin either? If it does not go to Jin, then it must be in Chen or in Chu ... Over the vast land under heaven shouldn't it go somewhere? Otherwise what is the will of heaven? If it were in Jin and I did not go there and have a try, how could I reconcile myself to the thought of the result in the future? A *junzi* sticks to the Great Way and considers other things as peripheral. I can't hang overhead here for long or I will become an old gourd!"

With these words Zigong knew the master had made up his mind and would not listen any more so he let the matter drop.

A few days later Confucius and his disciples got up as the cocks crowed in the morning, hastily washed before setting off. They pressed on in the lingering rain of autumn with its muddy roads, first to the west and then to the northwest. Before dusk they arrived at Zhongmou, a city on the east bank of the Yellow River. A strategic military landing location, the city was part of Jin's territory. It overlooked the Yellow River from its east side and bordered the states of Wei and Zheng.

Since the soaked men were worn out with fatigue and hunger, they chose to stay in town for the night before crossing the river the next morning. It was a rainy night, pitch-black with no moon and stars in the skies. The master and disciples lit torches, which flashed and sparkled in the night fog and mist along the winding road. Their torches emitted black smoke that curled into a cloud of fog which drifted and then dispersed in the air. When they reached town and went through the long dark gateway, startled bats flew out, with frightful twitters.

Confucius bade his disciples to be silent so as not to disturb the residents at their late hour of arrival, so the men covered their mouths with their hands, smothering their discontent. Strangely the town gate was wide open but there was no sentry. Only a bald eagle, which, with a croak, flapped its wings and flew away, greeted the shocked travelers.

The town was quiet, its streets deserted and doors wide open, a sign of the law and order that prevailed. Confucius was perplexed by the quiet. All of a sudden, his chariot jolted and caught on something. The shaft horse pulled several times, but the chariot did not budge. Gongliang Ru, who drove the chariot, leaped off and shouted with alarm. Under the wheels was the dead body of an old man with gray hair and beard, his face smudged with blood and dirt and his head almost severed from the body except for a strand of skin on the neck. One of his arms was tangled in the hub and spokes of the chariot. Suddenly a disciple riding on the next chariot cried out in horror. The other disciples rushed over with lit torches and saw the gruesome carnage. The household doors all stood wide open, and the ground was littered everywhere with the bodies of women and children. Bodies lay soaked in the rain, the ground flowing with bloody water. On the street several heads hung from the branches of trees, long hair floating in the air, unseeing eyes half open. The heads were of men.

At that moment Zilu returned from his scouting and in a fluster reported that earlier in the day the town had been captured and all its residents massacred, the young able-bodied men as well as women, children and the elderly. No one was spared, even the chicken and dogs. The town was deserted.

It turned out that the town's magistrate, Fo Xi, was a domestic subject of Fan, a court minister of Jin. When his formal host rose in rebellion against Zhao Yang, he decided to show his support at his town of Zhongmou. Zhao Yang sent troops to fight against the insurgents of Fan and Zhonghang. The rebellion was crushed, and Fan and Zhonghang fled to the town of Caoge in Wei.

Then Zhao Yang led his troops and lay siege in Zhongmou, capturing Fo Xi. The town, with the Yellow River as its natural barrier, was not easily captured. Fo Xi resolved to fight to the death in defending the town. He ordered his troops to defend the ferry crossing and riverfront in hopes of keeping the Jin troops on the other side of the river. However, a unit of troops unexpectedly came from the southeast, assaulted the town from behind and captured it as the defending soldiers dispersed. Fo Xi fled with no one knowing his whereabouts. Undefended, the residents of the town were slaughtered at will.

Confucius listened, as he stood in the rain, and heaved one sigh after another.

Zilu said, "Master, do you know who the commander of the troops was that led the massacre?'

"Who?"

"Yang Hu."

Confucius was stunned, the name sending shivers down his spine.

Zilu continued his story. Years earlier Yang Hu rose in insurgence in Lu and schemed to take the life of the Ji. After his plot was aborted he fled Jin and went to Zhao Yang where he was also the mastermind of prince Kuai Kui of Wei's plan to attack the capital of Wei with his disguised troops. Since he failed to take the Wei's capital he assaulted Zhongmou from behind the town and killed everyone in order to return to Zhao Yang and take credit for his deeds.

Confucius said nothing, unable even to sigh this time.

That night Confucius dared not stay in the town. He led his disciples through the night back to the bank of the Yellow River. There on the muddy banks of the river they hurriedly set up camp, pitched a tent and formed makeshift beds. They lay down to sleep, their body soaked.

The following morning Zigong woke up and found no sign of the master in the tent. Worried, he got up to look around. He saw his teacher standing on the river bank in the morning fog and looking ahead at the surge and flow of the water of the Yellow River.

Zigong walked up and heard the master murmur, "Probably I'm doomed to being barred from crossing this river."

Zigong said, "Yang Hu is in Jin. Master, you can never go there."

Confucius nodded and said, "Zhao Yang couldn't keep virtuous subjects like Dou Mingdu and Shun Hua. Only rogues like Yang Hu took his fancy. It seems Jin is not far away from the civil strife." Then he looked up into the sky and sighed, "The land is vast under heaven. Is it true that we will have nowhere to go?"

Chapter 16   A Virtuous Minister
(The Chronicles: Confucius at the Age of 36)

Yan Ying, prime minister of the state of Qi, had just finished his court affairs when he was informed of Zhongni's arrival. Yan Ying pondered on whether he should see the scholar or not, while putting back on the court robe he had taken off only moments earlier. He paced up and down his main room for quite a while before giving the order, "Get the dinner ready."

He had never liked scholars. Definitely this man from Lu, named Kong Qiu, would not strike his fancy, either. As the leading figure of the new school of Confucianism, he had suddenly become widely acclaimed, with a fairly large influence. Three years earlier when Yan Ying accompanied Duke Jing on a visit to Lu he heard that this man taught disciples in the yard of his home. He gathered a bunch of idle men, preached benevolence and filial duty, practiced rites and music and made a show of himself. It seemed inconceivable that this man eventually founded a large school full of students. There were even people who considered him an idol and trekked a thousand *li* to meet him. One could not keep oneself from bewailing that social norms of good behavior were declining day by day, and people's morals were not what they used to be.

Besides Yan Ying had another reason for disliking Kong

Qiu. He heard that in the aftermath of Lu's upheaval, Kong Qiu fled to Qi and sought refuge in the home of court minister Gao Zhaozi. At that time Yan Ying thought he was a runaway who could hardly manage to relieve his own plight so he did not pay much attention to him. Later Yan Ying was taken aback to learn that Kong Qiu, like a loach slipping into every opening, met with Duke Jing at the recommendation of Gao Zhaozi and told the ruler his ideas of the rule of benevolence.

It was said that this meeting went well with much talking and laughing, and Duke Jing was so convinced by Kong Qui that he promised to grant Kong Qiu an area called "Nixi" for him to develop into a "Rule of Benevolence Special Zone."[1] When Kong Qiu came to Qi he did not call on Yan Ying, the prime minister first. Instead he met with the duke. "How could he look down his nose at me?" was the question in Yan Ying's mind. Gao Zhaozi was a close subject of Duke Jing, but in Qi it would have been very difficult to get something done without the prime minister's approval, even if the duke permitted it.

That Kong Qiu had not called on him since his arrival in Qi and now suddenly wanted to see him, Yan Ying wondered what Kong Qiu had up his sleeve. He guessed wildly at the visitor's motive and weighed his own next move before deciding to see him. Not only did he want to see him but he also decided to give him a dinner.

More than seventy, Yan Ying served Qi as prime minister for fifty years from the reign of Duke Ling to that of Duke Zhuang to that of Duke Jing, a subject for three succeeding heads of state. In the midst of his tenure the state was peaceful, people were safe, the military was strong, and he became well known, widely acclaimed by his people and

---

[1] "Rule of Benevolence Special Zone," used to invoke the twentieth-century economic development zones in China, such as "Shenzhen Economic Development Zone" and "Tianjin Economic Development Zone."

highly admired among dukes of the states.

As prime minister he had one drawback—his short height. Less than five feet, he looked like a child. Every time he was on a visit to a foreign state and attended a review of the guard of honor he could not make a show of his state's strength. However, this weakness was offset by his extraordinary capability of handling business routines.

Years earlier the duke and officials of Chu humiliated him by cutting a hole in the city wall beside the main tall gate and letting him go through it when he visited the state, in hopes of making fun of him. When Yan Ying arrived he saw the town gate shut for humans to walk inside but the hole was open for dogs to worm through. Pretending to be surprised he said, "Why have I arrived in a country of dogs? No gate except a dog's hole?" When the officials of Chu heard his words they were ashamed and they hurried and opened the gate. They had learned a lesson: a man's height was not necessarily proportionate to his intelligence.

Though in power, Yan Ying socialized with people cautiously and behaved quietly. His prudence was shown in his industrious and thrifty management of the household. He ruled at home that the concubines were prohibited from wearing silk clothes and horses were not fed with maize. He also set a good example by wearing a black gown of cloth over the court garment of silk so as not to wear out the official uniform which was state property. Although he ate meat daily, he limited his food consumption to only one dish, disregarding the monotony of his meals.

Yan Ying's abode was located in a rundown alley in town. The place was sunken and wet, the roofs low, and the rooms cramped. In addition it was close to the morning food market, with all the bustle, noise, dirt and dust. It certainly had no appearance of the mansion of a prime minister. Although Duke Jing talked to him a few times and suggested that he move into a new residence, he did not listen, saying that living in an impoverished neighborhood gave him opportunities for learning about how the people lived and what they thought. Living close to the morning food market made him well informed as to fluctuations in food prices. There could not, in fact, be a better location for a prime minister. The duke was so moved that he ordered a large residence to be built on the outskirts of the town for Yan Ying when the prime minister was visiting the state of Jin. When he returned, Yan Ying simply would not move into the new house. Seeing no alternative, the duke let Yan Ying stay in his old place and granted him the new house as his vacation home.

Now Zhongni walked into the low, cramped house, for which the prime minister was famous. With a tall, stout build the master had to duck his head and elbow his way into the room. Inside he could not even straighten his back and outstretch his arms because he would hit the roof beam with his head when he stood erect. Therefore he had to curl his body and shrink down. At this sight of the visitor Yan Ying was satisfied. The prime minister's house was simple, crude, old and shabby. Inside the main room were incomplete sets of tables, chairs and other furniture, bare walls with the paint entirely peeling and wheat stalks sticking out from inside the wall at all angles. Each time visitors came to Yan Ying, they were shocked at the sight of his home, and this was exactly the effect that Yan Ying desired to impose on the outside world. He was set on turning his house into a site for teaching the spirit of hard work and simple living in the future.

The two men met as host and guest, one old and one young, as one bowed and the other bent, the bodies up and down constantly; one intended to show respect for the learned and virtuous while the other wanted to revere the old generation and righteousness. The movement went on and gained momentum so mechanically that they could hardly bring it to a close. They seemed to be competing against each other in showing who was more courteous. Zhongni bowed eight times in a greeting of the junior, and Yan Ying returned the greeting with nine times of bending, to which Zhongni immediately added one more bow in reply.

In the midst of greeting, Yan Yang scrutinized Zhongni. He had a broad-forehead with a straight nose and wide mouth, slender eyes and upright pupils. He did not appear like a young villain nor did he seem as deceitful and treacherous as imagined. Yan Ying relaxed from his original suspicion.

As they were seated the host said aloud, "The duke of Qi said you are an unusual talent. Today I see it is true that you are young, energetic, and promising."

Zhongni responded in saying, "I'm flattered. I'm flattered. A few days ago I was honored to enter the court and met the duke. His Excellency deigned to talk to me and ask about political affairs."

Yan Ying said, "I wonder how you answered those questions? I'd like to listen and learn about some different perspectives."

Zhongni said, "I talked about the monarch as a monarch, the subject as a subject, the father as a father and the son as a son."

Nodding his head, Yan Ying said, "A good answer! If the monarch does not behave as a monarch, the subject does not behave as a subject, the father does not behave as a father and the son does not behave as a son, the country will definitely not look like a country and the family not like a family."

They found they had common ground so the conversation expanded to more topics, ranging from the Three August Ones and the Five Lords[1] to the currently reigning dukes,

---

[1] "The Three August Ones and the Five Lords," the legendary rulers of remote antiquity in Chinese history including Fuxi, Shennong, and Suiren or Zhurong for the Three August Ones, and Emperor Huangdi, Zhuanxu, Di Ku, Di Yao and Di Shun for the Five Lords.

leaving almost no issues untouched on. Admittedly they were both righteous. Like heroes, they thought alike.[1] Their interests were generally on how to be loyal to the monarch, how to run a state, how to collect tax and rent, and how to educate masses.

As the conversation went on they started to treat each other with heartfelt respect, and, though they had not gone through times of weal and woe, they believed they could engage heart-to-heart.

Zhongni said, "The Great Way had been deviated for long over the land under heaven. The rites and music are entirely lost, wars are waged one after another, and society is in disorder. If the duke of Qi is willing to apply policies of benevolence, restore the rites and music, and appoint virtuous and talented persons to government positions, the dukes of all states will be emulating his rule and great order throughout the land will be achieved soon. To practice the benevolent government I will take the lead. The duke of Qi has promised to grant me the field of Nixi as an experimental area. I'm here to seek the assistance of Your Excellency the prime minister."

Yan Ying listened and showed no feeling or response. Then he said, "That's good. Why didn't you come to see me earlier?"

At this Zhongni hesitated for a few seconds before saying, "I learned of you as prime minister of Qi long ago and longed to meet with you and listen to your instruction with respectful attention. But I was puzzled with one problem and could not figure out the answer so I did not venture to call on you."

Yan Ying was curious and asked, "What's the problem that has perplexed you? I'd like to learn about it."

---

[1] "Like heroes, they thought alike," a pun in Chinese on the saying, "Great minds think alike."

After a moment of hesitation Zhongni said sincerely, "I've learned that a *junzi* should be loyal in serving the monarch. Loyalty helps fasten the alliance between the monarch and subject, stabilize society, move the gods, run the state well and bring order to the land under heaven."

Yan Ying responded, "What you said is absolutely correct. I've set much store by the word 'loyalty.'"

Zhongni said hurriedly, "As prime minister you've been loyal and respectful to the dukes of Qi and made a name for yourself in the universe. The fact baffles me that you've worked in three consecutive dynasties of the state without any trouble. It is true that one should be loyal to his ruler through to the end. Is it also true that one can be loyal to three rulers through to the end?"

At these words, Yan Ying looked a little uneasy and he blushed. His eyes stayed riveted on Zhongni for a long time before he was sure, as his complexion grew smooth again, that Zhongni appeared genuine and sincere with no sign of ridiculing him. There was a moment of silence before Yan Ying said in a calm voice, "If one serves three monarchs whole-heartedly he serves with heart and soul. If one is absent-minded in serving one monarch in life, that is a half-hearted service."

Zhongni was stunned. He turned these words over in his mind for a while. Then it dawned on him. He, struck the table and said, "I believe you are a virtuous prime minister of the state. How could you be virtuous but not loyal? It's my fault to blame you wrongly that you were less than upright. I'm not good at mathematics. I only knew drawing inferences about other cases from one instance but was ignorant of drawing one inference about one case from three instances. I did not understand the dialectical relations between one and three."

Now Yan Ying understood the reason Zhongni took so

long to come and see him. Yan Ying smiled generously and said, "Without witnessing Yan Ying's conduct, reproaching Yan Ying in terms of his personality would be probably a slip on the moral character of a learned man."

Yan Ying's voice was soft and gentle as floss silk, but his message was hidden inside like an awl.

Zhongni, hearing these remarks, flushed with shame. Flustered, he rose immediately, bowed and apologized for his faults, "It was sheer conceit on my part to make improper comments behind the back of Your Excellency as prime minister. I'm gauging the heart of Your Excellency with a *junzi* measure. It is my verbal offense to you."

Yan Ying laughed. He waved his hand and said, "Early in my life I met with scholars and thought highly of them. Later I met with them and became suspicious of them. Maybe I was conceited as well?"

As their conversation evolved to this point, the mist of misunderstanding was eventually dispelled between them, if the original grudges were not all buried, and the atmosphere became immediately relaxed.

At this time a servant came in, lit candles and reported that dinner was ready.

The prime minister's family dinner, though the table was loaded with wine and food, was pretty simple. Drinks were diluted rice wine, like slops. The entree contained boiled soybeans and stir-fried bean sprouts, plus rice with minced meat. The minced meat came on one tiny plate and was supposed to be shared between the host and guest. In fact this was a sumptuous, luxurious meal by the family's standards. It was said that Yan Ying once entertained a special envoy at dinner on his visit, sent by the duke of Qi. Not bothering to have extra dishes cooked, he simply split his food of that day on the plate and gave half of it to his guest. Consequently neither of them was full. The special envoy returned and reported to the duke of Qi, who thought the family of the prime minister had a tight financial budget and wanted to grant it some allowance. But Yan Ying rejected it by saying the duke gave him adequate grain ration and he was not hungry. He suggested that the extra food be granted to those people in need. His words moved the duke so deeply that he was unable to eat his meal for the rest of the day.

Zhongni took a seat at the dinner table. He saw, on the table, a cup of light wine and two dishes of soybean and bean sprouts. He was touched and said, "I did not know Your Excellency is leading such a plain life. The other day the duke of Qi consulted me on government. I replied that good government stems from sparing use of material resources. I am surprised to see Your Excellency has already taken the lead in practicing it. With such an example for the state as a whole, how could the state budget be in deficit? How could the economy not be brought into an upturn? How blessed the people of Qi are!"

Yan Ying said, "Corruption and waste are very serious crimes.[1] I dare not be corrupt nor dare I waste anything."

Three toasts were made. Despite being diluted, the alcohol in the wine was strong. After a few cups, their stomachs warmed and their hearts heated as the conversation became more harmonious.

Yan Ying asked, "You the master have traveled and made friends over the land under heaven and must have met with many extraordinary men."

Thinking for a while Zhongni replied, "Yes, I've been traveling and teaching for years. Indeed I met some very talented persons."

Yan Ying requested, "Who are they? Would you please talk about them to me?"

---

[1] "Corruption and waste are very serious crimes." a quotation by Mao Zedong and also a popular saying in China in the 1950s and 1960s.

Zhongni said, "Laozi, from the archives of the king of Zhou, is a man of profound thought and original perspective. He thinks of what one has never thought of and speaks about what one has never spoken of. He is extraordinary. In fact he is the dragon living among humans. When one sees a bird, one knows it can fly. When one sees a fish, one knows it can swim. When one sees a wild beast, one knows it can roam. As to the dragon, it rides the wind and clouds and soars to the skies. No one is capable of understanding it. When I saw Laozi it seemed that I were seeing a dragon."

Hearing his words, Yan Ying looked up to the sky with an expression of reverence.

Zhongni continued, "In the state of Tan, Tanzi is erudite and accomplished in learning. He is omniscient and can answer all questions concerning heaven, earth and humans. No one can be his equal. He is the snake living among humans. I once made an inquiry to him about the official titles in the previous dynasties. He explained them from the origins of Emperor Huangdi and Emperor Yandi, referred to the evolutions of Gonggong and Zhuanxu, and elaborated on the transformation of Taihao and Shaohao.[1] To my understanding to say Tanzi's knowledge reaches the ancient tribes of the four corners of the earth is not an exaggeration."

As he listened Yan Ying nodded and smiled with an air of admiration.

Zhongni said, "With respect to today's talents of running the state, Zheng has Zi Chan and Jin has Shu Xiang. But I have not had the opportunity for meeting with them. In addition," putting down his chopsticks, he cupped one hand in the other before the chest, continuing, "There is Your Excellency of Qi. You serve the duke, know when to eat humble pie

---

[1] Yan Di, also know as Shennong; "Gonggong," a legendary figure in ancient China, which is said to be human-faced, beast-bodied and red-haired, riding on two dragons; for Emperor Huangdi and Zhuanxu, see note 3 on page 51; Taihao and Shaohao, in ancient China "*hao*" is referred to as the firmament, Taihao referring to the north and Shaohao referring to the south.

and when to hold your head high, and you behave in society with working efficiency and principles to stick to. In your political career you have the consciousness of grass roots. To administer the government you have local grounds. You can be ranked as the cream of the current crop of politicians, truly a worm living among humans. I did not show proper respect. Today I hold you in high reverence."

Yan Ying stared blankly, as he listened, with a change of complexion. Likening him to a worm was rather disrespectful, let alone talking about grass roots and local grounds! He held up his anger, smiled and proposed a toast as he did, saying repeatedly, "Interesting! Interesting! The consciousness of grass roots, the local grounds."

In the meantime, Zhongni, a little intoxicated with the wine, blushing scarlet and very excited, believed he was drinking with a congenial friend so thousands of words were not enough. As his tongue gradually ran out of control he was unaware that he had inadvertently offended the prime minister.

The next morning Duke Jing of Qi asked Yan Ying about Kong Qiu, telling him that he promised to grant the learned man from Lu the area of Nixi to give him the opportunity to practice the rule of benevolence.

Yan Ying listened. Sitting on the fence in response on the issue, he told the duke that it seemed that no man from Lu had ever been appointed to a position in Qi. It was appropriate to act cautiously.

Duke Jing said, "I like his idea of 'the monarch as a monarch, the subject as a subject, the father as a father and the son as a son.' If the monarch does not behave as a monarch, the subject not as a subject, the father not as a father and the son not as a son, I will not be able to eat my meals."

Yan Ying suggested, "His idea of 'the monarch as a monarch, the subject as a subject, the father as a father and the son as a son probably implies something else. He scoffed at your failure to adopt the crown prince as the heir to your throne and fulfill the duties as monarch and father. Therefore he put forth this idea of 'the monarch as a monarch, the subject as a subject, the father as a father and the son as a son.'"

Quite awhile passed with Duke Jing's wearing an unhappy appearance. Then he broke the silence, "His idea that 'good government stems from sparing use of material resources' sounds very good."

With a smile Yan Ying said, "Your Excellency was deceived. Scholars are arrogant, their behavior is funny, and they like to talk big. For generations they have never completed the learning. For one hundred years they have never thoroughly understood the rites. Instead they are attired in splendid gowns, perform complex rituals, and conduct costly funerals. They often go down in bankruptcy and seldom succeed in accumulating wealth. How could they have faith in the sparing use of material resources? This man's thoughts should not be advocated. He should not be appointed to an important position. Your Excellency should take a closer look."

After hearing this suggestion, Duke Jing was rather clear, feeling he had become a wise head of state and no one would be able to pull the wool over his eyes anymore. Sobered up, he felt tired and, yawning, put Zhongni and his business out of his mind. This lasted more than two decades. Twenty years later when the two state heads of Qi and Lu met at Jiagu, Duke Jing met Confucius once again, reminded of the promise he made long time ago to grant the scholar the area of Nixi. Nixi was a land with rich and fertile fields and tens of thousands of households. Its annual taxes would have amounted to tens of thousands of pieces of gold, a promise worth a huge amount of wealth. Luckily he did not live up to his promise.

Chapter 17　Chen
(Spring and Autumn Period: 4th Year of Duke Ai of Lu's Reign, 491 BC)

The following spring Confucius finally arrived in the state of Chen with his disciples.

The day they entered the capital city Wanqiu, the sun shone brightly on peach trees in red and willows in green. With a town layout that was round on the outside and square inside, the town was in a poor, neglected state, its walls low and its streets aging and worn out. It was quite a simple, ordinary sight. But in the sunshine, the dilapidated alleys and lanes and the roofs on the uneven houses seemed coated with fresh paint, presenting an impression of newness. In the streets ragged, dejected pedestrians became spirited as well, coming, going, jostling one another and giving the town a revived vitality.

Confucius, along with his disciples, strolled down the streets. He felt inspired, his confidence restored that though the road ahead was tortuous the prospects were bright. His ambition to stabilize and run a state and bring order to the land under heaven was like the spring breeze that irresistibly swept through the universe once again.

Up to this moment of arriving in Chen, it had been five years of trekking back and forth among various places since Confucius' first departure from Wei. He was now more than sixty and could not afford to wait, so the urge in his heart to accomplish his mission was even stronger.

Duke Min of Chen learned of Confucius' coming and was delighted. He dispatched a chariot to meet him. Chen was small and located in a remote region and rarely had the honor of a visit from a well known learned man like Confucius. In addition, the duke had a question to pose to Confucius which his officials had been debating for days on end with no conclusion.

A couple of days earlier a dead vulture was found inside the palace. The body of this bold vulture was pierced by a one-foot-eight long arrow, made of the wood of the chaste tree and the arrowhead made of sharpened stone. The vulture fell on the steps in front of the court main room at night. In the morning when a maid saw it, she shrieked, dropping the chamber pot she carried in her hand. By midday the event was widely known in the palace, but, before the matter became clear, no one would dare to touch the bird. The dead vulture was still on the steps, causing trouble for the officials who arrived for the morning court affairs since they had to walk around it.

When the news was reported to the court, Duke Min was a little startled, concerned it might be an ill omen from heaven bringing a warning to dukes and subjects. All sorts of comment arose, too, among the officials, some suspecting the threat by an assassin and others guessing an inner court scheme. Despite their wild guesses, they all felt uneasy and suspected something sinister.

The special envoy of Duke Min brought Confucius to the spot of the event. The vulture was still lying there on the steps, its wings stretched out, its talons bent, both eyes closed and its body emitting a peculiar odor. Confucius covered his nose with his hand and got closer for a look. After a hesitation he said, "It's a dead vulture."

Two maids who stood by covered their mouth to subdue a giggle.

Looking more steadily for a while Confucius went on, "This vulture was killed with the arrow."

One of the maids snorted with laughter.

The special envoy of the duke, who came along, frowned, asking, "How come the vulture died here?"

Confucius said, "Pull the arrow out." An imperial bodyguard took it out from the vulture's body. Confucius took it in his hand and scrutinized it for a long time before observing in a slow voice, "This vulture came from afar."

The special envoy was at a loss and asked, "How do you the master know that?"

Pointing to the arrow Confucius explained, "The arrow is not an ordinary one. Its shaft is made from the wood of the chaste tree, and the arrowhead is made of sharpened stone. It is the arrow that is used in Sushen. Sushen is one of the ethnic minority tribes located in the northeast. In ancient times when King Wu conquered the Shang dynasty, his troops marched through the areas of all the ethnic minorities around China and established relations with Sushen. When the states and tribes paid tribute to the king, they presented their local produce. Sushen gave this long, stone-headed arrow as its tribute. This vulture was shot one thousand *li* away from here."

The special envoy listened as he nodded and gasped repeatedly, much impressed. He then plucked Confucius' sleeve and asked quietly, "Is it a good omen?"

Confucius hesitated for a while before replying, "Good omen. Good omen. This vulture flew to Chen with the arrow of Sushen. It must have carried a deep meaning. It stresses the virtue of the late King Wu of the Zhou dynasty. The late king Wu ruled the country with virtue and granted his eldest daughter Daji the Sushen arrow. Daji was married to Chief Hu of the Yu Tribe, who was granted the fief of Chen. According to the rites of the Zhou dynasty, treasures were offered to dukes of the same clan for feelings of kinship, and tributes were granted to dukes of different clans for stability and unity. Chen was a state of a different clan so it was bestowed the Sushen arrow. If there is anything suspicious about this, please check the state warehouse. Probably there are still some of them in stock."

The special envoy of Chen's duke was convinced and moved with veneration and admiration. He immediately sent people to look at the assortments of things kept in the state warehouse to see whether they could find some of the Sunshen arrows there. Before long one servant came to report there were indeed a few of them found there.

When Duke Min of Chen heard his special envoy recount this happening in detail, he too was greatly astonished, not just by Confucius' erudition that the learned man was more familiar with the history of Chen than he himself as the ruler was but also by the fact that his interpretation turned a sign of disaster into a propitious omen. Confucius was definitely a talent that the state urgently needed, so he ordered a dinner to be fixed in honor of Confucius.

Confucius was dressed in his official best and walked haltingly into the palace. Due to old age, he moved forward in small steps, staggering to his feet and swaying a little once in a while. Fortunately he had trekked about all these years with constant physical exercise so his legs and feet remained robust. Therefore when stepping into the palace, he still retained that quickness of a bird outspreading its wings and gliding on the air.

As he greeted the duke of Chen, Confucius noticed the state head was young, with fine features and an uplifting look. He had the appearance of a wise ruler. His confidence rose a little in Chen. He recalled his journey to Chen that brought him through innumerable hardships and hazards. Now he finally had a chance to meet with the duke of Chen and dwell on his ideas for running a state. Chen was a small state, and Confucius thought it would only take one month, before he was put in power and no more than three years, before the state rose to prosperity and the land under heaven was brought to order.

The duke raised his cup in a toast as they both drank the wine. The duke then praised Confucius' profound learning. Confucius rose from his seat, walked close to the duke, made a long bow with hands clasped and said, "I'm flattered. I'm flattered. A *junzi* should live and learn until he breathes his last."

The duke allowed him to be seated again and said, "I heard years ago when people dug a well in the Ji Mansion in Lu they dug up a monster. Nobody could tell what it was except you the master."

Again Confucius stood up and bent in a long bow so low that his hands were barely above the ground and replied, "That happened a few years ago. They found a pottery *fou*, in which there was a strange pottery beast.[1] People all thought it was a breed of dog. I was the only person who believed it was a member of the goat family."

"Why?" Duke Min asked, aroused with interest. He was curious by nature and interested in information on all subjects, particularly odd learning and strange ways of behavior such as whether the sparrow was able to fly with its eyes closed and how many legs the centipede had. He liked to read books of all sorts and especially to use his brains memorizing things. But he never wasted his mind on thinking.

Confucius said, "A terrestrial monster is the *kui*, if it lives in the woods; but *wangliang*, if it lives in the mountains.[2] An aquatic monster is the dragon, if it lives in the water; but *wangxiang*, if it lives in the river.[3] A monster living underground must be the ground goat. That was why I believed that unearthed monster was a goat."

The duke of Chen marveled and sighed in admiration, "Your learning is profound. It is better to see once than hear one hundred times."

Confucius replied modestly, "I'm flattered. I'm flattered. But the ignorance of one object would disgrace the scholar."

At his words the duke was further convinced of the master's

---

[1] *fou*, a narrow-necked earthen jar.
[2] *kui*, a legendary wild beast looking like a dragon with only one foot; *wangliang*, a kind of man-eating monster living in the mountain.
[3] *wangxiang*, a legendary beast living in the river.

CᏂ= WANGXIANG

193

accomplishments. He gestured for Confucius to sit again and told the servant to add a soft cushion to his seat.

One man invited to help entertain the guest at dinner was court minister Ji Xian, who was the leading official historian of Chen and the duke's attendant. He was also very accomplished in learning and knowledgeable about history, to the extent that he was able to answer all questions raised to him and even took the initiative to give an explanation on one issue that might prompt a question. In a similar circumstance he would be the one who fielded concerns at the table. But today in front of Confucius the conversation left him with no chance to contribute. This made him uneasy. Upon hearing the master's words, Ji Xian could not help but rise and ask, "You seem omniscient. I'm humbly ignorant and have a question to consult with you."

Confucius realized someone would be a thorn in his side so he said calmly, "Please."

"The year before last Fu Chai, the duke of Wu, defeated Gou Jian, the duke of Yue and took the capital Kuaiji. His troops dug up some bones of a huge body in the Mount Jishan. The body was so large that one limb filled up the complete chariot. The duke of Wu sent his envoy to us to ask about what kind of bone was so large. You're well learned and must be able to give an answer."

"They were the bones of the body of Fang Feng of the Xia dynasty. One year the tribe leader Yu met with the gods of mountains and rivers on the top of Mount Jishan. When Fang Feng arrived, Yu killed him and buried him in Mount Jishan."

Ji Xian asked, "What kind of god was Fang Feng?"

"Fang Feng was the ruler of Wangwang, who guarded Mount Feng and Mount Yu. He was a clansman of the Li family. In the Zhou dynasty his people were surnamed Changzhai, that is, today's Tall Men."

"How tall are Tall Men?"

"Jiaoyao are the shortest people, no more than three feet. The tallest are the Tall Men, ten times the height of Jiaoyao men. Three multiplied by ten is thirty feet."

Ji Xian was silenced. Quite a while passed before he raised another question suddenly, "Why did King Yu kill Fang Feng?"

Confucius smiled, "King Yu ruled the gods by decree, just as the king of the Zhou dynasty ruled the dukes by decree today. Fang Feng arrived late. If he had not been executed, how could the laws have been maintained over the land under heaven?"

Snubbed and silenced Ji Xian sat down, his head hanging low, as if he were turning attention sideways, dipping his chopsticks into the food on his plate and sticking it into his mouth. At this moment the duke was listening with rapt attention and, a little intoxicated with a reddening face, banged the table with his fist and cried, "He deserved death! He deserved death!" Holding the wine vessel high he presented a toast to Confucius, "Come on! Let's down another one!" Confucius felt obliged at the request of the duke so he drank another large drink, exceeding his capacity for wine. It never occurred to him that his shrewd exchange with his host at the dinner not only offended someone but would also bring him a fatal disaster in the future.

The meeting with the duke of Chen was over but nothing came out of it later on. It turned out that the duke of Chen asked Ji Xian, after the dinner that day, whether Confucius should be trusted with a government post. Smiling secretively Ji Xian said earnestly that Confucius was a genius but could not be assigned a position. Astonished, the duke asked why this talented man should not be recruited. Ji Xian explained when Confucius lived in Lu the state was wrecked with the civil strife; he went to Wei and brought social unrest there too; he trekked through Song and left Song defeated; then he settled down in Zheng and Zheng was conquered; now he was in Chen and what would become of Chen? The duke pondered and then said it was true that he had been turned down for government position by dukes of all states and they must have had their reasons.

Ji Xian continued to say that Confucius had expertise in the terminology of grass, trees, fish and insects. His learning was comprehensive but was rather distracting and deviated from fulfilling political ambitions. At present Chen was pressed with a build-up in military power. With a formidable enemy threatening the country human life was an issue of supreme importance and could not be slighted. If Confucius were enlisted to help govern, Chen would soon be in ruins.

The duke's face changed color as he shuddered at these words, rejoicing he did not give a position to the wrong man. Chen was a small state. It was independent but struggled among powerful states and ordered back and forth. It could not make decisions independently. A single slip would cause punishment. In recent years Jin and Chu fought against each other over border disputes, which automatically subjected Chen to constant invasions, with Jin's troops invading across the border one day and Chen's military sweeping through looting and rioting the next. The duke of Chen was forced to flee his state time after time. It was impossible to settle down and live, let alone to run the state in peace and stability. How could he be in the mood to care for grass, trees, fish and insects, despite the fact that those were his favorite pastimes? To be concerned with the state and welfare of his people first, he had to send Confucius away and store him like the Sushen arrows kept in the warehouse. Several months went by as Confucius awaited news from the duke's court of Chen. Seeing that no official appointment came, he knew he had encountered an obstacle again. He was anxious but at the end of his resources so he continued to wait. To make matters less upsetting the duke did not totally forget about him. Instead he sent people to the master's place once in a while to raise a wide range of questions like modern TV programs of knowledge competition, which bombard the audience with one question after another.

In the midst of his idle stay Confucius spent time each day discussing the cultivation of moral character with his disciples. In truth, with no government to run as a career and no family to take care of at home, he was left only with the business of cultivating his moral character. One day Zilu asked Confucius how to cultivate moral character and how to become a genuine scholar. Confucius paused, at a loss for words, before replying that the ultimate goal boiled down to Three Strengths, namely, virtue, intelligence and strong physique.

Then Zilu asked again, "How do you explain the Three Strengths in detail?" Confucius expanded by saying, "They require the virtuous person to be worried about nothing, the intelligent man to be ignorant of nothing and the brave man to fear nothing. These Three Strengths are more easily said than done! I'm not able to reach these standards."

Zigong, sitting by his side, said, "The master is very modest. The master himself is an example of the Three Strengths."

Confucius continued, "The Three Strengths are no more than cultivating moral character. But the reason one cultivates his moral character is to bring order over the land under heaven. Scholars travel over the land under heaven and serve in the government and for the public. They are classified in three categories. First, there are those who do not disgrace the commission of their duke and work hard in serving their state. Second, there are those who show both filial piety to their parents and love and respect to their elder brothers and behave as moral models in the neighborhood. Third, there are those who always stand by their word and act to bring plans to fruition. Their promise is worth a thousand pieces of gold."

Zilu cut in, "No matter whether a scholar should have the Three Strengths or whether scholars are classified in three categories, the quintessence is pressing on courageously in doing things, unyielding and staunchly, as hard as a rock. That is truly a scholar."

With a smile Confucius said, "It is certainly good to be as hard as a rock. But if a man considers himself infallible and is vain and stubborn in adhering to his own opinions as hard as a granite, he is at most a substandard man."

Listening quietly from the side, Yan Yuan thought the meaning was deep so he rose immediately to fetch his burin and block and take down each word. Then Zigong raised another question, "What do you the master think of those men currently engaged in government today?"

Looking up to the skies Confucius sighed, "A dipper and pail! The capacity of one *dou* and two liters. They are small men. How could they be scholars?"[1] He spoke of his current predicament which made him heave one sigh after another.

As the teacher and students chatted, Ran Qiu rushed into the room with the shocking news that the ancestral shrines of the duke of Lu had burned down. In the past few years when Confucius journeyed around the world Ran Qiu followed him. Influenced by listening to the master's instruction and watching his behavior, he gained proficiency and experience in getting along with people and displayed extraordinary political capability. These days he often took time off to go to Lu quietly, first to see his old mother and second to find out the situation in his home state. Now he was just back from Lu where he met with Nangong Jingshu in the capital.

Learning of the burning of the duke of Lu's ancestral shrines, Confucius said at once, "They must be those of Duke Huan and Duke Xi of Lu?" Ran Qiu was stunned, his eyes wide and round, "It's odd. It's odd. The master has become immortal. How could you know it like a prophet? Yes, what burned were the shrines of Duke Huan and Duke Xi."

Confucius said, "The will of heaven cannot be disobeyed! That year Duke Huan of Lu killed his elder brother and usurped the throne. Duke Xi slew his younger brother and took over the state. The shrines should not be dedicated to them after their death. Even if built they would even-

---

[1] *dou*, a unit of dry measure for grain in ancient China equivalent to 10 liters.

tually be burned down." The disciples were dazed by his words. In the past they only heard the master talk about the will of heaven and believed it would look like the master himself, beaming with benevolence and amiableness. The idea of peril and horror never crossed their mind in conjunction with the way of heaven. Now they immediately held it in awe.

"Thanks to Nangong Jingshu who fought the fire," Ran Qiu went on, "Otherwise the whole town of Qufu would have burned to the ground."

"Why didn't the clan Jisun come to their assistance?" Confucius asked.

"It was in chaos itself. Ji Huanzi died not long ago," Ran Qiu replied.

"Ji Huanzi is dead?" It was Confucius' turn to be astonished.

"Yes, he died ten days ago and was just buried."

Sitting there Confucius dropped into a long silence. That year Ji Huanzi took the duke of Lu, in plain clothing, to erotic dances. At the base of the town walls girls from Qi wiggled, their skirts fluttering, while, at the top of the walls, the duke and his subjects chatted and laughed with joy. It all seemed like yesterday. In the blink of an eye the songs stopped, dancers disappeared, the wine was gone, people were out of sight, and Ji Huanzi went to the nether world.

"Who succeeded Ji Huanzi in power?" Confucius asked again, as if inadvertently.

"Ji Kangzi, a son of Ji Huanzi. His given name is Fei, fat as he is," Ran Qiu answered.[1] After a pause he saw no response from the master and then said in a low voice, "Ji Kangzi called me back to Lu. I'm wondering whether I should go or not."

Confucius stared at Ran Qiu for quite a while before something

---

[1] *"fei,"* the Chinese character meaning fat.

suddenly dawned on him. He said, "Go back there. Go back there." So saying he rose and paced up and down in the main room. "Go back. Definitely go back. You are all young disciples coming from your hometowns. Though often presumptuous and unruly you all have ambitions and high motives to forge ahead. Through these years of studying with me you have made great literary advances and have become quite capable and experienced in handling daily affairs and human relations. With a bit of work experience you will surely become pillars of the state! I have little left to teach you. Return to your homes! Return! But only if you don't forget the career goals you originally strive to achieve!" He said with a wave of his hand. Toward the end when he finished, his emotions still ran high, and his hand waved continuously.

Zigong witnessed all of this as he stayed quiet by the side.

A couple of days later Ran Qiu took his leave of Confucius for Lu. Zigong came to the end of the path to see him off. Before Ran Qiu got on the horse Zigong plucked his sleeve and told him, "I think the master is having some thoughts about returning home. After you are back in Lu work in this regard through your connections."

Ran Qiu said, "It is said that before his death Ji Huanzi regretted too. People said when he was seriously ill his chariot went through the tall town gate where he had ventured out in plain clothing along with the duke of Lu and watched the dances. Once there, he sighed and said if Lu failed to rise in power it might be due to the offense he gave Confucius. He particularly urged his son Ji Fei when he ran the state, to bring Confucius back to Lu. The opportunity would possibly arise, but it would all hinge on Confucius, who was somewhat stubborn, making the outcome unpredictable."

Zigong said, "I understand. Do not worry about what will happen in the future. When you return to Lu and are trusted with an important position, do your best to encourage the duke of Lu to bring Confucius back to the state."

At these words Ran Qiu nodded and mounted his horse. With a hands-clasped salute he pressed the horse with his legs and galloped off to the east toward Lu.

Before long, the town of Wanqiu was stormed by the enemy. This time the troops marching into town were not those of Jin nor were they those of Chu. They were brutes from the south. Early that morning, just before dawn the master and his men were still asleep. Suddenly they were awakened by cries from the streets, "The Wu troops are here! The Wu troops are here!" Instantly the sound of weeping, cries, shouts, and the neighs of horses came from all directions. Confucius quickly got up and slipped into his garment while asking his disciples to find out what was going on outside. Word was brought back that it was true that the troops of Wu were bearing down on them.

Earlier that year the war between the states of Wu and Yue had ended after Fu Chai, the duke of Wu, led ten of thousands of troops to capture the capital of Yue. Gou Jian, the duke of Yue, was defeated and had to beg for peace in disgrace. He had to go to Wu, his hands tied behind his back, and serve the duke of Wu as a home slave. He also yielded Yue's beauty Xi Shi as part of his tribute to Wu to secure in return an opportunity to sleep on brushwood and eat gall.[1] Fu Chai's troops rode in on a tide of victory and intended to flex their military muscles to the fullest. They took no break as they overran regions to the north. They aimed at Chu rather than Chen. But as they swept through the town of Wanqiu, they stopped for a look instead of bypassing it. When the town folk got up that morning, their streets were filled with southern savages, their hair worn down and their bodies tattooed, who gabbed and chattered in an alien language. Though they did not kill people and set fire to property, they went on a rampage

---

[1] "sleeping on brushwood and tasting gall," a well known Chinese saying derivative from the story of Gou Jian, the duke of Yue, who underwent self-imposed hardship after his defeat by Wu and eventually brought his country back to power to wipe out the national humiliation.

of beating, smashing and looting everywhere. Panic-stricken, the residents ran in all directions for refuge.

Seeing the chaos in town, the disciples all urged Confucius to leave Chen for the neighboring Cai for the time being. The master turned the suggestion down, saying that offering sacrifices was scheduled that day in the court and he had to show up. As he said this he donned his garments and rushed outside heading for the palace. When he arrived at the main room of the state ancestral shrine he saw sacrifice streamers hanging high and utensils set up. However, the room was empty.

A quick inquiry informed him that the duke of Chen had fled the night before. At the side of the main room a few elderly musicians sat, playing one tune after another from the ceremony's repertoire, perfunctorily but faithfully, despite the absence of the leading officials. At this critical moment the music was played slightly out of tune. Standing there and listening for a few minutes, Confucius realized they played the music taken from "Shaoyue."[1] With a mixture of feelings welling up in him Confucius said, "I'm surprised to hear music of this caliber at times of turmoil and in the chaos of war!" Thirty years earlier he was in Qi and listened to the music "Shaoyue." He was so enraptured with the melody that he lost his sense of taste for meat for three months. Now this same music gripped him again as he stood there motionless. His disciples feared the music would lead him to the long-standing sacrificial formality of kneeling down three times and kowtowing nine times, delaying their departure and causing them to be stuck there. So, allowing no objection, they pulled and pushed the master out of the shrine and got him onto the chariot. They sped out the southern gate of the town, amid throngs of runaways and fled southwest.

---

[1] a music composition devoted to the emperor of Shun.

Chapter 18 The Musician
(The Chronicles: Confucius at the Age of 38)

The spring rain fell on and off until dawn. Sitting in his main room alone, Shi Xiangzi quietly listened to the pitter-patter of raindrops on the eaves, first rapidly and then slowly, originally incessant and later sporadic, and finally tapering off. Then, through the plant-carved window lattice, he heard, outside in the bamboo woods, the bamboo shoots pushing through the soil with creaks of "*chih-chih*" and the bamboo joints sprouting with thumps of "*teng-teng*" He heard a squirrel skitter down a pine in the yard and into a growth of grass. The next moment he heard a couple of flutters of a sparrow hawk, "*hu-hu*," turning and flapping in the wind.

He was old, blind in both eyes. Now the only way that he learned about happenings around him was through hearing. Sitting on the straw mat, he looked withered, bony and sallow, like a chunk of charcoal, as flames of life almost sputtered out to ashes.

Shi Xiangzi was a Musician on the *qin*, a string-plucked instrument in the state of Lu. He had been the best stringed instrumentalist in the Ji Mansion and led its band. One day when he served there years earlier, the host scheduled a performance of music on large bronze chimes. Shi Xiangzi disapproved of the idea and said the household of a court minister like Ji was only entitled to stone bells, not the bronze ones.

This infuriated Ji Wuzi, and he fired him. Since then the musician had lived in an impoverished neighborhood, scraping by giving music lessons. Occasionally life pushed him to his limits, and he stooped to trading his playing pieces on the streets, such as "High Mountains and Flowing Rivers," for copper and a few knife-shaped coins.

Now he heard a burst of footfall in the distance, a sound that, to him, was plausibly a thunderclap rumbling far on the horizon, roaring and soul-ravishing, and, simultaneously, he heard the drumbeat that sounded the night watches, pure and distinct with each stroke. The footsteps were of four men, he could tell, intermingled and hasty, and went from distant to near. One of them walked steadily, assuredly, and with a clear rhythmic pacing, at first fast then slow. He was certain that Zhongni was coming.

Zhongni's customary stride was straight with measured, evenly-pressed steps. Occasionally his gait included stamps every other three steps and leaps every other five, distinctly rhythmic and in an unmistakable manner.

Years earlier Shi Xiangzi taught Zhongni to play the *qin*. At that time Zhongni served in the Ji Mansion, first as a warehouse man and then a herdsman of cattle and sheep. At times when the cows and sheep slept he stole away to the musician's home for his lessons.

He was an earnest student, practicing industriously. In the past he had dabbled in wind and percussion instruments and played with confident rhythms. Now his execution on the *qin* came, periodically, in abrupt finality, notes identifiable but maladroitly linked, somewhat erratic and lacking a melody.

Three years passed and he continuously played the same piece, composed anonymously, the one he had started with. An etude for the beginner, this music was simple in melody with no variation. It was for new students to familiarize themselves with the strings and move their fingers and wrist. But Zhongni took it differently; he played with concentration and deep feelings, enraptured, as though inebriated. This composition was played over and over, as if a CD were played incessantly, until it seemed like noise. Such painstaking practice went on for a while before he was asked to learn a new piece. But he was unwilling to, saying he was not yet good at the meters. Another round of hard exercise ensued, and he became adroit at the rhythm. When advised to move on to new work, once again he would not budge, on the grounds the current piece's essence still eluded him. He plunged into more hard work. A few more months passed. This time he could play to the meter and understand the theme of the music, but he still refused, despite repeated requests to change, saying he had not been able to shape in his mind the fundamental image that the composition conveyed. Consequently he practiced the piece for ten years until the time when he had to flee the turmoil-stricken state of Lu to the state of Qi as refugee. Evidently his playing skills remained elementary.

The sound of footsteps came closer and closer, coming into the yard and then to the doorway.

"Watch the steps," Shi Xiangzi said.

"Yes, I'm watching," said Zhongni.

"Come here. Be seated on the mat," said the host.

"Thanks, I am." The words sounded like Zhongni.

"Is it you, Zhongni?" asked Shi Xiangzi.

"Yes, it is." Zhongni replied, saluting his teacher with the bow of a student, "I've come back from Qi."

"Is the young master Zhongsun back too?" Shi Xiangzi turned his head to the right.

"Yes, I'm here," Zhongsun answered. He had taken *qin* lesions from Shi Xiangzi, too, in the past.

"Is Zeng Dian with you?" Shi Xiangzi moved his head

leftward.

"Yes, here I am" was the prompt response from Zeng Dian, another former student of Shi Xiangzi, who used to sneak out to the tutor's place to learn to play the instrument during a period of a few days when working as chef in the Ji Mansion, between daily chores of frying, roasting, stewing and boiling.

"Shi Xiangzi, I listened to the 'Shaoyue' in Qi," said Zhongni excitedly. "It's extraordinarily melodious."

"Really?" Shi Xiangzi smiled. "Tell me something about it then."

"It starts in a rich timbre," replied Zhongni. "It's mellifluous and smooth, unfolding in a blaze of color. The melody proceeds to ride on an enrapturing current of sound, notes surging and pitches ebbing, carillons resonating and strings rattling. One moment it is like a boundless expanse of azure sea water under a bright blue sky. The next it resembles a raging storm. Then it strikes one like crystal-clear water running in rivulets down the hillside. It comes in a rich conglomeration of tones but presents an incredible ensemble. The finale gushes loudly to a grand close, the music vibrating and lingering, like a soft thread of silk in the air." Moving his hands up and down as he depicted the bewitchment of the music, Zhongni was utterly enthralled. "'Shaoyue' is spellbinding. One listening to it makes a course of pork a cheesy food. I've not had a taste of pork for three months. But I'm not hungry in the slightest, nor do I drool over it. On the contrary I'm full of vim and vigor."

"Is it true?" Shi Xiangzi was smiling. "The sound of nature is soothing. One listening is as good as taking vitamins."

"Since I listened to the 'Shaoyue' I have understood music." Zhongni went on, still unable to curb his excitement, "I can play that piece well now, I believe."

So saying, he sat in front of the *qin*, lay his hands on it, quieted himself and, holding his breath, started with strokes of his hands.

It was the same old piece. He played with confident rhythms, notes firm and decisive, but maladroitly linked. When he finished the piece, a hush descended over the group. Zhongni uttered no word, either, obviously carried away by his own playing.

"The melody sounds like a flight of steps, high and low. The harmony resembles a straw mat, crisscrossed," Shi Xiangzi said as he broke the silence. Each time Zhongni had been there for his lesson before this, he reminded his student of the stairs and mentioned sitting on the mat. But his words, alluding to playing the instrument never got through to Zhongni. Now he would not wait any longer. To fulfill a teacher's duty, he chose to express his meaning explicitly by saying, "When you develop a sense of melody and understand harmony, you are able to play it well, just like you ascend the stairs and sit on the mat, and then you are truly in the inner chamber!"

"I saw the King Wen of Zhou," Zhongni said suddenly, eyes flashing and sparkling, as if he hadn't heard Shi Xiangzi's words.

"Where did you see him?" Shi Xiangzi was taken aback.

"In the music," replied Zhongni, as he rose, his eyes gazing ahead and piercing through walls, over yards, and into the distant parts of the world. "He's standing alone in the wild, tall in physique, dark-skinned, strikingly-featured, with an awe-inspiring bearing. He's looking ahead over a broad skyline with rapt attention, like a king scanning his vast territory ... If he is not King Wen of Zhou, who else is he?"

Shi Xiangzi was greatly stirred and deeply touched. He stood up, solemnly expressive, and saluted Zhongni with a deep, formal bow. "Excellent! True words of yours. I'd always wondered whether this music was the long lost *To King*

Wen.[1] I asked many *qin* players for an answer, but none of them could reply. Today your words have lifted the cloud over my mind."

The young master Zhongsun and Zeng Dian, who sat in the room listening, were moved to tears. They were so excited that they were about to shout "long live King Wen" as if seeing him themselves.

Still standing there motionlessly Zhongni gazed forward, his heart in the faraway wilderness ...

The footsteps of Zhongni and his students faded away in the distance. Shi Xiangzi was left alone, sitting in his room, a hush taking rein once again. In the his life, he had taught countless students, among whom Zhongni was mediocre in acquiring a sense of rhythm. However, it was Zhongni who was capable of comprehending the quintessence of the music, the theme and overtones. As a music teacher Shi Xiangzi had nothing to offer him with respect to instruction. Certainly Zhongni's skills at this moment left some room to be desired. In addition, his hand, injured in playing, would defy further effort for improvement. With this thought in mind Shi Xiangzi heaved a sigh and shook his head.

Then he heard some faint rustles from the north of the city shoot up into sky, letting out screeches, like metal and copper rubbing against each other. The sound hovered overhead indefinitely. They jarred and burned his ears and sent a chill down to his heart. A feeling of agitation immediately arose inside him.

The rustles smacked of murder.

---

[1] *To King Wen*, a music composition about the achievements of King Wen of Zhou.

Chapter 19 Cai

(Spring and Autumn Period: 4th Year of Duke Ai of Lu's Reign, 491 BC)

As Confucius fled from the calamity, his laments streamed out along the road. "The land under heaven is truly in chaos. The duke doesn't behave like a duke, and the minister doesn't behave like a minister. The state will not remain a state. The state will not possibly remain a state!" But Confucius himself no longer fared like a *junzi* any more. Early on he could take a ride, standing in the carriage, hands on the bar in front, maintaining an upright posture. Later the roads were thronged with people, and the carriage could only inch forward at a snail's pace. He had to climb down from the carriage and ride a horse. However, the hassle offered, if not much, a sort of diversion. After a short distance, the horse came to a halt as well. Confucius then had to alight and walk along with the swarms of ordinary travelers. Caught in the crowds, he pushed to the left, shoved to the right, and thrusted his way ahead while fending off a surge from behind. Elbowing past one crowd after another and working his way through the moving mass, he wanted to reach the front of masses who were all traveling on the same route. By the time he reached Shangcai, capital city of the state of Cai, he was reduced from a *junzi* to a refugee, his face coated with dust and his clothing in rags. For days he had not brushed his teeth and his body emitted a strange odor. His formal robe appeared more like a heavily patched garment of coarse cloth, worn out and threadbare, its sleeves torn loose. On his head the official tall hat was bent to one side, the fastening tassel broken. He had to hold it steady with both hands. Along the way he did not forget to instruct Zilu walking beside him as his bodyguard, "The *junzi* dies with his official hat on, let alone in his flight from disaster."

The last thing the master and disciples could expect, however, was that no sooner had they fled to Shangcai of Cai from Wanqiu, capital city of the state of Chen, than did the troops of Wu arrived and began their siege on the city. Inside Shangcai, chickens and dogs ran about, and every household was panic-stricken. The duke of Cai had disappeared without a trace long before. Some said he had gone into hiding, others said he had committed suicide, and still others believed he had run to the state of Wu to surrender. A small country, accustomed to the tyranny of stronger powers, Cai had grown savvy with the tactics for surviving dire situations. Years before the duke of Cai paid tribute to the state of Chu with gifts, a fur coat and a jade pendant, to the duke of Chu; but the Cai's ruler forgot to submit a similar contribution to Zichang, the de facto prime minister of Chu. As a result the duke of Cai was detained in Chu by Zichang for three years. Later the duke of Cai threw in his lot with the state of Jin and sent his son and sons of senior officials to Jin as hostages as a token of friendship. When Chu and Jin were at war with each other a few years earlier, Cai was besieged. The duke of Cai was frightened. He strongly opposed the war. He then moved his capital city from Shangcai to Zhoulai and did not move it back until the dust settled. But he was totally unaware that he would soon come under attack by the troops of Wu, who had come all the way from the lower Yangtze valley.

When Confucius set foot on the capital city of Cai, the country lacked a ruler. He thus had no target for selling his ideas of benevolent government and the rule of virtue. Since going on with his aimless venture would be too risky, Confucius took shelter with his disciples just south of the town until a further decision could be made. As luck would have it, at this time plenty of houses were available to rent.

Hostilities left life in flutter and as dull as dishwater too. Confucius often sighed, "Three meals a day but nothing completed! What a long day to while away! A game of chess would help relieve our boredom." He gradually became agitated. One day he saw his student Zai Yu taking a nap around noon in the wing of the house. Growing angry, Confucius loudly reprimanded him in front of the other disciples, "Zai Yu, what rotten wood he is that cannot be carved! What a wall of dried dung he is that cannot be fixed with the trowel! What time is it now, and he's still in bed?! The land under heaven is in such a state of chaos and he's still asleep?!" The master's outburst of genuine rage stupefied the students and each dared not breathe.

Meanwhile, Zai Yu's loud snoring drifted in from inside the room, and he showed no signs of waking. This sight fanned the flames of the teacher's anger . "This sort of disciple, what could I say about him?" he said. "I would not say a word anymore! From now on, I won't believe anything he says. I used to judge one only by his words. Now I'm going to judge by one's deeds." Confucius stalked into the hall and banged the door shut behind him, and did not come out for some time.

Yan Yuan was there, watching and perturbed. He rushed into the room where Zai Yu was sleeping and nudged him. Awakened, Zai Yu, rubbed his eyes and asked, "Are the Wu troops invading?" Apparently he did not wholly lack concern for the state's welfare.

Zai Yu was a senior disciple of Confucius dating back to the Master's time in Lu. He had followed the master for over ten years, and had no serious faults nor obvious stain to mar his character. His only weakness was fatigue. It seemed he was never fully awake. He could sleep whenever he wanted, falling dead to the world wherever he was. He spoke little and and even dozed off in class. Though he appeared weary at times, he was not muddle-headed. He was capable of reasoning and logic and occasionally posing clever questions in class. Confucius once discussed, at a session of lecture, stepping forward bravely for a just cause. Zai Yu sat at the corner of the room, napping. Then his snore snapped as he opened his eyes and asked aloud, "If a man falls into a well and you plunge in to rescue him, you will surely die with him. But your deed is benevolent. If you chicken out and watch the dying man, you are not benevolent. Should you or shouldn't you plunge into the well?"

Confucius was stumped by the question. He pondered for a moment before muttering, "Why would one have to take such a rash action? One should think first at the side of the well and then figure out a solution, shouldn't he? Go and find a cord of rope. Or use a long bamboo pole. One need not plunge into the well. A *junzi* may be trapped by others, but he should not act like a loggerhead, should he?" Zai Yu nodded off before Confucius completed his response. Thus Confucius' frustration with Zai Yu started to mount long ago. The fact that Confucius threw a tantrum at his student thus was not wholly unjustified.

Days were not only souring but also increasingly thorny. To say that Confucius and his party "lived on three square meals a day" was an exaggeration. In fact, for three months the taste of meat almost faded into oblivion. Years earlier when Confucius was staying in Qi and listening to "Shaoyue," for three months, he ate meat without relishing its flavor. Now he was in Chen and had listened to "Shaoyue" again, but no scrap of meat passed his lips in three months. He could survive on a vegetarian diet. But he had stopped receiving an income now, and he increasingly had difficulty coming by melons, vegetables and fruits. At mealtime, typically a group of dozens of his men hunched over a small basin of rice and a scanty dish of vegetables. The courteous offering of food was only no sooner paid to each other than the gourd ladles, spoons and chopsticks jumped at the center and every last edible bit was swept away in the wink of an eye.

The teacher and students were grilled as the winter was dragging to a close and spring was around the corner. The hard time even made

Confucius nostalgic for the days when Fan Chi was with him. He guessed that Fan Chi, if with them now, would be able to till the wasteland and grow crops and vegetable patch so that they, both teacher and students, would not go hungry. Unfortunately Fan Chi did not come south with the group. Instead he went up alone and returned to Lu to see Ran Qiu.

Remembering how Fan Chi once inquired about crop planting and gardening made Confucius regret ridiculing this student. It was even more wrong for him to insult his student by calling him "a small man." It seemed that the truth was undeniable that a *junzi* could be worth his salt in living at times of peace, with the official salary and subsidy. But when caught up in the plight of war, a *junzi* had to eke out a livelihood like "a small man."

In the meantime, Confucius continued his lectures, but his talks started to stray from the point, as he said the masses could not be ethical without faith. A *junzi* in power could run the country without his personal guards and salary, but he should keep his word to the people. In comparison the disciples grew absent-minded, at once worried about the threat of the advancing Wu troops and flurried by the hunger, thinking that they would be too feeble to flee if the invaders were there, hence wavering in their confidence in Confucius' benevolent government and rule of virtue.

"Master, we've been traveling around the world and talking to the dukes of various countries. But why aren't they convinced by our ideas?" It was once again the voice of Zai Yu, who today felt little himself, amazingly awake in class and brisk with his thoughts. He frequently stood out among his fellow students for his unorthodox views and, unflinchingly, often laid them bare in public, which got on Confucius' nerves. Since the last time he snoozed by day that annoyed Confucius, he had spoken out more freely, as if he just might as well smash a pot to pieces since it's already cracked.[1]

---

[1] "Smash a pot to pieces since it's already cracked" is a popular Chinese saying meaning "to write off one's situation as hopeless and to act recklessly."

It was a sharp question that hit home.

"This issue, I don't quite understand myself ...," said Confucius.

"Frankly put, the Master's doctrines are like the sun and moon in the sky. How can one turn a blind eye to the existence of the sun and the moon?" Zai Yu continued. "There are times when the sun is blocked by clouds or comes through and the moon appears in full or as a crescent. The Master's doctrines might be rendered with blemishes?"

These words displeased Confucius. "When the Great Way prevails, it is because it's the way of Heaven. Therefore the four seasons evolve and one hundred species come into being. What's wrong with Heaven?"

Zai Yu had no intention of budging an inch. "If the way of Heaven is correct, then it's a human flaw. Probably Master is wrong somewhere? Perhaps there's a hole in the doctrines?"

Even more so than before, Confucius was fuming, "What hole could I have? At fifteen I set my heart on learning. At thirty I took a stand for grand doctrines. At forty I freed myself from different schools of thought. At fifty I understood the Decree of Heaven. At sixty my ear was attuned to the doctrines with a desire to do better. Now I am almost seventy. I have my own way but never exceed the limits of convention. I would wake up at dawn to learn but would not die at dusk to my regret. If I committed errors in attaining the doctrines, that's an act of deceiving Heaven!"

"I was not saying the Master was wrong. I was trying to deduce a conclusion," Zai Yu, seeing that his teacher was infuriated, immediately mellowed his tone of his voice lest something happen to the old man in his rage. But the expression he wore still indicated that the more truth was debated, the clearer it became, and he would stick to his position and argue his point strongly. "If the Master is not incorrect, then that is the fault of all dukes under heaven."

Confucius was confounded. A moment later he heaved a sigh: "A man can enrich doctrines, but not the other way around. A man can be born wise, learn to be wise, be driven to learn in straits, or be not stirred to learn even in straits. The man who is born wise is a sage. I am not a sage, but I've learned to be wise. If a man is driven to learn in straits, he is teachable. If a man is not stirred to learn even in straits, his situation is hopeless." At a loss for a while, he went on, "Dukes under heaven, are they not stirred to learn even in straits?"

CON.

CON.

MAN.

The talk was cut short by a sudden outburst of shouting from outside the window, "The city has fallen! The city has fallen!"

At this instant in darted the disciple Gao Chai, "Master! Master! Someone is inviting you to dinner."

Accepted as a disciple by Confucius in the state of Wei, Gao Chai, thanks to his short physique and ugly features, had never been one of the teacher's favorites. Confucius believed that a man's intelligence was like his features and that his talent was like his height. But judging others by appearance would leave him vulnerable to gossip. In addition, he would be disturbed if he ended up as a teacher without a following if he nitpicked over choosing students. Thus Gao Chai had been allowed to be with him over the years. That year, when traveling through the state of Song and being pursued by Huan Tui who wanted to kill him, only two disciples, beside Sima Niu, had entered the capital city of Shangqiu, Gao Chai being one of them. Since then he had kept his eyes peeled for this student. Seeing Gao Chai bluster in front of him now, Confucius was annoyed and asked, "The city has been taken. Who would invite me to a dinner at a time like this?"

MAN.

Gao Chai was panting in his haste. He gasped before retrieving his voice, "It's the military general that led the invading troops. He heard about your being here and said he must see you, because he admires you for your great name and doctrines of benevolence and righteousness."

"Really?" A beam of astonishment and delight lit up Confucius' face. "It's inconceivable that I'm known even here in the southern tribal territory. Evidently Heaven does not seal off all exits to me. The Great Way does not lead to a dead end. There is always someone under heaven ..."

"Master, the troops that are taking the city are not from Wu. They are from Jin," Gao Chai cut in.

"The Jin troops?" Confucius was dumbstruck.

"The Wu troops withdrew. The Jin troops advanced. They have just seized the city and are burning, killing and looting ..."

"Who's leading the troops?"

"Yang Hu, that's what they said, one of Master's old friends from Lu."

Confucius was stupefied as if turned to stone. A while passed as he gazed forward with a blank stare. His pathetic state was nerve-racking when the disciples were all quiet except Zilu, who was bold enough to wave his hand in front of Confucius' eyes and ask, "Master, are you okay?"

Confucius brought himself to his senses and replied, "I'm alright. I'm alright. Let's take off."

Hastily the teacher and students packed their bags and set out at once. They left Shangcai and journeyed southwards toward the state of Ye.

Chapter 20 The Villain
(The Chronicles: Confucius at the Age of 48)

Yang Hu bumped into Zhongni on the street. The use of
the words "bumped into" is only partially true. Yang Hu had
made a few calls on Zhongni but never found him at home. It
dawned on Yang Hu that the scholar was deliberately hiding
from him. As the year drew to a close, Yang Hu made another
trip and brought with him a roast suckling pig as a gift. Un-
derstandably Zhongni was not in this time either. Yang Hu
left his gift with the gatekeeper and told him the food should
be eaten while warm. His understanding was that people
of Zhongni's sort, bookworms crazy about the rites and etiquette of visits, must make a return call after being called
upon. Sure enough, this morning when he left home Yang Hu
was secretly told that Zhongni had taken advantage of Yang
Hu's absence from home and was on the way of repaying his
call, carrying a wild duck in hand to repay the favor he had
received. With a grin Yang Hu waved his carriage in the re-
verse direction. Thus the two carriages met at a crossroads
just a stone's throw from the entrance to the Ji Mansion.

As an official of the Ji's household, Yang Hu for some time
used to be called Yang "Huo."[1] After the old master of the
House, Ji Wuzi, died, the new master, Ji Pingzi, did not live

---

[1] "*Huo*" means "goods" in Chinese.

long before his own death. Now the most powerful man in the House, Yang Hu,[1] replaced his "Huo" with his original given name "Hu." When Ji Pingzi had died a year earlier, his son Ji Si succeeded him as head of the family, namely Ji Huanzi. Strangely, though Ji Pingzi was arrogant and overbearing, his son Ji Huanzi, in contrast, was weak and worthless. Ji Huanzi had a trusted assistant named Zhong Lianghuai, who in the past never let any opportunity to oppose Yan Hu slip by. Now, with Ji Pingzi dead, this assistant of Ji Huanzi saw himself finally able to challenge anyone in the House and so provoked Yang Hu even more blatantly.

At the funeral of Ji Pingzi, Yang Hu thought it would be proper to make the burial with precious jade of the state of Lu in compliance with ritual conventions. However, his idea was rejected by Zhong Lianghuai, who embraced a new world-view and believed that the imported jade should be buried instead as funerary objects. Yang Hu was about to kill Zhong Lianghuai by burying him alive with the deceased Ji Pingzi. But Yang Hu was stopped by a family official named Gong-sun Furao, who urged him to "prioritize the overall situation, maintain stability and unity" and instead disregard the arrogance of the man for the moment.[2] Later, at a feast hosted by Yang Hu, Zhong Lianghuai once again begot a sting when he turned down the toast to him proposed by Gongsun Furao, offending the latter and embarrassing Yang Hu as well. Gongsun Furao came and talked to Yang Hu that "yanda" should be rigorously carried out and handled sternly and quickly.[3] Mulling this over, Yang Hu decided it was a good idea, and so he sent for men to place Zhong Lianghuai under house arrest.

[1] "*Hu*" means "tiger" in Chinese.

[2] "Prioritize the overall situation and maintain stability and unity" was a popular saying used by the government in contemporary China during and after the Cultural Revolution (1966 – 1976).

[3] "Yanda " is an abbreviation for the policy of severely punishing those who commit serious crimes in contemporary China.

218

When word of the capture of his favorite assistant reached Ji Huanzi, he became enraged. He went to reason with Yang Hu, who decided to detain Ji Huanzi as well. Later a bilateral agreement was reached that Yang Hu would set them free and Zhong Lianghuai would be driven out of the Ji Mansion, never to be hired again. Willingly Ji Huanzi swore an oath of alliance with Yang Hu by smearing his mouth with the blood of a sacrifice and became sworn brothers for sticking together through hard times in the years to come. For Yang Hu, this commitment was definitely not worth the paper it was written on. From then on Ji Huanzi never dared show his rage, while inside the Ji Mansion no one had a say but Yang Hu.

In the state of Lu the clan Jisun was the most powerful, influential family, and Yang Hu was the most powerful and influential man in the Ji Mansion. Yang Hu became unquestionably the most important figure in the state. This reality went without saying, as bright as the sun and moon. However, for some unknown reason, no one except Yang Hu could make sense of it.

Yang Hu knew his limitations. He was not shy of power, as far as he was aware, but he had a bad reputation. The matter of reputations, like capital, called for care at the cost of time and money. He sought power all his life and never did a single thought about reputation flash through his mind. Occasionally he was seen during idle hours, but those leisure times quickly found their way in a battery of heinous actions. He was too engaged to spare any energy for worthy deeds. It was probably too late to mend his ways by this time. With these thoughts turning over and over in his mind, he was eventually left with the sole remedy of making a purchase. One simple way to gain a good reputation was to rub elbows with sages and borrow their prestige. Certainly Yang Hu would not borrow something and refuse to return it, nor would he use it for free. All he wanted to do was afford official positions and salaries in exchange.

He now had his eye on Confucius. To Yang Hu's surprise, this man of the illegitimate son of the Kong family, who had once come to the feast at the Ji Mansion to eat free food and had been herded off by Yang Hu, had now become a renowned sage, raising platforms, giving lectures, teaching the rudiments of reading and writing, and preaching doctrines. This Zhongni even rounded up hundreds of disciples and enthralled audiences by the thousands; he went to great lengths talking dukes into buying his ideas and enacting political reform. Yang Hu at this moment knew he should take a fresh look at Zhongni. Admittedly, he felt some of the ideas Zhongni touched upon were unpleasant to the ear, such as "The youngest prince is throned while the state is in the power of the minister." What made Yang Hu even more infuriated was that this poor wretch, whom he once let his dog chase around, was unwilling to return and serve the clan of Jisun, that is, Yang Hu himself.

There was no doubt Yang Hu was currently in a predicament—his need for a favor from others—so he had no choice but to show courtesy to ordinary men.

He had two reasons for calling on Zhongni. First, he would take advantage of Zhongni's highly acclaimed name. Birds of a feather flocked together. Rubbing shoulders with a sage, he would emerge as a man of a similar caliber. Second, through Zhongni's mouth, he would make known to the masses of Lu the truths that looked as self-evident and easily seen as the sun and moon. The masses should be educated, and to show them those truths, Zhongni obviously had a weightier tongue than that of Yang Hu himself. To achieve these two outcomes, Zhongni should be first prevailed upon to serve him. With Zhongni's consent, Yang Hu would swap his willingness to give up the grievances he had held on Zhongni's past offense and considerations for Zhongni's family background and strike a deal on any terms of conditions, ranking positions and an attractive salary, or anything to be exacted on him. In this regard, Yang Hu was never parsimonious.

Seeing each other in the street, Yang Hu and Zhongni both quickly descended from the carriage and stood at a distance. They were both tall and heavily built, one dressed in a yellow fox fur coat and the other attired in a plain-colored robe of cotton cloth. Cupping one hand in the other before their chests, they saluted each other.

"It's the last thing I expected to meet you here," Yang Hu greeted, forcing a smile. Seeing Zhongni made Yang Hu spiral downward again into a pit of low feelings. The man Yang Hu saw appeared a stranger but reminded him of a former encounter with him that he had had in the past. It seemed as if he were staring into a mirror but found it reflecting the image of someone else, who was of the same height as he, if not taller. Yang Hu was accustomed to looking down at people. But now he had to look straight ahead, or even a little up. He felt a dull sting in his heart.

"I did not think I would meet Your Excellency here," Zhongni replied, with an astonished and blithe expression. His astonishment was true but his blitheness was feigned. He was on his way back from dropping off the wild duck at the Ji Mansion, relieved that he had avoided Yang Hu. But a sudden twist of fate let him stumble across Yang Hu head-on in the street.

"Come on! Come here," Yang Hu warmly waved to Zhongni with a faint tinge of arrogance. "I have something to tell you."

Zhongni shuffled a couple of steps forward and then stopped.

Yang Hu questioned, "A *junzi* embraces benevolence and wisdom, doesn't' he?"

Zhongni answered, "Yes. To seek benevolence through

wisdom is what the *junzi* is devoted to accomplishing."

Yang Hu asked again, "A man possesses the talent for state governing and rescuing people but turns a blind eye on the chaos of a neighboring country and unrest at home. Can he be called "benevolent?"

"No," Zhongni replied.

"A man wishes to have something done in life," Yang Hu went on. "But he has frequently let the opportunity slip away. Can he be called a man of wisdom?"

Zhongni's answer was a "no" again.

Yang Hu said, "I'm speaking this way to show my high ideals and to encourage both of us. Days and months fly by. Time and tide wait for no man."

A silence fell as Zhongni withheld his reply before he said unhurriedly, "I understand the meaning of Your Excellency. Yes, you're right. At fifty, one knows the will of heaven. If I have a chance, it is time for me to leave home, go into politics, assume a position and get something done."

Having said this, Zhongni hastened to take his leave with hands cupped. Apparently he had no intention to carry on the conversation.

Watching Zhongni's carriage turn around and roll into the distance, Yang Hu sneered, thinking he would sooner or later teach those aloof and haughty scholars a lesson. They felt proud of themselves as "sages" and wished to stand up to state rulers and dukes, defying orders from him, Yang Hu. One day he would throw the book at them and make them shake like a leaf in front of him. Otherwise he would butcher them and salt them so as to turn them into real "salted men."[1]

Of course right now he had his hands full and no time to settle their hash. He must first complete one big item of

---

[1] "Salted men" in Chinese is a pun for "sages".

business.

This big item was to make Ji Huanzi vanish from the world.

It was the day for the annual ceremony of offering sacrifices to ancestors by the Jisun clan. As in the early years, it would be held at the Garden of Pu outside the eastern entrance of the city, where the family had its ancestral shrine. Ji Huanzi would preside over the ceremony. But the thought never came across Ji Huanzi's mind that the sacrifice to be offered this year was in fact himself, not the cattle and sheep.

Ji Huanzi was about to offer himself at the altar.

Yang Hu ordered Gongshan Furao to make the arrangements. The guards were secretly replaced at the Garden of Pu and security was tightened at all entrances and exits. Inside the ancestor's shrine, additional efforts were taken to have more trusted troops deployed, and they crouched along the hall and behind curtains and hid themselves beside doors and posts. If things went well, Ji Huanzi should have already been captured at his shrine by this time, and he, Yang Hu, would simply march over and facilitate the sacrifice, an offering ceremony once and for all.

It never occurred to Yang Hu that when he arrived at the Garden of Pu, Ji Huanzi had already escaped the trap.

A slight lapse let Ji Huanzi get away by the skin of his teeth and Yang Hu fail on the verge of success.

It turned out that upon his arrival at the Garden of Pu, Ji Huanzi noticed something unusual at the place and refused to enter the gate for dear life under the pretext of needing to urinate. It did not spring to anyone's mind that the restroom of the garden had a rear door that gave access to the woods behind the shrine and that rear door had been left ajar and unlocked that day! Ji Huanzi was in the bathroom for quite a while before Yang Hu's guards began to fidget around. "Was he relieving himself? How come he was taking so long?"

They dashed into the restroom and found that Ji Huanzi had disappeared. Immediately the chase started, but it was too late.

The instant Ji Huanzi darted out from the latrine he fled the Garden of Pu, leaped on a horse and galloped away. He later took sanctuary at the residence of Meng Xizi.

Outraged, Yang Hu smashed every sacrificial utensil at the Ji shrine to pieces, howling, "Gongshan Furao ruined my chance!" Without hesitating, he sent troops to storm the Meng Mansion. The Meng Mansion was not easy to capture. Yang Hu's attack was routed. Like the saying "An army in flight is like an avalanche of mountain rocks," Yang Hu saw his troops scattering and deserting him. The state of Lu became a poor abode for him. He fled alone and embarked on a course of aimless wandering, living in exile.

Yang Hu first trekked to the state of Ji, where Duke Jing refused to receive him. Then he turned to the state of Song and found himself persona non grata there, too. Finally he made his way to the state of Jin, in which he was able to stay but had to work blood, sweat, and tears for Zhao Yang. Yang Hu's life was a far cry from the indulgences he enjoyed when serving at the Ji Mansion in Lu. During the few years that followed, the dismayed man was drenched in the stream of enduring humiliation and hardship. Yang Hu felt that to be a villain was easier said than done, while to be a villain worth his salt was even harder.

A decade later, Yang Hu took orders and led troops in invading the state of Cai. After conquering its capital city, he learned that Zhongni happened to be there as well. He felt a flare of nostalgia for past days. He sent for Zhongni, wishing to get together and talk about the glory days of the past. That day at the Garden of Pu years earlier would have steered a totally different course for Yang Hu's life if the rear door had been locked. Zhongni's later years put him in the same shoes of Yang Hu, when the sage was at the helm of the Lu state and failed in his endeavor to purge the country of the "Three pillars." Two dashed high hopes! However, Yang Hu was startled to learn that Zhongni, on hearing about his coming, was scared into flight. His old temperament had endured through these intervening years!

Chapter 21 Ye
(Spring and Autumn Period: 5th Year of Duke Ai of Lu's Reign, 490 BC)

When lord Ye met Confucius, his first utterance was the question, "Have you ever seen the dragon?" Slightly stunned, Confucius replied, "No. I know there is a legend about it from ancient times. But unfortunately I did not grow up at that time." Lord Ye was a little disappointed, "Zilu once quoted you by saying, 'One should be insatiable in learning and tireless in teaching.' Obviously I thought you must have been very knowledgeable about dragons." "In my life I am essentially so dedicated to learning through plain living and pursuing enjoyment so as to be free of worries," Confucius immediately clarified, "that I have become too old to learn more. I'm ignorant of monsters, supernatural forces, immortal beings, and gods, let alone the dragon."

The remarks at once dampened Lord Ye's spirits. Lord Ye was well known for his fondness for dragons. Inside his abode, the mythical reptile was everywhere, painted on walls, engraved on pillars. He wrote poems and rhyming prose and hung them in his rooms. This affection even showed up in the examination questions he designed for the evaluation and promotion of officials.

Originally surnamed Shen, named Zhuliang and styled Zigao, Lord Ye was a senior official in the State of Chu. Since he was given the territory of Ye for his service by the Duke of Chu, the State was under his reign. As a monarch of a small population in absolute subordination to the State of Chu, he was hardly preoccupied with official routines. Therefore he turned concern and interests to dragons, this prehistoric, legendary monster. He craved seeing it day and night. One day he was seized by an illusion that he saw a real dragon wiggling through the window and into his room, ten meters long, with golden scales covering its body. It staggered around Lord Ye's room and creeped over his bed, scaring him out of his wits. This anecdote gave rise to an idiom, "Lord Ye's love of dragons." But this experience only solidified his belief in the existence of dragons.

Confucius arrived with his disciples in the territory of Ye the day before yesterday. Due to the rugged route at the foot of mountains, the hard travel and occasional detours took the group more than twenty days to reach the destination. Learning about their arrival, Lord Ye came out at once to meet Confucius. But Confucius' smattering of dragons turned out to be rather frustrating to the lord who originally sought an absorbing chat. To smooth over the embarrassing pause in the conversation, Lord Ye coughed and, absent-minded, raised another question, "I wonder what sort of research you do in general?" "Government," Confucius said. Lord Ye further asked, "I'd like to listen more." Confucius replied, "It is letting those close at hand satisfied and those in the distance come over. In other words it is the study of making subjects happy and other countries submit to your rule." Baffled by these words, Lord Ye mulled them over before soliloquizing, "Despite the small size of my country, it is a shrine of dragons. If there is a dragon exhibit, I'm sure it will entertain locals and draw crowds of visitors from other states."

However, the lord was still pondering the dragon show when another issue occurred, that of a lost lamb. A few days ago a lamb strayed out of the lord's mansion. It disappeared after someone said it rambled into the residence of Confucius and his disciples. Then the news reached Lord Ye.

One evening, Zeng Shen came to see Confucius, tears rolling down his cheeks, and said, "My father ate the lamb." Taken aback Confucius asked, "How did you know?" Zeng Shen replied, "Last night I saw him drink and eat mutton." His father Zeng Dian's liking for drinking and eating meat, particularly lamb, was not new to the Master. Zeng Shen continued, "My father told me he did not know that it was Lord Ye's lamb. He thought fortune had struck him with a stray lamb. So he stewed it. I intended to inform Lord Ye and, at the same time, requested my father go and confess his transgression. But he refused to go. He even wanted to keep it between us. I thought a *junzi* should value righteousness above filial affection. But he dismissed my belief by remarking that a filial son should not give up his parents. Today I reflected on it three times and yet I still cannot resolve it so I'm here for your advice." Tears again began to well up in his eyes.

Hearing these words Confucius found himself at a loss. Zeng Shen was not talented as a boy. At five he only learned to read the characters "之 *zhi*" and "无 *wu*" and to count numbers up to ten. When he turned 10, his learning showed no progress. His stupidity incurred plenty of stick beatings by his father, aimed at making him into a useful man. The first time he got hit, he stood around the corner of the street, weeping and explaining to passersby, "I reflected on this three times but could not make sense of what fault I had committed." Later when the beating became a daily routine, he grinned, saying to others, "When parents are delighted with one's behavior, one should be satisfied and remember their affection. When parents reprimanded one, one should be scared but not be resentful." The hard years of his early life left no impact on his adulthood. Finding him so filial, Confucius took him as disciple long before. Thus Zeng Shen became a fellow student with his father, spared for endless corporal punishments.

Slow but steadfast, Zeng Shen would ponder perplexing issues repeatedly. Gradually the habit of racking his brains three times a day formed. Sometimes the ritual of three times was not enough for a solution. Then he would add another one or two times. Among young disciples, he had the most thorough understanding of "benevolence." This realization brought him to recognize another two characters: "loyalty" and "forgiveness." This learning process did not stop until he understood many other characters, "filial duty, kindness, faith, respect, courage, honesty, firmness, thriftiness, integrity, modesty, endurance, admiration, cautiousness, gentleness, openness, and the sense of being ashamed."

Aware of his being caught in the dilemma between loyalty and filial duty, Confucius tried to console him, saying, "Please go home now. I will meet Lord Ye tomorrow and see what I can do about it."

The following day the Master went to the lord's place and inquired, "Is it true that your honorable residence has lost a lamb?" "Yes, it is," answered Lord Ye, "It's only three months old, young and delicate." Confucius remarked, "I've a disciple called Zeng Dian. He ate a lamb yesterday. But we have no idea whether it is the one that you lost." Lord Ye replied, "That's simple. You can just check with his son. Over here in this state, whenever someone steals the lamb, his son will certainly reveal the truth. One should be honest."

Confucius felt slightly uneasy. He coughed and responded by saying, "In my home state folks have different morals. Though honesty is commendable, father and son should cover up each other's offense, and this practice is valued as honest. I suggest you not send one to probe the occurrence." So saying, he reddened, slightly ashamed of his explanation. Lord Ye paused before responding, "Truly, what huge differences there are in the conditions among states!" Then, waving his hand, he continued, "Alright. Alright. It's nothing but a lamb. Now let's get back to the topic of dragons."

A couple of months had passed while Confucius stayed as a guest of Lord Ye. He found his host's interest in dragons not something he shared. Now he was further bothered with the annoyance of the lost lamb. His days began to drag on. At this time news came that the troops of the State of Jin pulled out of the city of Shangcai. Confucius decided to take his leave of Lord Ye and returned to the State of Cai.

The group departed and traveled back on the same route, first in the east and then in the north after a detour. However, the travelers had no sooner left the city of Yi than they got lost, able to distinguish between the east and west but getting confused about north and south. In front of a river, they could not locate the point of crossing they had gone through on their way to the area of Ye. Then they saw two men on the hillside in the distance, one tall and one short, pulling a plow forward on the field. Although both pulled hard, the forces they exerted on the plow were not even, with one greater than the other, making the plow trace a zigzag. Both clad in the long gown of plain cloth, they appeared like senior officials from town instead of farmers living on the field. Confucius was certain that they were some learned hermits so he sent Zilu ahead to greet them and ask for directions.

Zilu walked forward and extended his formal greetings and respects to the two scholars. Then he requested their honorable names. The tall man, frowning and pulling a long face, replied with displeasure, "My humble name is Chang Ju." The short man was delighted and grinned, saying, "Mine is Jie Ni." Zilu realized they gave pseudonyms. Chang Ju meant sustained depression, while Jie Ni signified disrespect for the silly ruler. Which recluse would rashly let his real name known to others?

Zilu inquired about the point of crossing.

Chang Ju asked, "Who's the man holding the reins over there?"

"Kong Qiu," Zilu replied.

"The one from the State of Lu?" Chang Ju further asked.

"Yes, it is he," Zilu confirmed.

Rather vexed, Chang Ju said, "He should be acquainted with it! Doesn't he travel around the world, teaching kings about governance? How come he doesn't know where the point of crossing is? Otherwise what's the point showing off his learning?" Then he turned around and refused to talk any more.

Standing there Zilu was embarrassed. At this moment Jiu Ni came over with a smile and asked, "Who are you?"

"I'm Zilu. My formal name is Zhong You," Zilu replied.

Jie Ni said, "Oh, I heard about you. You must be a disciple of Confucius."

Zilu said, "Yes."

Jie Ni observed, "The world's enormous. It should take its own course in development. Who's able to impose his will on it? One is to learn from us living a solitary life in the mountain instead of following some conceited person going around among states and selling his ideas. How do you think?" Then he too left Zilu and went back to join Chang Ju in plowing.

Zilu was frustrated, disappointed with his failure to learn about the location to cross the river and encounter with the jeers. He returned to the Master and recounted what had happened. This left Confucius perplexed and speechless. He let out a long sigh and said, "If the world had adhered to the Great Way, why would I have attempted to reform it? How could I have associated myself with beasts?!"

All of a sudden the point of crossing was found. With Yan Yuan, Zigong and others, Confucius was first ferried over the river leaving Zilu behind. Usually Zilu led the way and the Master followed. This time the small riverboat could not sit many so he let his master go over in the first round.

A moment later when he reached the other bank Zilu found himself alone. Looking around he saw an old man saunter over, holding a walking stick in his hand and carrying a straw basket on his back. He walked up to him and inquired about his master's whereabouts. But the old man quickened his pace as if he did not see him, mumbling to himself, "If he is neither able to toil with his four limbs in the field nor tell apart the five cereals, how could he be called Master?" He strode up the hillside to a terraced field of crops. Planting the walking stick into the soil, he picked up a hoe and started hoeing the field. How dare Zilu bother him with another question? Later, when he found Confucius, he recounted the happening. The Master listened and was lost in thought. Quite a while later he said to Zilu, "He is another hermit. This shows the State of Ye is not only a dwelling of dragons but a home of recluses. They all demonstrate the head and conceal the tail!" Then he sighed and continued, "Their dismissal of me as ignorant of farming is justified. At times of war and chaos, who has ever thought about the need that a learned man encounters to labor in the field so as to make a living?"

Zilu was still in the shroud of disappointment of the day. After dark, the Master and disciples went to a family in a remote village and decided to stay for the night. Lying on the straw bed with the Master, Zilu could not refrain from raising the question to him, "We can forget about being rejected by those dukes. But why do these hermits frown upon and jeer at us too?"

The Master replied, "Hermits are worthy men! They lead a solitary life at the time of turbulence for four reasons. The first is that they want to get away from the chaos of society. The second is that they desire to stay away from a particular place. The third is that they choose to turn away from others' frowns of displeasure. The last is that they refuse to listen to others' taunts. We are constantly on the way among the states and try to persuade one duke after another. Certainly they display no respect toward us.

Zilu said, "Should a man of virtue be considered not righteous if he chooses to lie low rather than taking an official position? The moral principle is held up if the son is filial to his father. Should ethics be given up if the minister does not subject himself to the monarch? Isn't a *junzi* selfish to choose to live away from the turmoil of the society for keeping a good reputation? It's for the sake of preaching the Great Way that you master choose to assume official responsibilities instead of staying in solitude, isn't it?"

Confucius heaved a sigh and said, "Yes. If I do not preach the Great Way, who will do it?" Then, smiling wryly, he continued, "A *junzi* holding an official position is fulfilling his duties. Even if he knows it is impossible to spread Heaven's decree over the land, he should not refrain from his responsibility. Probably I'm one of those who try to accomplish that which cannot be done."

Zilu understood his master was recalling Zilu's past experience in the State of Lu. That event happened when Zilu went outside the city on business and was held up late. As a result, he stayed in the outskirts of the city for the night. The following morning when he entered the city the guard at the city entrance asked where he was from. He told him that he was one of the Confucius' followers. The entrance guard laughed, questioning, "Is it that one who is bent on accomplishing what he knows can by no means be done?" After Zilu got back home and told Confucius about it, the latter was not irritated. On the contrary he was pleased, taking it as commendation and believing in the solemnity and sorrowfulness of one's living. By that time, at the zenith of life, Confucius was Chief Legislator and acted as prime minister in charge of the Lu's affairs.

That night Zilu dropped the matter. He blew out the lamp and, listening to the howl of the gale outside, went to sleep until dawn.

Twenty days later Confucius and his disciples returned to the capital city of Shangcai. The mayhem reduced the city to rubble, debris, dilapidated walls and charred houses. They were all greatly saddened and deeply distressed at the sight. As they drew closer to home, they saw the alleys full of fine horses and extravagant carriages stretching all the way to the main avenue. An inquiry about it informed them of the special envoy of the King of Chu who had arrived and awaited respectfully for long. Only then did it dawn on them that the emissary from the state of Chu had been waiting for such a long time.

Chapter 22   The Monarch
(The Chronicles: Confucius at the Age of 50)

On a snowy, gusty night, Duke Ding of Lu did not summon Kong Qiu by impulse alone.

Since his ascent to power, Duke Ding was frequently woken by the crowing of roosters, not the crows at dawn, but rather those uttered at the triumph of cockfighting. In a trance, he watched Ji Pingzi dash into his palace brandishing a sword. Ten years earlier, Duke Ding's elder brother Duke Zhao had been chased by Ji Pingzi to the State of Qi after the latter had lost a cockfight and ever since had been terrified to return. A few years earlier, his brother died in the territory of Marquis Hou, leaving Duke Ding in power and thus ending several leaderless years in the state of Lu.

It was not easy for the Duke of Lu to rule. It was a tough job, characterized by both domestic troubles and international worries. The domestic troubles were caused by the "three pillars:" the clan of Ji, the clan of Meng, and the clan of Shu. The clan of Ji was particularly problematic, as its influence rising, and it had single-handedly seized power over the state. The international worries stemmed from the State of Qi. Qi and Lu were neighboring countries, as close together as lips and teeth. At times they were on good terms, while at other times, when relations soured, they became bitter foes. Over the years, Qi became stronger than Lu, which made peaceful relations tough to maintain. Border incursions were common, with Qi's troops crossing over into Lu for no apparent reason, occupying lands, laying waste to farms, capturing women and seizing property. And then, Qi would promise to maintain a lasting friendship with Lu for future generations to come.

Late that night Duke Ding once again was awakened suddenly by the crowing of a rooster. Frightened, he became startled and wide awake. His imperial chambers were blanketed in silent, dim candle light with bed curtains hanging motionlessly, but there were no roosters and no people. Sleepless and plagued bt insomnia, he agonized over the state of his country and people. It was at this time that he sent for Zhongni to meet in his palace.

Duke Ding had long since heard of Kong Qiu. He was a learned man from a simple background, and yet had vast influence, capable of bringing people together. He had attracted a group of over a thousand disciples. Regardless of where he taught, his call could rally ten percent of his audience behind him. His reputation gained the respect of Ji Huanzi, and even the power-hungry Yang Hu badly desired to bring him into his faction. What was most laudable about the remarkable man was his innate loyalty. A few years earlier, when Lu was without a ruler, he steered clear of officialdom and stayed at home, a recluse dedicated solely to writing books and poetry. He likened himself to the pine and cypress trees during frozen winter, surviving by sheer austerity and rectitude alone.

Duke Ding realized that the dual threat to his rein from both Yang Hu and the "three pillars" actually provided him with an opportunity to restore his authority over the government. Who would be able to help him restore order? Kong Qiu came to mind.

Now, at this very moment, Zhongni stood before him, his

head and shoulders covered with snowflakes, with a thin layer of ice formed on his eyebrows. He sneezed loudly. It then finally dawned on Duke Ding that it was snowing outside. Not wanting the duke to have to wait for him, Zhongni had chosen to walk instead of waiting for his carriage. With nearly one foot of freshly fallen snow on the ground, his shoes were soaked through.

Duke Ding of Lu was no longer a young man but he was still impetuous and demanded immediate results. Without any delay, he asked directly: "Do you have a single piece of advice for how to build a powerful country?"

Zhongni was well aware that the reason he had been summoned in the middle of the night was to undertake a momentous responsibility, and so he chose his words carefully. He thought for a while before offering a guarded reply: "No. Perhaps, though, there is a statement that goes, 'It is neither easy to be a sovereign nor a senior official.' Isn't understanding the difficulty of serving as a ruler itself a recommendation for establishing a powerful state?"

Duke Ding listened but was mystified by his response and so raised another question, "Is there, then, one particular statement for bringing down a country?"

Zhongni reflected on his question and offered another cautious remark, "Again no, there isn't. But there is another statement that comes close: 'Subjects speak and behave to please their ruler no matter whether his words are correct or not.' This means that the ruler's pleasure stems from the total submission of his subjects. If the ruler's words are correct and all his subjects act accordingly, isn't that how it ought to be? If the ruler says something improper and no one rises in opposition, wouldn't that be a situation that could bring down a country?"

Still baffled and struggling to fathom what he meant, Duke Ding wrung his hands and asked further, "How should the king give orders to ministers and how should ministers serve the king?"

Again, Zhongni hesitated before replying: "The king should treat ministers according to the ethical code, while ministers should serve the king with loyalty."

This answer delighted the duke, who thought to himself that Kong Qiu was a truly loyal official, one who fully understood the proper relationship between ruler and minister. Smiling, he said to Kong Qiu, "Good! This sentence is just what I wanted. I like loyal ministers and loathe rebellious ones."

As he spoke, Duke Ding anxiously paced back and forth in front of his bed, his fat body wrapped in a loose bedrobe with long untied belts dragging along on the ground. Clad in court dress, Zhongni stood neatly aside, with his head bowed and his eyes fixed on the duke's robe dragging on the ground, and wondered whether or not he ought to make a suggestion about this.

"Ji Pingzi has gone too far!" Duke Ding grumbled indignantly, "When I held a memorial service for Duke Zhao, there were only two dancers left in the whole shrine. The others all went to the residence of Ji and joined in the celebration for his birthday. How dare he have a dancing performance with eight rows of eight dancers each inside his home, I will kill him sooner or later!"

Hearing these words, Zhongni chimed in with indignation, "If this can be tolerated, is there anything else that cannot be tolerated?"

"Fortunately he died and can no longer push me around," Duke Ding said. "Ji Huanzi is also despicable. Recently Yang Hu has rebelled against Ji Huanzi and the clan of Ji is in chaos. I'm trying to restore the prosperity of my ancestors and rejuvenate the imperial order. But what should I do?"

Seeing the king's resolve to restore law and order in the

court, Zhongni proposed, "If the land under heaven is in order, the supreme ruler formulates rites and types of music and issues orders to suppress rebellion. If the land under heaven is in disorder, dukes assume the position of supreme ruler in addition to all these responsibilities. Nowadays the state of Lu is ruled not by you but rather by senior officials who formulate rites and types of music and issue orders to suppress rebellion. If Your Majesty wants to rebuild the country, you have to start from the ground up."

Duke Ding appeared confused by his speech, as though he did not fully comprehend his meaning. He grew tired of pacing and then slumped on the edge of the bed, saying, "Please explain your meaning."

Pausing shortly, Zhongni then continued: "In order to maintain an order at home, external affairs must first be taken care of."

Eager to learn more, Duke Ding pressed, "How should I manage external affairs?"

Zhongni replied, "Form an alliance with Qi, make peace with them a priority, then transform conflict into a review of troops, and transform wars into negotiations."

Applauding, Duke Ding acclaimed "Wonderful!" He remembered that his elder brother, Duke Zhao, had died long ago and that there thus would no longer be any barriers standing in his way to forge an alliance with Qi. He then asked, "How will I be able to maintain order at home?"

Zhongni responded, "A country cannot have two rulers. But the power of the State of Lu is shared by the "Three Pillars." This is why there is social unrest. As the old saying says, 'A minister should not be allowed to command troops, nor should a senior official possess even so much as a small town.' Your Majesty should regain power over the territories conferred onto those ministers and disarm the troops of senior officials so that they cannot maintain the military strength to raise a rebellion."

Duke Ding fell silent for a moment, knowing that this was all easier said than done. If unsuccessful, he once again would be forced to flee to Qi. All of a sudden, he recalled the nightmare he had earlier that morning, and it filled him with courage. Rubbing his fists and palms, he exclaimed, "Let's do it!"

That night the two of them chatted until the wee hours of the morning. At dawn they finally agreed on the guiding principles of the country. By the time Zhongni left the imperial palace, the snow had stopped and rays of sunshine shone through the clouds as the city echoed with the crowing of roosters. However by nightfall yet another blizzard struck, followed by several months of lingering haze over the country.

A couple of days later, Duke Ding delivered an imperial edict appointing Kong Qiu the magistrate of the capital city of Lu. Although he was fifty years old, Zhongni unfortunately had little experience as an official and consequently had to start at the lowest level. The magistrate of the capital city, a grass-roots position, was in charge of a key region and therefore played an extraordinarily significant role. For Zhongni this represented a training opportunity. One year later he was promoted to the position of Deputy Minister of Works, in charge of the construction, examination and approval of engineering projects. Before long, he rose to the post of Chief Justice and held a concurrent position as head of the board of rites. His three successive promotions led to his imperial appointment as prime minister, a powerful position, acting as regent for the king.

Chapter 23   Chu
(Spring and Autumn Period: 6th Year of Duke Ai of Lu's Reign, 489 BC)

On their way to the state of Chu Confucius, along with his disciples, was stranded in the wilderness, and a band of rogues blocked their way out. With no sign of a village or house in sight either ahead or behind them, they were in a place surrounded by rocky, barren hills. The only route leading to the state of Chu was rugged and uneven and had been taken by a group of outlaws who were in front of the master and his students. Another group of rogues pursued them from behind. Zilu had succeeded in leading a few young fellow disciples who had been able to hold them off for a couple of days.

Originally Confucius thought he had run into a group of highwaymen. This region was located between the states of Chen and Cai with no designated border or clear ownership, and so outlaws appeared frequently. Warfare fueled plunder and turned robbery into a daily occurrence. Usually travelers were released unharmed so long as they surrendered their money, just as travelers pay the road and bridge tolls in today's society. But a further look refuted Confucius' initial thought. It was strange that these outlaws were all prisoners, just released recently after serving their sentences of forced labor. They still wore prison uniforms and shouted out to kill him. Confucius realized that, though he had given lectures among states on benevolence and righteousness and had gained a degree of fame in the process, it was still quite unlikely that his name would be known by a bunch of rascals living in remote mountainous lairs. Obviously this ambush had been designed by someone.

That day news spread quickly throughout the capital town of Chen, Shangcai, of the King of Chu's invitation to Confucius with huge sums. As a large state, Chu was true to its word. Its special envoy, impeccably attired and richly ornamented, appeared with noble deportment in a dazzling chariot and in the company of a huge entourage. The impressive procession went through the downtown, causing quite a stir that made the whole town turn out. It was said that the money that the special envoy had presented was spectacular: a large heap of shining gold coins. He told Confucius that the King of Chu had heard about his great name and was willing to offer him a fief of 700 *li* to invite him to take the position of senior official so as to implement policies of benevolence. The offer was well received by Confucius who, after expressing appreciation, told his disciples to pack his books and bedding and get ready to meet the king the following day.

The whole town was excited by the news except for one man, who felt incredibly uneasy. This was Ji Xian, the leading attendant of duke of Chen. After the troops of Wu took the capital town of Chen, Ji Xian fled south and found his way to the state of Cai because the husband of his wife's sister, Du Neng, served in Cai as a senior official. One time Ji Xian had lost face at a banquet when Confucius outwitted him in an argument. Though the topic was insignificant, Ji Xian took it to heart as loss of dignity in front of the duke, and so he secretly wished that Confucius and his followers would be killed at some point along their journey, either by the troops of Wu or beasts in the wilderness.

Now that Confucius had been invited by the sovereign of Chu, Ji Xian felt that he could not wait ten years, the amount of time that a *junzi* usally took to get revenge. Not wanting to miss this chance for action, Ji Xian talked to Du Neng and pointed out that it would not benefit Chen and Cai if Chu allowed Confucius to assume an official position. The two men were also aware that Confucius had lived for a long time in Chen and Cai, and was very familiar with the corruption and incompetence of the officials in the two countries. Now Confucius, a learned man, once in Chu, would be sure to tell the ruler of the Chu court about the corruption he had seen in Chen and Cai. With Confucius in power, Chu would surely become strong and Chu and Cai would perish. Having worked as court officials for years, Ji Xian and Du Neng were wary and thoughtful. In the interest of Chen and Cai, they decided to kill Confucius on his journey. As a senior official in the state of Cai, Du Neng lacked the power to dispatch troops. But he was in charge of the jails. One night he released a group of prisoners, granting them a special amnesty. The prisoners were given cudgels and were sent on a relentless manhunt for their designated targets. Two days later they arrived east of Sleeping Ox Mountain and besieged the hill on which Confucius and his men were stranded on their way south.

Though hard pressed in the wilderness at this critical juncture, Confucius remained calm. He was a little agitated due to hunger. A couple days later, the shortage of food became serious.

It was the third day that the master and students were surrounded and the first day that they had nothing to eat. They had left home for the journey in a rush and thus had not brought along enough food. To make it worse, the continuous warfare among states ravaged the area, leaving villages and households emptied without a sign of life. The food the traveling group carried was all gone after the first few days. Now forced to stay at such a wretched place, the starved men found nowhere to go to relieve their plight. The master and disciples, over ten of them, survived only on water fetched from a nearby brook, and could not move one step further.

Concerned that the aging master was exposed to the coldness of rain and wind, the disciples set up a tent against a rock at a low point of the ridge and made him lie down to rest. Zilu, holding a long sword, stood watch outside the tent day and night. In truth he had not an ounce of strength left, but nevertheless kept a vigilant air.

Even then, Confucius did not give up teaching. His students, weak and feeble, either slouched against trees or lay on the ground. Barely able to focus their attention on his lessons, they listened to their teacher's words while dreaming about steamed buns and rice. That day the master's instruction was on personal integrity. Zilu was the physically strongest of all but suffered the most from starvation. His stomach rumbled and he wore a worried look, feeling that he could no longer be a *junzi* without food. Then he asked his master, in a faint voice, "Master, why should we have to endure this sort of suffering?" Seeing that he was disheartened, Confucius replied, "A *junzi* can endure hunger but a small man cannot." Zigong was the only disciple that could still hold himself up, and he stood bracing himself against a large tree. Hearing the master's remark Zigong felt inspired, looking determined and standing straight. Confucius saw him and called out his name, saying, "Ci, do you think I am a learned man?" Zigong replied, "Yes, master. Don't you think so?" Confucius, shaking his head, said, "No. I'm just one that can hang on to the end of what I've done."

Zilu was too hungry to hang on. He ran up the hill into the woods. He dug up some wild herbs, picked mushrooms and brought them back to the starved group. However, after eating them the men all grew sick and no one knew whether the wild herbs were inedible or the mushrooms were poisonous. They starved for days on end. Today the diarrhea almost pulled their intestines out. Unable to recover, the disciples dropped to the ground one after another, with no strength left.

Confucius saw no way to carry on his lessons and he did not press them. Instead he started playing his *qin* and singing songs and odes to enliven his students and enhance their morale. The music and singing, however, ran off and on, sometimes even suddenly pausing on a resounding note, and, moments later, gradually restarted, leaving the listeners totally disconcerted. Still the entertainment diverted the men from the pain of hunger. It turned out that Confucius had eaten the same substance, and so now it was his turn to suffer.

Though just early autumn, it was chilly and windy. At night mountain valleys and woods echoed with the roars of tigers and wolves.

On the fifth day of starvation, no one could move a muscle. Confucius could not go on with his performance, either. The excitement died down and hush descended over the group, which was seized with a sinking sentiment.

Propping himself up, Confucius feebly sat on a rock. Landed in such a plight of despair, he became quite worried. It was a critical juncture. He knew his men were even more anxious.

He asked Zilu to come over and said, "*The Book of Songs* says, 'Wild oxen and tigers roam in the wilderness.' We're not wild oxen and tigers. Why should we be stranded in the wilderness? The lyrics seem meant for us. Is it because we committed some fault that we should fall into such misery?"

Zilu had eaten the most wild herbs and mushrooms and so he fell sick the most frequently. At this moment he was so faint that he could barely form clear thoughts. But he blurted out, "I guess we must have not cultivated our moral character to the level of true righteousness. Therefore people do not trust us. We've not procured wisdom, either. Therefore we've never truly accomplished anything successfully."

Shaking his head, Confucius said, "Is this true? If the masses all had trusted righteous men, there wouldn't have been sages who died of hunger like Bo Yi and Shu Qi. If intelligent people had brought to fruition all they desired, there would'nt have been able senior officials who were executed like Wang Zi and Bi Gan."[1]

He then summoned Zigong. Zigong, propping himself up by leaning

---

[1] Bo Yi and Shu Qi, two brothers, were princes of a state and famous men in the Spring and Autumn period. Wang Zi and Bi Gan were two loyal subjects of the Shang dynasty who were executed by the tyrant Emperor Zhou.

on a stick, shuffled his feet, taking one step at a time. Confucius repeated the same question to him. Zigong, mulling it over for a while, replied, "My teacher, is it because your ethics are set too high to make sense to the masses? Perhaps that is why they are not widely accepted. Maybe we might try to bring down our standards a little to see what happens?"

Immediately Confucius shook his head again, "No. A good farmer sows seeds but does not care about reaping the harvest; a gifted craftsman enhances his skills but does not follow trends. A *junzi* cultivates his innate qualities according to principles, preaches his doctrines, and promotes law and order under Heaven. Why should he expect to receive anything in return? Harboring presumptuous intentions, a man apparently cherishes low aspirations!"

At this instant, Yan Yuan, lying aside, chipped in, "Our master's doctrines are high and profound, that's why the land under Heaven finds them so hard to accept. Why does it matter whether they are accepted or not? Their unpopularity is a testament to the truth of a *junzi*!" With a fragile physique, he was basically a lesser eater; he had experienced years of hardship and so he could endure starvation fairly well. In the past he had survived on just a bowlful of rice and ladleful of water. Today to sustain hunger for a couple of days on end was not unbearable to him. Holding a chisel and cutting block in hands, he spoke while continuing to record everything uttered by the master. As he continued to speak, his tone became excited and indignant. "It's disgraceful of us, his disciples, to fail to grasp firmly our master's doctrine! It's disgraceful of dukes and ministers in the land under Heaven to fail to apply our masters' ideas to their states' governments! How dare they refuse? How dare they all refuse? The masses' refusal to accept them is a testament to the truth of the master's beliefs!"

"Well said!" Confucius listened, his eyes beaming with pride, and said to Yan Yuan, "A distinctive part of becoming a *junzi* is living in poverty. But gentlemen do not remain poor forever. Hui, in the future you will be the first of my disciples to be rich.[1] By that time I will manage money matters for you."

The men all laughed. Some of them, too weak to laugh, stifled giggles and held their bellies.

Zigong burst out laughing too. He then asserted, "Master, we can't wait here for death! We have to figure out a way."

Confucius said, "When we reach the state of Chu, everything will be fine."

Zigong said, "Of course. But the problem is we may not be able to get there. We've got to find a way to get out of here."

Confucius inquired, "Do you have any ideas?"

Zigong thought for a while and said, "When we were in the capital of Cai, I heard that the king of Chu led his troops north and later had them stationed in the area of Chengfu. I reckon that place is not far from here. If one of us can reach the troops of Chu and request their help, we'll certainly be able to escape."

Confucius said, "Given our current predicament, we have no other alternative." So saying, he gave the last bits of food to Zigong. "You're the only one who can accomplish this mission. We're counting on you to save our lives."

Zigong stood up, his body straight. He stretched, smoothed out his clothes, and brushed the dust off. With effort, he managed to kowtow, saying, "As your disciple, I will not let you down."

Two days later, Zigong returned, wearing new clothing, his face glowing with health and vigor. He looked as if he not only had taken a bath but also had eaten his fill. He brought back large amounts of food, dried meat and vegetables. The starving men on the hilltop were at their last gasp. When they saw the food fetched for them, they could barely manage to get up and eat it.

---

[1] Hui is Yan Yuan's given name.

Zigong said to Confucius, "Master, the king of Chu has dispatched troops to help us! Those villains fled upon hearing the news, covering their heads like rats."

Confucius looked up to the sky and gave a long, loud cry, "Heaven has eyes and is unwilling to watch us starve to death in these desolate, barren hills!"

Zigong hesitated before saying, "This time, despite the fact that we have been rescued with the assistance of the king of Chu, we'll probably not be able to go to Chu."

Taken aback, Confucius asked, "Why? Is there another gang ahead?"

Zigong grinned and replied, "No. Certainly I did not mean that. I simply heard the king of Chu would give you a warm welcome. But Zixi, the minister of internal affairs of Chu, was rather displeased. He's opposed to the king's grant of seven hundreds of *li* to you. He said that you pretend to preach for righteousness but actually are ambitious in an effort to steal power, just as King Wu of the Eastern Zhou dynasty did, who achieved his success in the name of King Wen of the Eastern Zhou. If you go to Chu now, there would be tons of trouble waiting for you there, possibly even death."

Confucius fell silent. The stillness continued for a long time before he slowly uttered, "Where should we go if not to Chu? So long as the king of Chu is willing to allow me to take charge of his state affairs, I have absolutely no desire to emulate King Wen, let alone King Wu. But why could Chu not be able to become another empire, like the Eastern Zhou dynasty? When one state rises in power, the whole land under heaven will be governed in order. The effects should be evident in one year; and in three years the rejuvenation of the who state should be complete. If only the king of Chu would trust me with the court duties …"

At twilight, Confucius stood alone at the edge of a rocky precipice atop the hill, gazing at the sun falling behind the mountain range that rose and fell in the distance. He was lost deep in meditation. Far away behind him stood Zilu, who refrained from disturbing the master. Aware that dusk was falling rapidly, Zilu quietly walked forward.

With a sigh Confucius soliloquized, "If I failed to carry out my doctrines in Chu, there would be no possibility of realizing my dreams in the whole land. Then I could only go to the eastern regions, inhabited by marginal tribes, and those poverty-stricken, sparsely populated areas." Turning around, he then said to Zilu who was walking up, "Otherwise, I could travel by raft on the sea to the lands of the unknown. You, my student, would you be the only one to go with me by that time?"

Deeply touched by Confucius' trust, Zilu replied, "Master, I will follow you wherever you go, no matter whether we travel through fire or water." At this point the student became more fervid, "If a *junzi* is unable to be diligent, endure hardship, not fear death and take delight in simple living, what's the point of fostering the ethics of righteousness? Unfortunately I'm not good at swimming and am sure to drown in water. If I ride on the raft, I'm afraid I would be the last one to be able to rescue you in an emergency. I'll start learning to swim from now on so that I can protect you in the future."

Smiling, Confucius responded by saying, "Have we been left now at the end of our resources? I don't think it'll be too late to learn how to swim then."

Confucius and his disciples hit the road again. After another ten days of arduous journeying they finally crossed the mountains and arrived at Fuhan, a key town just north of the state of Chu. Beholding the town walls in the distance, with banners and flags fluttering, the travelers, both master and disciples, were thrilled. Entering the town, they found black banners and flags everywhere and the garrison troops in white mourning apparel, generals and soldiers of the garrison clad in uniforms of sackcloth with white kerchiefs covering their heads. Inside the town, the streets and alleys were deserted, all the shops closed and households' doors hung with strips of white gauze. Moments later the travelers' confusion was gradually dispersed by news they picked up on the street. The king of Chu had just passed away at Chengfu, and his coffin was being brought back to the capital town.

Confucius was stupefied. He stood upright on the chariot, looking up into skies. His chariot rolled to a stop at a crossroads, blocking the traffic.

"How could the king die at this critical moment? Was it predetermined by heaven that my doctrine is doomed to failure?" Confucius was unable to understand the will of heaven. However, he was fully aware that another opportunity for achieving his ambitions had slipped away.

Meanwhile a tall, skinny man staggered along across the street. He had long hair scattering over his shoulders and was dressed in shabby clothes, with a bold, frustrated air. He looked simultaneously like a wizard and someone on the sacrificial altar, but it was hard to identify him. Unrestrained and wildly arrogant, the man strode ahead singing heartily. The song was sonorous, but the lyrics were ambiguous and went something like this,

The phoenix! The phoenix!
You've retained your virtue.
Your advice cannot alter the bygone,
But it is not too late to put it forth for tomorrow.

The man walked up to Confucius' chariot and, seeing that the road was blocked, he yelled, "Get away! Get away!"

Confucius stared ahead blankly, deep in thought. The yell shook him to his senses. He saw that the man was deranged in appearance but possessed delicate features. He was struck by the man's resonant voice and profound verse. The master rushed forward without a moment of hesitation and greeted him with a bow, "My humble name is Kong Qiu.

May I know yours?"

Paying no heed to the greeting, the man, pointing to the chariot, shouted, "The street carriage. The street carriage," meaning the street should be cleared of the chariot immediately.

Confucius misunderstood him, thinking the man had revealed his name. Due to the man's heavy Hunan accent, Confucius took his pronunciation of "street" as "reception."[1] Assuming that the man was surnamed *Jie* and his formal name was *Yu*, Confucius made a prompt response, "Mr. Jie Yu ..."[2]

Running out of patience, the man reckoned that he had encountered an intolerably annoying man, and so the man muttered impatiently, "Enough! Enough!" And then he squeezed through beside Confucius' chariot.

Confucius intended to say more, so he alighted, bowed to the man and asked another question, "Is the song you sang just now a composition in the style of Chu? It's probably not collected in *The Book of Songs*. May I know its title?"

To avoid endless quibbling over the matter, the man shook his head, repeatedly saying, "Enough. Enough." He walked past the chariot and continued on his way.

"'The Song of Enough'? I heard about the song 'All Good Things Must Come to an End' but have never learned anything like 'The Song of Enough." Even more bewildered, Confucius took it seriously and inquired further, "Is this song intended satirically or metaphorically?"

Those in power today,
Are perilous, perilous, perilous!

The madman threw out another vague poetic line of the song and

---

[1] Hunan, a province in south China.
[2] "*Jie*" means "street" or "reception" in Chinese. "*Yu*" means "carriage" in Chinese.

floated into the distance.

Confucius stepped forward to raise more questions, but the man had disappeared.

It was a sunny day in autumn, the sun at noon illuminating every corner of the town. The streets were deserted with no soul stirring, and the town was frozen in stillness.

A flock of wild geese flew silently across the sky in the formation of the character "人," and gradually vanished south.

Standing at the crossroads for a long time, Confucius was lost in thought.

Chapter 24   The Dukes
(The Chronicles: Confucius at the Age of 52)

Duke Jing of Qi watched Yan Ying, prime minister of Qi, and Kong Qiu, prime minister of Lu, standing together and all sorts of feelings welled up in his mind. Yan Ying was over eighty while Kong Qiu was in his early fifties. Both serving as the masters of the ceremonies, they were in striking contrast; the former was short, doddered in movement, and propped himself up with a bent back; the latter was big and tall, vigorous in youth, and straight and towering like a tree.

Turning around, Duke Jing took a look at Duke Ding of Lu sitting beside him. The Duke of Lu, in his forties, was short and stout, though not in a dignified manner. He had rosy cheeks, with an unmistakably healthy appearance. Looking at himself, Duke Jing was advanced in years, completely silver-haired with his teeth either lost or loose. His hearing and eyesight were not good either. In addition, he was afflicted with lingering diseases. With great efforts, he made it to attend this summit. But sitting for a long time would wear him out. These thoughts made the Qi's ruler deeply worried about the future of Qi.

Now Duke Jing felt a little regretful, for he had not kept Kong Qiu in Qi years ago. At the time he recalled his promise to grant Kong Qiu territory to apply the rule of benevolence. Duke Jing also remembered his aspiration to establish a relationship with Kong Qiu just like "that of Ji and Meng." Ji used to be a high-ranking minister of Lu, while Meng a lower-level minister. The relationship between Ji and Meng was a relationship between a higher-ranking official and a lower-ranking one.

Fortunately at that time, Duke Jing accepted Yan Ying's advice and did not commit that foolish stupid mistake. Instead he declined to use Kong Qiu on the pretext of being too old as a state head. Later on, the duke completely forgot about Kong Qiu along with his promise to the scholar. By now over twenty years had elapsed, and the duke was getting old. He earlier actions all came back into his mind. Was it true that the elderly have a bad memory? It seemed that young men were sometimes more forgetful.

This Qi-Lu summit of alliance was to be held at Jiagu at the request of Lu. The resentment and grievances between the two states had never subsided in the past few hundred of years, and Qi always was more powerful than Lu. A stronger power, Qi frequently used military force to invade Lu, attacking towns, seizing territories, capturing groups of people and plundering property, as if Qi's troops gathered things from their own backyard. At a time of civil strife in Lu, Duke Zhao of Lu fled to Qi, which used opportunity to seize Yunyi, a major town of Lu. Then Yang Hu rose in rebellion. Later, when Yang Hu had been defeated and fled to Qi, he brought his host a few territories of Lu as the first meeting gifts, including Wenyang and Guiyin. As its rival to Lu, Qi became stronger and stronger. The weakening Lu could only compete and survive on its age-old history and profound cultural heritage. Today Qi sought hegemony while Lu wanted peace. Qi said, "If you permit me to control all the land I will allow you to live in peace." Lu had no way to maintain peace with Qi but to attend this bilateral summit of alliance to be held at Jiagu.

The south-facing square terrace for the summit was built

on the hillside above a valley with three floors and twenty-seven steps. That day, in the spring sunshine, flags and banners waved and a forest of spears and halberds stood erect. Standing at the highest point were Duke Jing of Qi and Duke Ding of Lu, the former on the right and the latter on the left, a clear sign of Qi's position of superiority. In the middle of the terrace were the two prime ministers who presided over the ceremony, Yan Ying of Qi and Kong Qiu of Lu. Below them, at the bottom of the terrace were the officials of the two countries standing along the steps according to a strict court hierarchy of ranks. Along the four sides were masters of ceremonies from the two countries. Beyond the guard of honor, groups of servants were waiting on their respective masters, some holding golden hand-washing washbasins, others carrying silver bowls of tea, and still others holding wooden chamberpots in case their masters needed them. The officials and servants of Qi were dressed in a variety of colorful costumes. But their counterparts from Lu donned the uniform black formal attires in light of the traditional dress code of the Western Zhou dynasty.

For this Jiagu summit, Qi made careful arrangements. Hundreds of sword-carrying headsmen dressed up as masters of ceremonies. Thousands of archery units, camouflaged in twigs and leaves, waited in ambush in the surrounding wilderness. Even more impressive, there were 100,000 troops positioned in the immediate vicinity around the valley.

Duke Jing of Qi originally thought he would make a display of force to threaten the sovereign of Lu. But Duke Jing's senior official, Li Ju, advised the ruler to take advantage of this summit, to capture the duke of Lu and put him under house arrest, just as Duke Zhao of Lu had been treated years earlier, so as to ensure a stable relationship between the two states. Duke Jing did not comment on the suggestion, though he considered it a wonderful plan.

After exchanging gifts, the two heads of state were seated. The ministers in charge of the two countries' military stepped forward, bent down on their right knees, held their fists in a general's salute and reported aloud, "The troops are ready for review. Your Majesty please begin!"

Duke Jing of Qi said, "Let it begin." Duke Ding of Lu said too, "Let it begin."

And so the review began.

Lu's troops took the lead, with a hundred soldiers marching in a square formation, clad in the brand new uniforms and glittering suits of armor. They goose-stepped gallantly by the terrace, chanting commands and saluting in unison, lifting their legs and turning their heads. In the sunshine, their dagger-axes, lances, spears and halberds sparkled brilliantly, and even at first sight, this demonstrated that the weapons were of low quality, made of inferior materials with silver decorations.

Lu's parade was closely followed by Qi.

With a wave of Duke Jing's hand, the battle drums were struck on Qi's side with increasing tempo and loudness. When the drum beating hit the peak, loud shouts exploded from a corner of the valley, shaking heaven and earth, and a crowd of savages dashed out, bird feathers planted on their heads, greasepaint coated on their faces, necks and shoulders bared, hair hanging down loosely and the whole bodies tattooed. Brandishing cudgels the barbarians charged over ferociously.

His blood freezing, the duke of Lu asked, horrified, "What troops are they?"

With a grin Duke Jing replied calmly, "They are prisoners of war from the ancient tribe state of Lai, inhabitants of border areas. They are well known for being fierce, tough and barbarous, capable of subduing tigers with their bare hands and killing humans within ten steps."

At this instant, the barbarians gathered in front of the terrace, screaming, showing their teeth and brandishing weapons up toward Duke Ding of Lu, who was within ten steps. One of them even made an attempt to race up the flight of steps to the top of the terrace.

Looking deathly pale, Duke Ding thought that if he was captured he would be eaten alive by these savages.

Meanwhile Duke Jing maintained his composure, a smile hanging on his face, as if nothing had happened.

At this critical juncture, Zhongni, who had stood below, dashed up the flight, taking two steps with one stride, to the front of Duke Jing. Lifting the sleeve in salute, he stated in a stern voice, "This summit is supposed to establish good neighborly relations. How could the threat of force be used? Please dismiss the crowd of savages!"

Duke Jing was astonished at the sight of Zhongni standing before him with an awe-inspiring expression. He did not expect the Lu's prime minister to rush up the steps in a flash. According to court etiquette, one should ascend the terrace by taking one step with both feet on the ground before climbing the next one. But Zhongni leaped onto the top in a couple of strides in defiance of the official rites.

At the foot of the terrace the uproar raged on. The order to halt was shouted by ministers of both countries, but the disturbance showed no sign of abatement. The brutes only fixed their eyes on Duke Jing for a command.

Seeing the embarrassment, the duke of Qi laughed and waved his hand. All of a sudden the noise ceased, like an electronic device unplugged.

Duke Jing made several more hand gestures, and the barbarians of the Lai tribe hung their heads and bowed, as they gloomily beat a retreat, bending over, pulling the lances and carrying the cudgels under the arm. The valiant air displayed moments earlier vanished like smoke.

In the meantime, the two countries' ministers of recreation walked up. With their left knees on the ground, they paid official obeisance by cupping one hand in the other before their chests and recited aloud, "The dancing groups and musicians are ready. Your Majesty, please give the command!"

Duke Jing replied, "Let it begin." So did Duke Ding.

Lu's band played the ancient musical composition called "Supreme Force," which was said to have been written for King Wu of the Zhou dynasty during his expedition against the Emperor of the Shang dynasty.[1] Now the solemn and dignified music was played with a tone of deep and unswerving determination, using mainly percussion, giant drums and gongs, accompanied by high-pitched horns. Most of Lu's musicians were gray-haired, weather-worn old men, who feebly beat their instruments and blew their horns off key. However, the composition's ancient theme of the composition still came through clearly.

Next was Qi's music and dance performance. But on the stage emerged a group of opera singers, in red and green attire, with the brightly-colored faces. They sang and swayed their hips. Among them was a dwarfish clown doing somersaults and making wry faces.

Outraged by this sight, Zhongni rushed up the flight of steps again, taking two steps in a single stride, leaping to the top of the terrace. He dashed in front of Duke Jing. Bowing in a polite salute, he requested sternly, "At the summit the proper etiquette for dukes should be conducted. Why should this kind of farce be staged to impose an insult? Please dismiss the singers and clown!"

---

[1] The "Supreme Force" is one of the six dance performances of the Western Zhou dynasty. The complete performance is comprised of six parts, "Dispatching Troops," "Conquering the Shang Dynasty," "Southern Expedition," "Strengthening the Rule on Southern Border Areas," "Separate Governing," and "Supreme Force."

With a swift change of expression, Duke Jing of Qi rose slowly. He reached a cup of wine and held it above the head. At that point the prime minister Yan Ying and senior official Li Ju fixed their eyes on their superior's cup, along with the hundreds of sword-bearing headsmen, disguised among the masters of ceremonies, thousands of archers waiting in ambush in the wilderness, as well as the 100,000 troops surrounding the valley in combat readiness. If the duke of Qi threw his cup on the ground, the soldiers would move to capture the Lu's duke and officials.

However, Duke Jing of Qi did not smash his cup.

His eyes were fixed on Zhongni long before he gestured, with a wave of hand, for the withdrawal of the singers. Turning around, he spoke to Duke Ding of Lu, "Qi is willing to form an alliance with Lu and live in peace forever!"

Rising immediately, Duke Ding of Lu grabbed his cup in a show of compliance.

At this time, Yan Ying, who had stood below, defying his old age, staggered to his feet and walked to the top of the terrace and said, "On the two state alliance, whenever Qi dispatches troops out of its country, Lu must send three hundred armored chariots in company."

On Lu's side, Zhongni rejoined at once, "In regards to the two state alliance, Qi should return the territories that it seized from Lu in the past, such as Yunyi, Wenyang and Guiyin. This will serve as a token of sincerity."

Staring at each other for a moment, Duke Jing of Qi and Duke Ding of Lu both responded by saying "yes."

After the summit, on their way back to Qi's home country, senior official Li Ju asked Duke Jing why he had opted to abort his original plan. Was it because the he felt compassion for Lu's ruler?

Duke Jing replied, "They have acted in an open and aboveboard way as a *junzi*. But you officials teach me the demeanor of northern barbarians."

Hearing these words, Li Ju, a little uneasy, said, "We shouldn't care about whether it's the behavior of a *junzi* or northern barbarians . If Lu becomes powerful, Qi will be in danger."

Duke Jing turned around to Yan Ying, who rode in the same carriage with the ruler, and asked, "What's your opinion?"

Mulling the question over for a moment, Yan Ying answered, "I, an old man, believe that if Lu is under the control of Kong Qiu, Qi will be threatened in the future."

Looking up to the sky and laughing, the head of Qi said, "How could I have been ignorant of this possibility? But Kong Qiu is a *junzi*. To deal with a *junzi*, why should one resolve an issue by force? We can obtain our goals by the means of the small man."

Chapter 25 Wei
(Spring and Autumn Period: 7th Year of Duke Ai of Lu's Reign, 488 BC)

In little more than ten years the town of Diqiu, capital of the state of Wei, had changed beyond recognition. Avenues and alleys remained the same as they had been, with stone paved streets and stores displaying signs up high. One fine, warm day after snowfall, the town emerged free from the prolonged period of war, with a bustling stream of horses, carriages and people upon the muddy roads. In the south of the town, the residence of Yan, once inhabited, stood slightly decrepit. But the old elm tree, tall, straight with dry branches, remained erect at the center of the yard, braving the chilly gusts of wind.

Yan Zhuozou was old. He had given up the butcher's trade long before. He made daily trips to the fair, where he sipped wine and observed the roadside festivities. After Confucius left, his schooling had ceased. The break from learning had left him with a rustier recollection of the characters he had learned. Of over three hundred poems from *The Book of Songs* he could only recite one line, "A beautiful, pure and virtuous girl is a suitable match for our lord."[1] But the misspelled character "qiu" remained incorrect. All these years he yearned for Confucius' return. On this return journey to Wei, Confucius and his followers decided to visit

---

[1] "A beautiful, pure and virtuous girl is a suitable match for our lord": in Chinese "*yaotiao shunü, junzi haoqiu.*"

Yan Zhuozou first and to stay with him for some time, which delighted the old butcher enormously. It was the Spring Festival. In anticipation of the party that was to come, Yan Zhuozou prepared a hog to pay a respect as a student to his former master.

The death of the duke of Chu halted Confucius' plan to travel to Chu once more. With the sudden turn of events he found himself stranded in the vast plains of central China with no place to stay. After a couple of days in the town of Fuhan, pondering his journey from there, Confucius decided to travel north, back to the state of Wei.

One windy autumn day, Confucius and his disciples set out on their return journey. They travelled for the entire winter and it was not until the beginning of the next Spring Festival that they finally reached Diqiu, the capital of Wei.

Duke Ling of Wei had long passed away. The new duke, Duke Chu, his grandson, was young, less than 15, but had been in power for four years. His father, Kuai Kui, was the former crown prince who had fled to the state of Jin. Kuai Kui aspired to return home and restore his fame and position but was prevented from doing so by the unanimous opposition of the state's officials and courtiers due to the unpardonable crimes of murdering his mother and betraying the state. The court's firm resistance led to reform of the hereditary system, deposing the crown prince and placing his grandson on the throne.

Nanzi, wife of Duke Ling of Wei, was still alive, but no more than an old lady, whose name had faded into oblivion. In the people's memory she had been beautiful in her early years, and occasionally they would talk about her at that time of her life. Few knew that she was now alone, confined in the court,lonely and passing time playing cards with her maids in the palace. The only tradition she had insisted upon was riding out in her chariot on the day of the country fair, at the beginning of each lunar month, without regard to wind or rain. She would have her horses and chariot prepared, select a beautiful shawl and ride to the market to appease the yearning for the grandeur of her past life, which had become mere memories of her present life.

Upon his arrival in Wei, Confucius intended to inquire about Nanzi. As they were both old, he felt that their relations would not invite any unwarranted suspicions from among the disciples. But on the few occasions when the he thought to look for Nanzi, Confucius found it difficul to raise the matter in public; though he thought of her constantly.

Confucius was disheartened by being unable to meet the duke of Chu, and this dampened his ambition to find work as an official. He felt old and his nostalgia for home increased with each passing day.

During their stay in Wei, the disciples were eager to put into practice the theories they had learned.

During this period of Wei, Kong Kui, a senior official, was in charge of governing the state. He was a royal kinsman of the court—the runaway crown prince, Kuai Kui, was his mother's brother. It was Kong Kui who had placed Kuai Kui's son, i.e. his own cousin, in his current position of Duke Chu of Wei. Kong Kui firmly supported the younger in the hostilities that existed between father and son. Furthermore, the level of closeness varied from relative to relative by reference to kinship and Kong Kui found it much easier to serve and relate to the young and ignorant cousin than his experienced and astute uncle.

Kong Kui quickly learned that Zilu was the bravest of all Confucius' students but also the least resourceful, a man easily controlled, and so he appointed Zilu manager of the household.

The day before he assumed his new position, Zilu came to Confucius for advice on government.

Upon entering the room Zilu saw his teacher absorbed in a book. So he did not dare speak but stood aside for a while, until Confucius had finished the bamboo slip and looked up. Zilu broke the silence, "If you, master, were in charge of handling the affairs of Wei, what would you do first?"

"I would first, set titles right," Confucius said immediately.

Smiling on the suggestion Zilu continued, "My teacher is truly pedantic. How could the correct title be reinstated in Wei? Can we possibly expel the current duke and bring Kuai Kui back to the throne?"

Confucius' face fell slightly, "Why do you say things like this? A *junzi* can be suspicious about any confusing matter but never speaks nonsense. For a country, if the correct titles are not established, arguments will not accord with truth. If arguments do not accord with truth, affairs cannot be handled successfully. If affairs are not handled successfully, the rites and music cannot be practiced properly. If the rites and music are not practiced properly, justice will not be served. If justice is not served, people will be at a loss at what to do. If masses are at a loss at what to do, they will speak and behave in an irresponsible way. If that happened, how could a country be governed efficiently? Therefore setting titles right is a matter to be dealt with seriously."

Aware that he had earlier spoken out of line, Zilu timidly bid a hasty retreat.

No sooner had Zilu left than Zigong arrived, trying to help the former collect advice from Conficious on good governance. It turned out that Zilu was discouraged by his talk with the master and disillusioned by the master's idea of dealing with official matters of Wei. He felt that the date assigned to take up the position was drawing near and what worried him was that he was unable to tell whether Confucius supported the ruling duke of Wei or the exiled Kuai Kui. If the issue of supporting either father or the son could not be ascertained, Zilu would not know if he should serve the ruling duke or not. A country should be run according to laws with things performed according to one's morality. Therefore, Zilu asked Zigong, his fellow student, to help seek advice from the master.

Since their arrival in Wei, Zigong had not entertained the idea of taking an official position immediately. Instead he had resumed his profession of being in business. He was born in the town of Diqiu so he had plenty of connections there. Additionally, Zigong had gained experience and knowledge from his dashing around all these years. This gave him fresh insight which he applied to his work and earned him considerable profit. He used part of his income to cover the daily expenses of Confucius, who had lost his official salary from the duke.

Wearing his usual new garment of silk cloth, Zigong entered, positive and full of energy. He first greeted the master and then spoke about a variety of things before approaching the main issue in an indirect manner.

"My teacher, what kind of people are Bo Yi and Shu Qi?" asked Zigong.

"Both are worthy men in an ancient time," replied Confucius.

"Then shouldn't the elder brother Bo Yi have complied with his father's request and yielded the state power to his younger brother?"

"He should have," Confucius answered but, quickly, raised a question to his student, "Shouldn't the young brother Shu Qi have turned down the offer?"

Zigong was silenced. After a while, he asked again, "I wonder whether the brothers begrudged one another?"

"He who strives for benevolence will surely have his efforts recognised. Why should they hold grudges toward one another?" Confucius said.

Standing there Zigong pondered before responding.

"I've understood."

Then he took his leave.

As he walked to the door, Confucius stopped him.

"All things evolve this way under heaven. Unfortunately, there are increasingly fewer worthy men, and it is more and more difficult to lead a principled life." Confucius sighed, "I do not intend to assist Kuai Kui to return here to rule the country. Nor do I refuse to support the current duke of Wei and request him to yield power to his father. I'm only worried that if titles are not set right in Wei, the state will fall into a state of chaos and social upheaval may ensue. Tell Zilu to be cautious!"

A few days later, senior official Kong Kui celebrated the seventieth birthday of his father Kong Wenzi by throwing a banquet at home and made special invitation to Confucius through Zilu. After the feast, Kong Kui asked Confucius to stay and led him into an inner room.

Walking inside Confucius saw a table groaning under the weight of a large pile of gold coins, their sparkling brilliance filling the entire room. This was not the first time that his eyes had crossed a great sum of money. That year when the special envoy of the king of Chu came to him with the official appointment, a huge trunk of gold coins was brought as a gift for him. But such enormous amounts of gold remained a rare sight to him. That trunk of gold had been dazzling. By comparison, this mountain of coins made him dizzy.

Seeing the effect that the gold coins had on his visitor, Kong Kui burst into laughter, "These are a gift to you from the duke of Wei. Originally the duke intended to invite you to join in the government as prime minister. After learning of your willingness to keep out of official circles, he changed mind and sent me here to offer this humble gift with a sole request that you make just one public statement."

Turning around, Confucius, with a cupped hand salute, expressed gratitude, "I'm but an ordinary person. What reverence the duke of Wei has shown to me! What public statement do you request from me?"

Losing no time to sit him down, Kong Kui explained, "Your moral character and standing are well known to dukes of the states, and your word is able to persuade dukes and ministers and alter popular views. The duke of Wei wishes you to say that the duke of Wei's action in driving his father out of the country is in the interests of the country and people, therefore filial and benevolent, and his ascension to the throne is legitimate."

There was a long silence before Confucius replied solemnly, "I find it improper to say that! He does not have legitimate title, and therefore my words will not reflect truth!"

Kong Kui was displeased, "Why does the duke's court revere education and foster men of talent? It has included and encouraged a great number of scholars. Should it not be able to count on these learned men to help deal with disputes and conceal embarrassment? Why do you think the duke of Wei would offer you so much gold?"

Stung by these words, Confucius rose from the seat and said with austerity, "All humans are greedy for wealth. If it can be pursued as an idol, one can worship or try to marry it; acquiring wealth through dishonest means is, by my standards, no more than floating clouds. This is a lot of money, but it cannot make me, as a commoner, give up my will and forsake my principles!"

These words having been said, he sent for his chariot and, without another glance at the heap of gold coins, took leave of his host at once. As he walked, dejected and somber, he thought, "Birds can choose the tree upon which to perch. But can a tree choose the birds that will perch on it? Birds can fly."

That night, just as Confucius had settled in, he was alerted and notified of the arrival of someone who had come from his home town, the state of Lu, and sought to meet him on emergency business. Confucius rose from bed, dressed himself and stepped into the main room of the house. A hard glance at the middle-aged man made him realize that, standing in the comer was none other than his only son, Boyu, whom Confucius had not seen for a decade. The son had changed a great deal in appearance, but, though he had gained weight, his brows, eyes, nose and mouth had remained unchanged.

The father met the son, both excited and lost for words. After a long while had passed, Boyu found his voice, "Father, my mother passed away."

"When did she pass away?" Confucius asked in astonishment.

"The day before yesterday. I hurried here that very night to bring you the sad news."

A faint expression of sorrow played on the face of Confucius, as many distant memories of those early years surfaced in his mind, such as the radiant dawn, the evening glow, the breeze blowing outside the windows and the rain drops washing the stone steps at the doorway; some of them remained clear in his memory and others dim and blurred. He was regretful of the high mountains and long distance that obstructed his way home. After a long moment of silence he said, "Li, my son, I cannot go home now. You should give your mother a good burial." With these words, he broke down and sobbed. "Had I returned to home a little earlier I probably would've been able to see her one final time."

His disciples saw their master crying in accordance with the rites and they too felt aggrieved and broken hearted.

Eager to return home to prepare the burial, Boyu set off that evening. Immediately after he finished his mother's funeral services, however, he too unexpectedly died, and thus was never able to see his father again, though Confucious was on his way back to his home land. The meeting between father and son days before, became the last time they would see each other in this world. Despite his early death, Boyu himself became a father that year. His son, named Ji and styled Zisi, was the final fulfilment of his filial duties to produce offspring to carry on the Kong family name.

That day, Zigong noticed Confucius' uneasiness at being unable to return home in time for his wife's funeral and was aware of his teacher's yearning for his hometown. Then Zigong wrote a letter and sent it secretly to Ran Qiu, who had returned to Lu a couple of years earlier and was at the time serving in the Ji Mansion.

When the mourning period was over, the disciples, worried that the master's health may have deteriorated from the grief, took him out in an effort to relieve his sorrow. It was the start of summer with the sun shining, gentle breezes blowing, plants blooming and trees growing tall with their long branches and leaves. On that day, a major fair was being held as merchants and vendors crowded the market, selling their fruits, the hawker's cries echoed out of stores, and street traders sold their goods. Townsfolk flooded every avenue and alleyway, holding up traffic from all sides. Their horse carriages came to a standstill and had to be kept outside the main street, so Confucius and his retinue alighted and made their way through stalls stacked with water melons, peaches, plums, apricots and dates. They picked and tasted fruits and were happy and carefree.

As the revelry continued, a chariot was sighted moving closer in the distance . It was a spacious box-wagon pulled by a team of four horses, with flower-carved and beast-engraved sides laid with gold and silver. The colors on the chariot had faded from the wear and tear of time and weather. The gold frame remained, however, despite the faded colours of the past. The opulent lifestyle of the early years was visible. It was like a young lady of class and standing who, despite her plain clothes and red string for securing her braids, carried an unmistakably distinguished demeanor. The curtains in the carriage hung low shielding the inside from curious glances.

The chariot came to a complete halt at the entrance of the market, after which there was no room to move and, as the occupant seemed unwilling to emerge from the chariot and walk, they remained stuck at the crossroads. The anxious driver called repeatedly, as the horses stomped and neighed impatiently.

The chariot was familiar to Confucius, reminding him of something long ago. A sudden breeze lifted the curtain, revealing an old lady sitting inside, dressed in fineries with a large red shawl draped over her shoulders. She gazed outside with knitted brows and a blank look in her eyes. Outside was a world with all the noise, traffic and bustle that, obviously, had nothing to do with her.

Confucius was dumbfounded. Instantly he recognized the lady riding in the chariot as Madame Nanzi. She appeared to have changed from being sweet and shy. But her features had retained the beauty of her early years.

Confucius stood there, stunned. The old lady glanced at him indifferently, and seemed faintly perplexed for a moment before slowly shifting her gaze in another direction.

The curtain gradually fell back to place.

Soon after, the carriage turned around and went back in the direction it had come.

Speechless, Confucius stood there, watching the carriage vanish into distance, visibly perturbed.

One year later, word finally arrived from Lu and the group of exiles heard what they had been expecting for a long time: the duke of Lu was summoning Confucius back home. The duke's decision was, undoubtedly, facilitated by Confucius' disciple Ran Qiu.

Since returning to Lu that year, Ran Qiu had stayed in the Ji Mansion. He first served as manager of the household through which his talent for government and leadership won Ji Kangzi's trust in him. Early that year when Lu was being invaded by Qi, Ran Qiu was made to lead Lu's resistance against Qi's troops as there was no military commander. He won the battle, defeating the enemy at Langdi and driving Qi's army out of the territory. His strategic competence was lauded and he became a war hero, considered the leading general of the next generation.

At the victory banquet, Ji Kangzi asked Ran Qiu where he had learned military strategy. The night before Ran Qiu had just received a letter from Zigong urging him to make arrangements so as to bring Confucius back to Lu. Thus, Ran Qiu answered that he had been tutored by Confucius. Hearing about Confucius, Ji Kangzi recalled the name. On his death bed Ji's father had declared to his son, "For the position of Lu's prime minister, none other than Zhongni should be appointed." Ji Kangzi did not know that Confucius was well accomplished in both political advice and military strategy as he had always considered him a man merely of education. "Is he able to fight?" the head of Ji asked in amazement. Ran Qiu said that he was unsure whether Confucius could actually ride a horse and fight on the battlefield; but, undoubtedly, his master was well versed in military negotiation and reaching a resolution with . Ji Kangzi was curious about this famous scholar's skills at war and further questioned Ran Qiu on Confucius' military proficiency compared with the well known "Thirty-six Strategies". [1]

Ran Qiu had originally intended to talk about something casually so as to touch upon the issue of Confucius' return home in conversation. Ji Kangzi's seriousness caught him by surprise. Ran Qiu had no other way but to go along with it. He emphasised Confucius' extraordinary use of military strategy that was quite different from those traditional tactics, as his teacher usually started by correcting names, then disseminating the idea among the people, and then finally reporting to ghosts and gods. More often than not, the enemy would retreat before the troops and horses under Confucius' command needed to be deployed, which was a much more efficient method than the "Thirty-six Strategies."

Upon hearing this, Ji Kangzi developed a profound respect for Confucious, and kept repeating aloud, "Incredible! Incredible!" He lost no time inquiring whether Confucious could be brought back home. After a moment of pondering, the former student of the master replied that it could be arranged; however, people of inferior moral character could not obstruct the *junzi* in administering state affairs, the ruler should not be aided by corrupt ministers. Ji Kangzi answered immediately, "That is simple. Tell me who these men are?"

Ran Qiu responded that they were the men that practiced corruption,

---

[1] Thirty-six Strategies, a set of military strategies developed in ancient China.

like Gong Hua, Gong Bin and Gong Ling, those whom his boss heavily relied upon. Ironically, all three had "Gong" in their surnames which means "public," but in reality, they went out of their way to seek private gains.[1] Ji Kangzi considered this for a while before deciding " I will let them go. I can find replacements if I need to, in the future." He raised his arm as he spoke and then made a downward movement as though chopping through a slice of meat. Thus, Ran Qiu had settled the matter of Confucius' return during his conversation with Ji Kangzi. At the meantime those men, whom Ran Qiu despised, were removed from the clan of Ji without further ado.

Ji Kangzi notified Duke Ai of Lu at once, telling him that Confucius was being invited back to his home town. The duke knew that Confucius was one of the ministers who previously served his predecessor Duke Ding and who had ordered the town walls of the three capitals to be destroyed. Duke Ai had wanted to reinstate Confucius for some time but did not dare to advance his idea. Now as it had been raised by Ji Kangzi, the duke would not reject it.

The news filled Confucius' disciples with joy at the thought that they would soon be back home. The thought of being free from the hardship of traveling without a fixed route was comforting to the students and gave them a feeling of residing at a permanent home. Zilu, however, had to remain behind because his position as manager of Kong Kui's residence was not one which could be easily replaced. Along with him, Gao Chai and a few other disciples were also to be left behind, as they also had official duties in Wei that could not be abandoned without careful consideration.

That morning, the disciples busied themselves with loading more than ten carriages with luggage. Zilu, Gao Chai and others all came to see them off. Before departing, Confucius counted his group and

---

[1] *Gong*, the Chinese character is a surname and also means "public."

noticed one missing. He counted again and was still one short. Upon closer examination, it was evident that Gongbo Liao had disappeared. At once, people were dispatched to find him. They searched far and wide but he could not be found. Most of the disciples agreed that they had not seen Gongbo Liao since the previous night. At this point, one of the door men reported seeing the missing disciple exit the door at dusk the night before and walk in a southwesterly direction. Upon hearing this news Confucius became suspicious.

Gongbo Liao had been one of Confucius' earlier disciples, whom he had formally accepted as a student in the state of Lu. However, Confucius could not remember where and when he had been admitted. Gongbo Liao constantly followed the master day and night, eventually earned him admission into the school.

"Gongbo Liao usually comes and goes like a shadow," Zilu said. "Master, please leave on your journey. I'll try to find him later."

Confucius knew of the prolonged conflict between Zilu and Gongbo Liao. One year when Zilu was in charge of the affairs of the Ji Mansion, Gongbo Liao slandered Zilu in front of Ji Huanzi. This happened again, when Zilu worked for Kong Kui of Wei. Luckily Zilu never took it to heart and did not hold it against him, displaying a true *junzi's* acceptance.

But where could Gongbo Liao have gone at this point?

All of a sudden Confucius recalled that in the year he passed the state of Song where Huan Tui sought to pursue and kill him, Gongbo Liao also left Confucius without a word. The runaway had not reappeared until the master and students had reached the state of Zheng. Those who had entered the capital town of Song that day had included Sima Niu and Gao Chai as well as Gongbo Liao. Confucius had previously harbored suspicions about Sima Niu and Gao Chai. But Gongbo Liao's name had never come to mind. All these memories left Confucius with a sense of foreboding.

Chapter 26 A Mean Man
(The Chronicles: Confucius at the Age of 54)

One moonless night Gongshan Furao led his troops in a long distance raid and besieged the dwelling place of Ji in which Duke Ding of Lu and Ji Huanzi were residing. At dusk, Gongshan Furao launched an attack on the palace, whilst the duke celebrated and feasted inside. The Duke, however, was warned of the sudden military attack and, terrified, he abandoned the feast and gave orders to the servants to, "Keep the wine warm" before fleeing the palace with his close officials, toward the Ji Mansion. Close at the Duke's heels, Gongshan Furao and his army chased them to Ji's dwelling place, spurred by the thought of capturing both the Duke and Ji Huanzi and removing them both from power.

In the early hours of the morning, the sky in front of the residence of Ji Huanzi was lit up in flames and the atmosphere rang with belligerent cries. The soldiers of Gongshan Furao ran at the gates with large rocks and torches in hand. Inside, Ji's soldiers tried desperately to resist. A few times, Gongshan Furao's men managed to ram the gate open a crack, but it was immediately pushed closed again.

Gongshan Furao possessed a unique name, with two characters comprising his surname and another two forming his given name, which sounded much like a hotel sign, notifying others not to disturb its occupants. He had, for many years, been a trusted aid and assistant in the residence of Ji Huanzi. But Ji had later found favour in another assistant, Zhong Lianghuai. Furious, Gongshan Furao offered his services to Yang Hu and served this new master as an assistant. Yang Hu first helped revenge him by driving Zhong Lianghuai out of the Ji Mansion. He then gave Gongshan Furao one hundred taels of gold and one thousand silver ingots, and finally appointed him the magistrate of Feiyi, which was a politically significant role as Feiyi was the capital of Ji Wuzi. On top of this, Gongshan Furao received the highest annual salary amongst all the officials. During Yang Hu's insurgence it was Gongshan Furao who schemed to capture and kill Ji Huanzi at the Garden of Pu. Unfortunately for Gongshan Furao, Ji Huanzi escaped—just as the adage goes: even the wise are not always free from error. At learning this, Yang Hu became extremely angry at Gongshan Furao and criticized him bitterly. Seeing that Yang Hu was defeated and the battle almost lost, Gongshan Furao immediately betrayed Yang Hu and sent troops after him until he had been chased away. Later, when rewarding people based on contributions, Ji Huanzi allowed Gongshan Furao to remain as the magistrate of Feiyi and granted him numerous heads of cattle and sheep so that he would have objects for sacrificial offerings when he conducted ceremonies of worship to the gods and ancestors.

But three years later, Gongshan Furao once again betrayed his master. This time he led the rebel army in attacking the capital of Lu, with the intent of assassinating the Duke.

Finally, the gate of Ji's residence was struck open. Gongshan Furao willed his troops forward, excited that success was imminent. At this time, it was reported to him that the duke of Lu and Ji Huanzi had retreated to the Terrace of Wuzi in defense and that they, along with their officials, were surrounded and trapped by Gongshan Furao's troops, unable to escape even if they could fly .

With a long sword in hand, Gongshan Furao strode into Ji's mansion. The layout of the place was so familiar to him. He knew it like the back of his hand. This Terrace of Wuzi had been built on a high platform, one hundred feet high, years ago, when the old master, Ji Wuzi, had celebrated his sixtieth birthday. It had been completely built from stone. Inside the terrace there was only one narrow flight of stairs that led to the top. After the gate was shut, the terrace was completely sealed from the outside world—even a mouse could not enter. The original purpose of the building had been to enjoy the view on high. Now, it had become the perfect refuge.

The insurgents attempted to enter the terrace but prevented from doing so as arrows rained down from above. At the top, in the terrace, people were crowded in a dark entangled mass, feeling as vulnerable and terrified as crabs unable to escape their fate in a burning pot. The idea of setting the place on fire came over Gongshan Furao since he could not enter the terrace by force. Without hesitating, he ordered his troops to set up piles of dry wood. Moments earlier he planned to capture the duke of Lu and Ji Huanzi alive. But now, he had to forego that idea. if he could not take them alive, Gongshan Furao would have to settle for their corpses; if he could not obtain raw meat, he would have to be satisfied with the cooked one.

What delighted Gongshan Furao was that Kong Qiu was trapped up on the terrace as well. In truth, Kong Qiu had been the catalyst for this mutiny.

Two years earlier Kong Qiu assumed the position of Chief Justice in Lu and, before long, had taken over the position of prime minister. When in power, Kong Qiu was intent on tearing down the walls of the state's three capitals, that belonged to the three clans of Jisun, Mengsun and Shusun. The clan of

Shusun was the first to witness its town walls of Houyi being destroyed and could do nothing but stand by and suppress their indignation.

The second target was the town walls of Feiyi, which belonged to the clan of Jisun. Before Ji Huanzi committed himself, Gongshan Furao had opposed, because Feiyi was his den and sphere; if it were to be destroyed, how could he be expected to refrain from anger? Gongshan Furao had immediately incited a rebellion. He had become accustomed to rebellion and would feel that his life lacked something if he was not involved in a rebellion. He rallied the clan of Shusun in helping him stage his resistance and led thousands of troops toward the capital of Lu in an effort to capture the duke of Lu so to control the duke's officials and Ji Huanzi. It would also be propitious to capture Kong Qiu alive as well.

In fact Gongshan Furao had been trying to entice Kong Qiu to act in alliance with him for all these years. Before him, Yang Hu had attempted the same but his efforts had been futile. Yang Hu had resorted to bribing Kong Qiu with material goods rather than wit and intelligence. Gongshan Furao, however, believed that success lay in targeting the man's weakness, for all men had shortcomings which left them vulnerable. Once their vulnerability was exposed one could pry open their weaknesses or pour temptation into their desires. Some people were fond of power, others were greedy for money, and still others were lecherous. These weaknesses made every man vulnerable to temptation.

By comparison Kong Qiu's fault was of a different nature: he worshipped Duke of Zhou. He was quite extraordinary in his obedience to Duke of Zhou and honoring the Zhou dynasty. In his official capacity at Feiyi, Gongshan Furao once pretended to restore all the rites of the Zhou dynasty in an ostentatious way, posting up slogans and setting up banners. It had all been ready but for the absence of Duke of Zhou. So,

Gongshan Furao had sent for Kong Qiu. After all, Kong Qiu was knowledgeable and if he found himself in a position to practice the rituals of the Zhou dynasty, Kong Qiu would be so overjoyed that he would not bother to question the validity of the whole thing. At that time Kong Qiu was righteous but felt restless as he had nowhere to put his knowledge and ideals to practice. Now that he had been invited to represent Duke of Zhou to restore the prosperity and ideals of the ancient dynasty that he admired and loved, how could he refuse?

Kong Qiu prepared to set off at once. He was also quoted as saying that though Feiyi was small, one could not be sure that it was not a city with great potential. Was it not true that King Wen and King Wu of the Zhou dynasty, at the beginning of their careers, came from the small towns of Feng and Hao, and were able to achieve success? The forward thinking learner further remarked, "They are summoning me now. Their deep sincerity should not be ignored. Are they not striving to restore to greatness of the Eastern Zhou dynasty?" Stifling their bemusement, his disciples raised no objections. Had Zilu not dissuaded him, Kong Qiu would have been well on his way to Feiyi to act as Gongshan Furao's "Duke of Zhou."

Piles of dry wood were ignited by the troops. A great fire erupted and billowed in the violent wind, crackling in a roaring blaze and producing mountains of dense smoke. The lack of firewood prevented the flames from reaching the top of the terrace, but the clouds of smoke continued to increase. Those on top of the terrace now began to feel the fire and were incinerated like roasted poultry.

Amidst the attack, Gongshan Furao heard someone call to him in a low voice. He turned to see a skinny man standing in the shadows of the trees, making a bow with hands clasped toward him. The flames flickered in front of his face, leaving his features dimly visible.

"Your Excellency, you must leave immediately," the man said. "By order of the Chief Justice, Left General Shen Juxu and Right General Yue Qi are leading ten thousand troops over here to this town."

"Where are they now?" Gongshan Furao felt unsettled. His head was swimming and legs felt weak.

"They are saying that this town is about to be invaded. In my humble position I am here to report back in case it is too late for Your Excellency to escape."

Hastily Gongshan Furao ordered his troops to retreat. He then turned around and made to flee. However, before he had run too far, he looked back and saw that the man was still standing there, motionless amongst the trees. Gongshan Furao asked aloud. "Why aren't you running away? Is it because ..."

"Let me humbly introduce myself. I'm Gongbo Liao, a disciple of Kong Qiu's so I do not need to flee." The man hid himself in the woods, his face still hidden behind the flicker of flames.

Gongshan Furao was taken aback. He vaguely remembered one informer that Yang Hu used to send to spy on Kong Qiu and his disciples and report back on their whereabouts and activities. The informer was often present at Kong Qiu's lectures and from there, learned a great deal about Confucian doctrines so that his mind was filled with ideas of "filial duty, respect for elder brothers, loyalty, honesty, trustworthiness" and "good temperament, kindness, courtesy, discipline and generosity." Later, the informer became a formal disciple and had been initiated into the school of Confucianism, thus serving as a spy for Yang Hu.

Gongshan Furao did not know the identity of this spy. Now he wondered, "Is this man standing before me that spy? Is it possible that, after Yang Hu was defeated, the informer decided to seek favour with me by delivering me from harm? Or does he want to help me escape because I know what he is scheming?"

However, the situation did not allow Gongshan Furao to ponder this any further. So he bade the man, "We'll meet again," before hurrying away. Meanwhile, his troops, who had appeared so brave and fierce moments earlier, now panicked, dispersed and fled the town. They had not travelled very far and had only reached the areas of Gumei before they were captured by the armies of Shen Juxu and Yue Qi and defeated. Gangshan Furao was the only one to slip through the net. He ran all the way to the state of Qi on foot. Fortunately, Gongshan Furao and Yang Hu, his former foe, narrowly missed each other, as the latter had fled to the state of Jin and settled there.

Gongshan Furao did not learn until many years later, that after he had been defeated, Feiyi had been destroyed, and the man who had directed the destruction of the city was none other than Gongbo Liao. Proud of his deed, Gongbo Liao expected a reward. To his indignation, Zhongni recommended Zilu for the post of manager of Ji's House. Later, he was upset further when the position of Feiyi's magistrate was given to Gao Chai at the recommendation of Zilu. It was said that Gongbo Liao then stormed out of the House of Kong and ran to Yang Hu, his old master who lived in the state of Jin, and rejoined his original unit.

In the meantime, the tearing down of the walls of the three capital cities that was being directed by Kong Qiu, was suspended at Chengyi, the capital city of the clan of Mengsun and, also, the last capital city of the three clans. The men from Meng pointed out that Chengyi was a town bordering the state of Qi. If the wall was destroyed, it would allow Qi's men to cross the border into the country. At that time, the head of the Mengsun clan was Meng Yizi, or Zhongsun Heji, who was on good terms with Zhongni. His younger brother was Zhongsun Yue, nick-named Nangong Jingshu. Both brothers were students of Kong Qiu. To see the town wall belonging to an acquaintance, one could hardly remain impartial and refrain from interfering with it. Therefore the task was abandoned.

Since arriving in the state of Qi, Gongshan Furao had been unable to move on from his initial set back and his frustration worsened each day. He first served as a receptionist in the house of a senior official Li Ju and was in charge of greeting and escorting visitors. Later, his master saw that he had a sturdy body, military accomplishments and no family responsibilities, so he was assigned to lead a group of men on street patrol and night watch. As he grew too old to perform these duties, he was sent to work as a gatekeeper at the town gate, living in the tower that stood over the gate, sharing his residence with swallows and bats.

One evening through the steady autumn rain, he saw a group of elderly vagrants huddling together inside the gateway to find shelter from the rain. The leader of the group was wrestling food from the hands of an old man. It was obvious that the leader was angry at the old man for taking the food so he had snatched it forcefully from the old man, striking the poor man's head with a branch to punish him. That old man was clothed in rags with long, disheveled gray hair. He clung desperately to the leftovers that he had tried so hard to obtain.

Gongshan Furao was not the kind of man who would allow this injustice to pass unpunished. He seized a dog-driving rod and strode over to break up the tussle. As he moved close enough to berate them, he caught sight of the chief, all skin and bone, and thought that he looked familiar. He scrutinized him. This man had a long face, pointed scalp, small physique and cross-eyed. Was it not Gongbo Liao? Gongshan Furao was startled but did not show this in his expression. But at this moment, while both were distracted, the old man seized the opportunity and devoured the crumbs in his hands. Content with the morsels he had just eaten, the old man looked up, his face filthy and his toothless mouth wet and crusted with mucus and saliver. Only his eyes betrayed a sense of loathing and wickedness.

Gongshan Furao was dumfounded. He recognized the man as Yang Hu, who, although much older than he remembered, still bore a frightening look. In astonishment, Gongshan Furao dropped the rod. He had learned that Yang Hu had originally approached and served Zhao Yang of Jin. He had led troops in attacking Zhongmou, defeating Fo Xi, a senior official of Jin. Later he had invaded the states of Chen and Cai in a retaliatory expedition. Furthermore, Yang Hu had also assisted Kuai Kui, the crown prince of the state of Wei, in a surprise attack on the capital city of Wei and helped to reinstate the prince to the throne, which had distinguished him as a remarkable war hero.

After the death of Zhao Yang a riot had broken out in the state of Jin. Yang Hu, unable to stay there, had gone to Wei. Soon the state of Wei was also plagued by social unrest, as Kuai Kui, the duke of Wei, treated his people like animals and forced them into hard labor that had caused a rebellion by the workers. Kuai Kui had escaped by climbing the wall to safety, while Yang Hu crawled through a cave in the back that was so low that only a dog could pass through. Along with Gongbo Liao and a few followers, Yang Hu took to flight and finally reached the state of Song. There, Yang Hu worked under Huan Tui, minister of war. But before long, Huan Tui was overthrown before Yang Hu had had the opportunity to make a substantial contribution. Huan Tui was exiled from Song and died in a foreign land, and the stone coffin, which had been elaborately designed and constructed for him, was left unused. After these setbacks, Yang Hu and his follow-ers found themselves in a wretched state, like homeless ani-mals, roaming the streets and struggling to make a living from begging. What astounded Yang Hu, however, was that Gongbo Liao, being the youngest, used his youth to take over leadership of the group and bully his former master. It thus proved the belief that, given the situation, all people are ma-nipulative and scheming. How difficult it was to see progress in this world! Gongshan Furao could not help but recall that night of murder and arson twenty years earlier. Had the night been darker and the wind stronger, the duke of Lu, Ji Huanzi and Kong Qiu would have burned to death in the terrace and he would not have been forced to become an old gatekeeper! Thinking this, he felt a surge of compassion for the beggars as "the fox mourns the death of the hare." He upbraided the band head and allowed the group to stay inside the entrance of the gate for the night instead of driving them away.

Chapter 27 Lu

(Spring and Autumn Period: 13th Year of Duke Ai of Lu's Reign, 482 BC)

Confucius returned to the state of Lu. He was home in glory, retiring to his birthplace as was the custom with the older generation.

A day before arriving at the city wall, he noticed a sea of banners and flags. He noted that it was an entourage sent by the Duke of Lu to the outskirts of the town to greet him, which cheered him up. To his surprise, the young Ji Kangzi showed up in person, an unmistakable sign of the high standard of the welcoming ceremony. When serving as Lu's Chief Justice years before, Confucius found Ji Kangzi to be no more than a young thug who loitered with his friends all day and walked around with his dog attached to a leash in one hand and an eagle attached to a leash on the other, and clamored along the street, creating total mayhem and disturbing the peace. It was hard to believe that fourteen years had passed and Ji Kangzi had turned over a new leaf and come to power, now governing the state of Lu and responsible for the safety and well-being of his subjects.

The welcoming ceremony was held outside the high Southern Gate of the city, the very same location where many years ago Duke Ding of Lu and Ji Huanzi watched provocative and lewd performances by the dancing girls from Qi. Fortunately everyone was so preoccupied by the welcoming ceremony that the embarrassing history of the site was overlooked. Confucius alighted from his carriage, refusing his disciples' attempts to support his arm, and walked to the city gate aided by a cane. At the gate Ji Kangzi, stout and portly, stood waiting respectfully. He was flanked by the guard of honor, military generals and troops brandishing swords and lances, in an impressive show of force. There arose the resounding eruption of a three-gun salute followed by ceremonial music, accompanied by drumming and loud cheers of the crowds that echoed throughout the vicinity. Watching Confucius shuffle over to him, senile and frail, , Ji Kangzi felt rather disappointed. In the dim evening twilight, he saw a dishevelled old man, moving forward slowly, stopping every three steps and bowing with clasped hands every five steps. The old man made his way over to him with an uneven gait and swaying. It was a rather perturbing sight and it seemed as though Confucius would not make it over to him before nightfall. Ji Kangzi was worried that Confucius might stumble and fall. Although he smiled, Ji was inwardly furious at Ran Qiu for having recommended such a useless old man to lead his troops into battle. Contrary to what Ji Kangzi had expected, Confucius, despite all his fame, had, in fourteen years, become as old as the mountains. Ji Kangzi had counted on the sage for defeating his enemies on the battlefield. Now, given Confucius' present state, he'd be lucky if the sage could even sit in a command tent and create military strategies for battles that were occuring thousands of miles away. The famed scholar would probably end up being viewed as the "Honorable old man of the State." With that thought, Ji Kangzi waved his hand, gesturing his inferiors to put away, for the moment, the one hundred gold coins prepared in advance, saying that upon his arrival Confucius should be treated with rites instead of money.

That night a lavish welcoming banquet was held at the Ji Mansion for Confucius' arrival. At the formal evening feast, Ji Kangzi, not completely disheartened by the seemingly futile situation with his guest, consulted Confucius on the art of war. Ji's concern stemmed from the recent border raids by the Qi's troops, which were a thorn in his side. He now placed all his hope on this learned man.

Confucius was clearly unaware of the overstatements Ran Qiu had made about his military accomplishment in front of Ji and responded modestly, saying, "The benevolent one is invincible. The benevolent performs the art of war in a straight way."

These words unsettled Ji Kangzi, who was restlessly eager to inquire, "What's a straight way?"

"The straight way," Confucius answered, "is the just way. An army dedicated to the just cause breaks all enemy resistance."

Unable to grasp the essence of the message, Ji Kangzi raised another question, "How can the cause be made just?"

Confucius replied seriously, "Leading troops is like governing a country. For a ruler to reign justly, he must set a good example with his own conduct. If a military general commands his troops in line with justice, will there be an enemy army that he's unable to conquer?"

Ji Kangzi was still in a daze. He was overweight and, usually, perspired when he ate. Confucius' remarks bewildered him and made him think harder, but this only made him perspire more. The perplexity overwhelmed him. He thought again. There was nothing wrong in what the sage had said, but they were futile in helping him to resist Qi's invasion!

Seated beside the host and guest Ran Qiu felt a surge of anxiety. He wanted to interject and lead the conversation toward a new topic but saw no opportunity. With no alternative he kept coughing and strained every nerve serving food and urging all of them to drink in an effort to divert Ji Kangzi's attention.

After realizing that his search for military strategy advice was failing Ji Kangzi proposed to discuss the way of curtailing domestic unrest. Recently his territory had been rampaged and plundered, making the rulers feel helpless.

The concept of justice balanced against injustice, however, totally engrossed Confucius. In response to Ji Kangzi's question, the respectable guest quoted from memory, "Repressing the crime of plunder is like reigning over a country. Again, setting a good example with one's own conduct should feature high on one's list of priorities. If gentlemen are not corrupt and avaricious, thieves will look up to them and mend their ways."

Upon hearing these words Ji Kangzi nearly choked. His face first reddened and then turned into a shade of purple, which may have been caused either by anger or suffocation. He did not regain his composure for a while afterward. At this time a tight budget was constraining both the State and his household, and he was considering increasing farmland taxes, which required that each village, on top of paying taxes, yield an army horse, two rank and file soldiers and three farm cattle. The preliminary enforcement of his new policy led to widespread discontent across the country. Confucius' comment seemed, to Ji Kangzi, to have a ring of irony directed at him that a state leader should work according to his conscience and be representative of the interests of the masses. However, his guest appeared earnest in expression and sincere in his words, displaying no sign of ridicule. Though unhappy, Ji Kangzi had to restrain his rage. That night he hastily wound up the banquet after three rounds of wine had passed.

After the feast, Ji Kangzi took Ran Qiu aside and castigated him. Ran Qiu had initiated this business for Confucius, who, however, obstinately prattled on without any diplomatic savvy. As Ran Qiu found it hard to defend himself, he had to offer suggestions for Ji Kangzi in the increase of farmland taxes so as to atone for his mistake. In the months that followed Ran Qiu worked tirelessly, coercing farmers to pay taxes, imposing fines and fees, and extracting money and wealth by force. Confucius was unaware of the complications in the matter, nor was he aware of the distress that Ran Qiu experienced. Instead he assumed that his disciple was giving whole-hearted assistance to the clan of Jisun in procuring wealth and had forgotten the principles of benevolence. He had denounced him to the other disciples angrily, declaring "Qiu is not my student. Every one of you should condemn him." Meanwhile Ran Qiu had attempted to make contact with his teacher, expressing his wish to explain the situation and rectify the misunderstanding. But Confucius refused to see him and consequently master and student grew apart.

A couple of days later Confucius went to the state court and called on the duke of Lu. At the meeting the duke consulted him about the state affairs. Confucius replied, "The secret to good government lies in the prudent selection of wise officials." Then he added, "It is essential to lay down and implement policies in maintaining a competent and efficient court of officials and military commanders. When your court is well comprised, just policies can be carried out efficiently; when your court is corrupt, your government falls to pieces." Upon hearing these words, the duke sighed, understanding that he was not in a position to appoint officials as a sovereign. All appointments were made by the clan of Ji. His position as the duke, was in title only and his reign had already come to an end. The duke's disheartened demeanour made Confucius believe he had said something negative to the duke and it reminded him of the numerous failures in his life of advising rulers across the land. It saddened him and made him reluctant to discuss the matter further. The duke and his subject sat facing each other in silence. A while later Confucius rose to leave. Not wanting to impose on him, the duke dispatched a servant to bring a chunk of meat, left-over for sacrifice a few days earlier, and gave it to Confucius. The learned man was touched in accepting the gift and his mind was filled with thoughts.

After his glorious return to his home town Confucius led an unburdened life. He did not know that his old age was the reason for his host's disappointment. Instead he believed that he was no longer consulted on state affairs due to his differing beliefs. Thus, rather than vying for an official position in the court he stayed at home burying himself in writing books day and night. He first set his hand to the editing of *The Book of Songs* and *The Book of History*, then collated *The Book of Rites* and *The Book of Music*, and finally wrote *The Spring and Autumn Annals*. *The Spring and Autumn Annals* was originally written as the history of Lu in biographical style, which recorded the state and court affairs spanning more than two hundred years starting from Duke Yin of Lu. Confucius, taking advantage of the opportunity to edit, incorporated his own commentary, both positive and negative and embedded in the writing all his thoughts, grievances and frustrations that had been present in those years of his life. Some of them, unable to be expressed openly, were intimated through words and phrases that he would coin, and expressions and innuendoes that he would employ. For instance, the dukes that he respected were called "*jun*," a monarch, while those that he disparaged were referred to as "*zi*," a son. Those rulers who rose to power by murdering their predecessor were all depicted as tainted with the crime of "regicide" that made them infamous. After he had finished writing, Confucius felt pleased with the preciseness and stylistic elegance embodied in his words and sentences and believed that those legitimately in power would undoubtedly be pleased at reading these books and be inspired to emulate the virtues, while those in power who were corrupt would, after reading the book, be frightened to defy their superiors and launch rebellions. On second thought, the scholar doubted that his complicated techniques of writing and use of unfamiliar terminology would impart these implicit messages to his readers. Thus, he would often explain the true meaning to his disciples word by word and sentence by sentence. Once in a while, he would sigh with emotion and say, "In the future I will be known by the *Spring and Autumn Annals* to those who can keenly appreciate my ideas. These *Annals* will also cause disaster to me by those who resent me."

On ordinary days Confucius would sit with his disciples on the Apricot Platform from dawn till dusk, relentlessly teaching and discussing his doctrines. Throughout every season of the year, the spring and the autumn, and through the summer heat and chilled air of winter, the teacher and students recited poems and chanted passages from books; they sat and conversed on breezy nights, when the bright moon would hang in the sky and the melodious *Sheng* pipes and string instruments would mingle with the aroma of culture in the courtyard. More than ten years before, in this yard, the gingko tree that had been planted by Confucius, had only grown to a man's height, with a trunk whose width measured two hand spans. But now it had grown to be a giant tree with its lofty spire saluting the heavens and a couple of smaller trunks growing up from its roots, surrounding the central tree and gave the plant a total breadth of more than three persons. It was a sight to behold with its huge, towering crown shielding off rain and wind and spreading a dense leafy shade, and with the fruit hanging heavily on its branches.

Out of admiration for Confucius, scholars from various states, near and far, convened in hundreds; those not fortunate enough to gain entry into the hall and inner chamber of Confucius' residence, were content with the privilege of viewing the courtyard and gate to see the reverent demeanour of their beloved sage. The number of visitors reached three thousand and it became a problem to feed and accommodate them all. Outside in the courtyard, there often stretched two long lines, one with the pilgrims waiting for their food and another to use the toilet. Due to the vast number of students, Confucius was unable to teach in person. It was suggested that Yan Yuan be recruited as a substitute for Confucius in giving lectures. Out of all of Confucious' students, Yan Yuan best understood the master's ideas. But this young man, who was extraordinarily hard working, was pushed to the limits of his physical health. Moreover, his work and prolonged malnutrition from a modest and self-effacing life left him suffering from a number of lingering diseases. He was bedridden for a few months and too debilitated to teach, but continued to be overcome with the desire to do so. Another student, close to Yan Yuan's caliber, was Zigong, who, though not as obedient to the master's teaching as Yan Yuan, developed his own insights, personal commentary and fresh interpretation on the lectures that he listened to. When selected to teach, however, Zigong, usually conceited and proud, shook his head and modestly declined, saying "This is no light matter. How would I be able to substitute for our teacher? Our teacher's learning is like the palace wall, tens of hundreds of feet high, while my knowledge would not be higher than a man's shoulder, and can by no means measure up to his." As he said this, he illustrated the proportions with his hands. Then he let out a sigh of regret, "When the teacher explains poetry and prose from books, the content generally make sense to us. But, when it comes to the way of Heaven and life, it bewilders the listener and we lose our comprehension."

At this time, Confucius was more absorbed than ever in the study of *The Book of Changes*, almost to the extent that he skipped meals and ignored sleep. He had started reading this classic at the age of 50 and it had been fully twenty years. But its ideas still eluded him. The only thing he had gained over the years was the increasing volume of his notes. All canons of learning under Heaven were covered in the six classics. He was well-versed in *The Book of Songs, The Book of History, The Book of Rites, The Book of Music,* and *The Spring and Autumn Annals* except *The Book of Changes,* which seemed uncomplicated but it was not. In this world the truth was self-evident. The feudal ethical code specified that a country should be run with the three cardinal guides, that were: the ruler guides the subject, the father guides the son, and the husband guides the wife. A person should behave with the five virtues, that is to say, benevolence, righteousness, propriety, wisdom and fidelity. It was the way to manage state affairs and bring peace and stability to the country so as to achieve Great Harmony. But, absurdly, no one—not the dukes and ministers of the upper classes, nor the common people, wished to follow this correct path. All these years he had trekked from one state to another, enduring all kinds of hardship and difficulty in conveying his ideas to rulers. Despite his patience and earnestness he had hit hurdles and his efforts had been undermined everywhere. Until this time, at the age of 70, Confucius could not comprehend the reason why he had faced numerous setbacks in life. Was it because he had failed to master *The Book of Changes*? Was there another force of Heaven in the obscure book that controlled the human world? Despite his old age, he now picked up *The Book of Changes* and began to re-read it. He labored through it more arduously than ever and resolved to identify, from the ambiguous language, some reference to the three cardinal guides and five virtues.

He had reviewed the book nine times and this was the tenth.

One day Confucius was preoccupied with reading in the main room. When he came to the 24th Hexagram "Fu (returning)" in *The Book of Changes*, a surge of agitation seized him, causing the divinatory figures and explanatory notes to dissolve and become blurred and abstract before him. Then, with a sudden sound, the leather cord that bound the bamboo slips, snapped apart.

Confucius was shocked. Immediately he concentrated on that part of explanatory notes:

> *He goes out, returns in condition*
> *and finds no fault with the visiting friend.*
> *He elaborates on his doctrines time and again*
> *and replies to the inquiry in seven days.*

As he deliberated over the lines and searched for the meaning, Zigong entered the room, followed by a few other disciples, all dressed in white mourning garments.

"Master, Yan Yuan's gone."

With a vacant stare at Zigong, Confucius made no response.

"Master, Yan Yuan's gone."

Confucius still did not respond to his student. Yan Yuan had been suffering from an ongoing disease and, six days before, had become seriously ill. Confucius was certainly not unaware of his state of health. But he would never have expected that his student would pass away so soon —to die earlier than the teacher himself.

After a moment of silence, he murmured, "Heaven's seeking my death! Heaven's seeking my death!"

Zigong had no idea why the master made such an ill-fated comment, nor did he dare query further. An instant later, he presented Confucious with a wooden case adorned with carved patterns and said, "Before his death Yan Yuan left this case with me and asked me to bring it to you." Inside that case were twenty fascicles of inscribed wooden slips, on which the seal characters were delicately engraved.

Zigong continued, "Yan Yuan said that they are the notes that he had taken on Master's teaching from your personal examples and verbal instruction in the past dozens of years of his schooling. He said that the teacher is knowlegable and his teaching dignified, when confronted by it, and complex when one tries to comprehend its message. The meaning may appear simple for a moment but confounding in the next. Often, the master's teachings were too difficult to understand immediately, so he'd had to note the lessons word for word, careful not to leave out any phrases and sentences or to give them his own improper interpretations. If the Master identified any errors or omissions in the text, he implored the Master to forgive him."

Confucius placed his hand on the wooden case and stroked fondly, tears sliding down his cheeks. He did not wipe his eyes as he wept. He looked up to the sky and was silent.

Zigong tried to console him.

Confucius responded, "If I do not grieve for Yan Yuan, who would I grieve for?"

The disciples proposed to give Yan Yuan a lavish funeral to honor him. But the Master opposed to the idea, replying "Yan Yuan lived a poverty stricken life and dwelled in humble abodes. He would not wish for a luxurious grave. It is better to have a modest funeral service for him."

That day Yan Yuan's father, Yan Lu, escorted by others, came to see Confucius. Yan Lu was one of the earliest disciples. Also advanced in years , he had a hunched back and shuffled forward, leaning on a walking stick and stopping every few steps to catch his breath. When he saw Confucius, tears began to well up in his eyes and his throat was choked with sobs before he could open his mouth. Yan Lu wished to purchase more expensive inner and outer coffins for his son. Given his destitution, he was forced to make the request to Confucius. Aware of his teacher's meagre income Yan Lu sought to beg his teacher to sell his cart and to use the funds for the coffin. Yan Lu had made that cart for Confucius years before. Now with all his belongings sold off Yan Lu was left with nothing; he had to come to Confucius for help.

Again Confucius could not help but weep, "Yan Yuan's your son. But I considered him my son, too. Unfortunately he died young. When an ordinary person dies the inner coffin fits the purpose and the outer coffin should not be made for him. When my son, Li, died he was buried in the inner coffin without the outer one."

Yan Lu wept, "As father and son, we have followed you for our whole lives. How could we not understand this truth? My son, Hui, had a cruel twist of fate. He was poor and never had a single good day in life. I cannot bear to see him suffering in poverty after death. I'm old and not long in this world. I just want to make some satisfactory funeral arrangements so that my son will be better off in the afterlife. This is my one last wish in life. I have no other hope. Could you please grant me this favor, this time?"

Confucius said, "I can not sell my cart! Not because I'm unwilling to give it up but because I can't go without it as a senior official of Lu. It's not in accordance with the rites to go on a journey with the duke without my own cart of transport. Besides, I would be unable to keep pace with a contingent of court people by walking."

Hearing these words, Yan Lu wiped away his tears and bade his farewell, "I'm sorry to have put you in an awkward situation."

Confucius gazed at Yan Lu's receding figure of sorrow, tears trickling down his cheeks, and said, "I'm sad, too. But I'm not in a position to defy the rites!"

At seeing the exchange between the two men, Zigong was deeply aggrieved. In secret, he sent some one to purchase a quality coffin and, in addition, made arrangements for a decent funeral with his own money. After learning of this, Confucius did not say anything but sighed.

Yan Yuan's passing aged Confucius considerably, both physically and mentally. First his eyesight deteriorated. Then his hearing began to weaken. Not long after, he noticed that his energy was failing and he began to lose his memory. Sometimes he sat there waiting for his lunch, moments after he had just eaten. Sometimes he confused his disciples' names and faces, mistaking Zeng Shen for Yan Yuan and Zigong for Zilu. He spoke less and less in his daily lectures. It was obviously more effective to simplify his ideas, however, he now forgot to complete his sentences and left the audience confused and wondering. A few times, he would doze off, abruptly ending the workshop with students. His deteriorating condition led senior disciples a dance, while the newer students complained at the level and amount of instruction they were receiving, believing it to be a waste of money. It became evident that discontent was brewing.

Fortunately Confucius finished selecting and annotating three hundred and five poems for *The Book of Songs*, editing one hundred twenty chapters for *The Book of History*, making textual criticism on the rites of the dynasties of Xia, Shang and Zhou, compiling *The Book of Rites*, rectifying score errors in the "Shaoyue," the "Supreme Force," the "Ceremonial Music," and the "Odes," and thus restored authentic meaning to the music. Meanwhile *The Spring and Autumn Annals* was completed on the chronicle of Lu's reign of Duke Ai. The period of the rebellion was yet to come and so there was a paucity of eventful materials to write about. However, *The Book of Changes* remained the most challenging to read and interpret. Those symbols of trigrams and hexagrams, with whole or broken lines which were one on top of another, resembled tadpoles. Though their forms gave clues about the text, their meaning were elusive in one way or another. He wrote volumes of notes including some commentaries entitled "Records," "Symbols," "The Rhetoric," "Implications," "On the Eight Trigrams," "Preface to the Eight Trigrams," and "Variants of the Eight Trigrams." But he always felt incapable of conveying the idea clearly and often failed to impart the implicit meaning even after selecting the correct word. He once said to the disciples around him, "If Heaven let me live on borrowed years, I would make a detailed and precise annotation on these trigrams so that they could be widely used for reading aloud, reciting and singing like *The Book of Songs* and *The Book of History!*"

Before long it was winter again, snow forming big flakes and falling to the howl of the gale. One morning, Confucius rose early and sat by the window reviewing *The Book of Changes*. Outside it was cold and the ground was frozen. Unfortunately, the fire in the cooking stove went out so it was chilly inside as well. The bamboo slips had frozen together, stiff and hard, and cracked when they were turned over as if they were about to split open. At this moment he was reading the 30th Hexagram "Li (clinging, fire)" and pondering the meaning when the cord that bound the bamboo slips, snapped apart again.

Confucius was surprised. The cord came apart at the position of the nine by four hexagram of change, at the point where it was written,

It comes all of a sudden, inflicting destruction from fire, death and desertion.

Confucius was terrified, feeling that it was forewarning that something frightful would occur, and was on tenterhooks for the rest of the day. By dusk nothing had happened and this left him feeling a little better.

That evening Zigong invited the master and students to a dinner of green onion dipped in brown paste. Knowing that the master was from Shandong and relished this sort of food Zigong bought a few kilograms of green onion from the market and mixed together a large pot of ground pork blended into brown paste. He requested the cook make quite a few pancakes. Then he made special arrangements by asking the young disciples, Zixia, Zizhang, Ziyou and Zeng Shen, to join him in having a festive and hearty meal with the master.

As Zigong had expected, Confucius found his appetite stimulated at the sight of the green onions, ground pork paste, and flower pancakes the size of cooking pot lids. He dipped the green onion in the paste, rolled up one pancake, and took a huge bite, chewing enthusiastically. No sooner was one pancake wolfed down than he reached for the second. During the meal, the gatekeeper brought the news of Ran Qiu's arrival and called on the master.

"You invited him?" Confucius was rather disappointed, casting a glance at Zigong. Since Ran Qiu assisted Ji Kangzi in collecting taxes Confucius had denounced Ran Qiu as his follower. The rejected student had subsequently made attempts to regain contact, all of which were turned down by the Master. In his final plea to be heard, Ran Qiu had pleaded that Zigong explain in front of his teacher that he had not ignored the teacher's philosophical teachings but had fallen short in the mission of implementing them. Confucius raised a question in reply, "Should one give up his beliefs halfway because of his incompetence?" He dismissed Ran Qiu and criticized his lack of strength and will to succeed. Zigong had tried to be supportive of Ran Qiu, but it fell on deaf ears.

"It was not my doing this time." Zigong said at once, "Perhaps he really has something urgent to discuss with you."

The gatekeeper said, "He said he had emergency business to report."

Confucius replied, "I'm still on the post of Lu's senior official and well informed of the state affairs. What emergency business of his should I need to hear?" Giving it a second thought, he finally said, "Let him come in."

Ran Qiu rushed inside, overlooking all etiquette and forgetting to bow. Furrowing his brows in displeasure, Confucius deliberately turned his face sideways, "What errand are you running for the clan of Jisun this time?"

"A coup took place in the state of Wei, Master," Ran Qiu replied.

A wave of uneasiness seized the Master. He turned his head quickly and asked, "At what time?"

Ran Qiu said, "Last night. It's said that the exiled Kuai Kui secretly returned to Diqiu and arrived at the capital city of Wei. He and his sister, Kong Ji, held senior official Kong Kui captive and launched the coup. The court was in chaos for the entire night. Duke Chu of Wei fled the country."

"What about Zilu? And Gao Chai and others?"

"I have no clue."

"Zilu is obstinate and would be ill-equipped to cope with an emergency," the Master observed. He recalled the broken cord and strange writing of the hexagram that had occurred that morning and his heart skipped a beat.

Ran Qiu then asked the master, "Do you know who it was who led Kuai Kui back to Wei?"

"Who?"

"Gongbo Liao."

Stunned, Confucius dropped his plate, causing the brown paste to spill over the sides and splatter onto the table. It became clear to him that

Gongbo Liao had plotted to kill Zilu for a long time. When Confucius and his disciples had set out to return to Lu, Gongbo Liao had left the group without saying goodbye. Did he go to the state of Jin? Yang Hu must have secretly plotted this surprise attack by Kuai Kui. The situation for Zilu was dire!

Part way through the conversation about Zilu, the teacher and students were interrupted by the report of Gao Chai's arrival. Gao Chai wore rags, his hair was disheveled and there were bloodstains all over his body. Clutching a long edged, broken sword in one hand, he lurched inside. Seeing the master, he dropped the sword, fell to his knees and let out a wail.

"Master, Zilu has been killed!"

The men approached him and helped him up on his feet.

Confucius sat down in shock, repeating to himself, "This is exactly what I was worried about. This is exactly what I was worried about."

Gao Chai wept as he recounted the events of the previous night, "Last night when the coup occurred Zilu and I were not in town. We were on our way to the outskirts for another matter but when we learned about the unrest, Zilu insisted that we head back to town. He said that one should be loyal to the provider of his meals, and one should overcome all difficult and dangerous obstacles that stand in the way of protecting this ideal. I was worried about him so I accompanied him to town. When we arrived, flames were lighting up the sky, the fields were littered with corpses, and the city was in turmoil. Kong Kui was forced to submit to the rebels. I pleaded with Zilu to leave immediately and told him that since our leader had surrendered there was no need for us to go to rescue our country. But Zilu wouldn't listen. He said that Wei was a large country and it would be a disgrace and a shame to hear that no one had stayed loyal to the sovereign or devoted to the state. He had then drawn his sword and run into the palace. He had intended to defeat all the insurgents and free the duke of Wei on his own. I was so worried that something might happen to him so I followed him into the palace. The palace, we soon found, had actually been empty for a while. The duke of Wei had fled a long time before, and nothing more could be done. Meanwhile, we had found ourselves completely surrounded by the insurgents. We fought them desperately and finally escaped. Zilu instructed me to go first but he himself got stuck inside, unable to escape. Before he died, he let go of his long sword, retied his hat tassels that had come apart and declared, 'The master taught me that *junzi* should die with his hat on ...' Before he finished speaking, he was brutally murdered by the enemy."

Gao Chai cried violently, choking with grief. Confucius could not listen any longer. He rose from his seat and turned his back to them. Wiping away tears and pointing to that large plate of brown ground meat, Confucius said gently, "Throw it away."

After Zilu's death Confucius did not read *The Book of Changes* for a long time. He was afraid of seeing another ill omen and knowing the will of Heaven. The following spring he took the book from the small rattan box again, to resume reading through it for the tenth time.

He read it carefully, slowly and gently turning over each bamboo slip. As he came to the last Hexagram, the 64th one, the new cord snapped apart again, undone for the third time. However, this time Confucius was not filled with anxiety or fear. He looked at the name of the Hexagram "Wei Ji (Incompletion)" and was lost in thought. A moment later he shook his head and mused to himself, "My undertaking has come to an end!"

What ill omen did this hexagram signal to him? Whom would it befall?

At this time an uproar broke out in town as word circulated that a man hunting on the western outskirts had captured a weird beast. It had four hooves and one horn, resembling a deer or a horse; yet it had scales covering its body that made it seem more like a turtle or a crocodile. No one in the town could tell what it was.

So, Zeng Shen approached the master for his thoughts on the beast.

Confucius asked him, "Does that animal have a body of a deer and feet like a horse?"

"Yes, it does."

"Does it have a single horn?".

"Yes, it does."

"Is its body covered in scales?"

"Yes, it is."

The master mulled over the description before concluding, "It's a kylin!"[1]

Zeng Shen recalled, "When the townsfolk saw this strange animal they were extremely frightened. They believed it was an ill omen so they drove it out of the town. The beast attempted to run away but slipped and fell into a river. It seems to be able to swim but right now it's struggling in the water."

Confucius replied, "The kylin is a benevolent creature. It has traditionally symbolized the coming of a sage sovereign. But there is no sign of the sage sovereign nowadays. The kylin unicorn was at the end of its lifespan and had fallen into the water." As he said this, the statement that had been spelled out in the hexagram moments earlier, sprang to mind,

If the little fox when almost over the stream wets its tail...

There was no way forward, and the river could not be crossed. Did the line statement forewarn of the adversity that would befall the kylin? Or was it referring to misfortune that would befall the master himself? At this thought, Confucius was solemn and said to Zeng Shen, "The Yellow River does not yield the 'River Sketch' nor does the Luo River pro-

---

[1] Kylin, or Chinese unicorn, is an auspicious legendary animal with a horn and scales all over.

duce the 'Book of Luo.' The phoenix has failed to appear and the kylin has been captured. These signs show that it's likely that I've traveled to the end of my life."[1]

Zeng Shen knew that the two books the Master mentioned contained the story of the rule of a sage sovereign and, that during the reign of King Wen of Zhou, the phoenix had appeared. The Master now felt too old to wait for the appearance of the sage sovereign. Now though the kylin had appeared, people were not aware of its signficance. What was worse, it had been chased out of town and fallen into the water trying to escape. This series of events were very distressing. Zeng Shen felt helpless and retreated into solitude and silence.

Since that day Confucius came to terms with how much he had aged. Even in spring and summer, he was unable to experience the same feeling of relaxation and tranquility that he had once enjoyed. His physique reflected a man burdened by loss and dejection. His writings on *The Spring and Autumn Annals* had been infinitely suspended, the last chapter written in the year the kylin was captured and not a word added since. No classes were taught after this time, either. When disciples called on him, he would only recount stories or events of the past or inquired about recent events with each of them. When there were no visitors, he just sat alone. Meanwhile, he developed the habit of sleeping during the day, just as his student Zai Yu, particularly fond of taking a nap after lunch. He would dream during these naps but seldom of the periods of Zhou. Sleep usually transported him back in time to the period of Lu, that had been filled with enthusiasm and pride. At times, he would question what life he would have led had he not left home, swept up in fervour due to that piece of sacrificial meat many years ago.

[1] According to "Implications: Part 1" ("Sici: Part 1") of *The Book of Changes*, "The Eight Trigrams" is found in the Yellow River, while the "Nine Measures for Fighting Floods" appears in the Luo River. It is an old saying that during the reign of Fuxi, a legendary ruler of great antiquity, a dragon-like horse leaps from the Yellow River carrying the book, the "Eight Trigrams," and a spiritual turtle emerges from the Luo River. Both indicate that the will of Heaven is incarnated in spiritual beings.

Chapter 28   Friends
(The Chronicles: Confucius at the Age of 55)

It was at the bordering region that Shi Yi caught up Zhongni and his disciples. The trek of the master and students was slow with frequent stops and many detours. The journey from Lu to Wei was about one hundred *li*. After four or five days of travel they reached a small village called Tun where Zhongni planned to rest for the night hoping to spend the last night in his town before crossing over the border the following day.

"It is fortunate for me that you have traveled slowly, so that, I as an old man, have been able to catch up and see you off," Shi Yi said to Zhongni. Shi Yi got down from his chariot and commanded his subordinates unload a couple of jugs of the Qu Wine of Lu from the carriage. It was the state's finest wine, delicious, mellow and fully-bodied, and one sip would make one tipsy.

"I am leaving my parents' home land so I am traveling slowly," Zhongni replied, with a sigh of regret. Zhongni was touched by the old friend's arrival from the capital town and grateful for the good wine he had brought to farewell him. His delay was principally due to a reluctance to leave his birth place; it was also due to a hope that the duke of Lu would change his mind and dispatch troops to call him back. Now the border was in sight and the master's long delays only served to bring his friend Shi Yi to him. Zhongni's heart was warmed but he was unable to mask his disappointment. Shi Yi and Zhongni had known each other as children. They had been neighbors and had grown up playing as friends. They had been tutored on the *qin* by the same teacher Shi Xiangzi. Shi Yi had been better than Zhongni and had been selected to be a professional *qin* player for the duke's court; Zhongni had not been as talented in the arts and eventually gave it up altogether to take up government posts, which finally led to the position of Chief Justice. Evidently, sometimes the student who does not show promise in class takes office.[1] Shi Yi and Zhongni, both modest gentlemen, revered and thought highly of each other. Furthermore they both observed the rites of gentlemen when eating and drinking together at parties, however, drinking wine remained a taboo. Because the friendship between gentlemen was considered "insipid" as water, they had only drank mineral water in the past. This time Shi Yi blatantly broke this rule by bringing wine to bid farewell.

That night the people at the village inn in which they were staying cooked a few dishes of wild fowl for the two friends to accompany the wine. Together Shi Yi and Zhongni drank the wine until the moon rose from behind the eastern mountain. They were both a little drunk, Shi Yi's eyes glassy and Zhongni's cheeks flushed.

Shi Yi asked, "Do you really have to leave? The fault lies with the sovereign, not with you."

Forcing a smile Zhongni heaved a long sigh, "Yes, though it is the sovereign's fault, could I have been free of fault? Could I have been able to stay on?"

A few days earlier, Duke Jing of Qi had sent the duke of Lu eighty beautiful girls and one hundred and twenty court-grown horses, which were put on display at the southern high

---

[1] One old saying goes, "He who excels in study can follow an official career." The author is being humorous here.

gate of the town. There were performances of love songs and dances, horsemanship and vaudeville, and the whole town, in tens of thousands, turned out to watch the performances. Ji Huanzi was the first there. The shows astounded him and rendered him speechless. Without hesitating, he brought the duke of Lu with him on his next visit. Duke Ding of Lu also was paralyzed and intoxicated by it all, his blood surging and pulse beating fast. He yearned to join in the revelry, which continued tirelessly for three days; he forgot to attend his morning court sessions and missed the grand ceremony to be held on the suburbs, too. Angry at this, Zhongni resolved to leave the country.

Shi Yi said, "They love watching young beauties, love listening to soft music and watching erotic dances, and love attending horse shows. It's not your business to interfere."

Zhongni responded, "The sovereign should behave like a sovereign and the senior official like a senior official. This is how a country should be run."

Shi Yi replied, "I think you only understand the etiquette of good behavior required of the sovereign and senior official. But you are not aware of the relationship between man and woman. The norms of good behavior of the sovereign and senior officials are derived from rationality. The relationship between man and woman is instinctive. How could the mind overpower instinct? Instinct is natural—the sexual desire, more ferocious than fierce floods and more devastating than raging flames. The consequences of nature cannot be reversed. Family affairs are this way as are state affairs!"

Zhongni was silenced. A moment later he looked up to the sky and breathed a long sigh, "The implementation of the Great Way was preordained, and so was its failure. Since my doctrine cannot be practiced in the state of Lu, I shall leave and travel to other states. I will preach according to my beliefs to see what the will of Heaven is."

All in all Shi Yi was a musician, gifted at playing instruments but unskilled at speaking. At this moment he was short of words for persuasion and consolation. He was familiar with Zhongni's stubbornness since the time they had been children, stubborn as a mule which refused to be commanded. Then Shi Yi took out the *qin* he had brought along with him and, amidst his intoxication, decided to play a farewell song for Zhongni.

Tuning the *qin*, he chuckled to himself, "We're like the old songs. I suppose no one is interested in listening to us."

He played an old piece. It had originally been a folk song from the state of Zheng, called "A Song of Grievance." It described a man whose heartlessness aggrieved his lover. Later the song was adapted in the state of Chu, where the message became more patriotic and the theme became more apparent through a clear melody. But the tune remained sentimental and plaintive.

Zhongni listened, the music stirring his heart and arousing in him a flow of emotion. He was moved by a torrent of thoughts. Intoxicated, he began to sing aloud to the *qin*. His sadness resonated in his deep voice. It was an old tune and he had replaced the original lyrics,

> *A girl's good looks may drive one to exile;*
> *A girl's charm may bring about the perish of a state;*
> *Leisurely and carefree, I'm whiling away a year.*
> *Leisurely and carefree, I'm whiling away a year ...*

His disciples were already asleep. His singing awakened them. One after another they emerged from the room and came to crowd around their teacher. They were accustomed to Zhongni's lectures but had never heard him sing. After he had finished, they applauded loudly.

Embarrassed by the applause, Zhongni hastily comment-
ed that he was out of practice and incapable of singing high
notes any more. However, the men praised his vocal talent,
assuring him that a lower tone was more suited to classical
songs.

Their comments encouraged Zhongni and he asked Shi Yi
to play another song, "A song of Mount Turtle." This piece described one's yearning for his hometown which particularly
resonated with the master at this time.

Zhongni's began to sing,

> *When I am gazing in Lu's direction,*
> *My view is obstructed by Mount Turtle.*

His voice was deep and melodious; the men listening
were touched and began to join in,

> *As I hold no ax in my hand,*
> *Mount Turtle dashes my aspirations.*

The sound of singing echoed loudly around them, rever-
berating through the ravines before fading away into the distance. The singers stopped singing but the melody continued
to be heard afar; It moved further and further away and startled flocks of birds that flapped their wings and screeched
into the night sky.

At this moment the autumn moon emerged, a crescent,
scattering the land with shafts of light.

When the singing had finished, they drank a last toast
and then retired to bed. The next morning Shi Yi accompanied Zhongni and his disciples to the outside of the village.
At a crossroads, they stopped. The main road cut through
a stretch of wilderness, on which a newly planted sapling

stood alone. This represented the boundary marker between the states of Lu and Wei.

"I can only come this far and must say goodbye to you here. If I went any further, I would cross the border," Shi Yi said to Zhongni.

"Can I entrust you with the state affairs of Lu," Zhongni asked.

"Yes," nodded Shi Yi, looking solemn.

"And would you be kind enough to take care of my affairs at home as well?" Zhongni asked again.

"Certainly," Shi Yi replied. "Rest assured, I will."

"Just one more thing," Zhongni paused, clasping his hands in a grave salute, "That should also be placed under your care, my old friend."

"Feel free to let me know," Shi Yi saluted in return. "I would never be negligent with any of your matters."

"If I die in a foreign state, I would like the duke of Lu to permit the return of my body to my hometown to be buried beside my parents' grave."

"Yes, I will do as you wish," answered Shi Yi, conscious that this would be their last moment together, as his eyes became moist.

They wished each other well and bade each other farewell before departing on their respective ways.

When Shi Yi returned to Lu, Ji Huanzi came to see him to ask what Zhongni had said when he was leaving. Shi Yi repeated to him what had been said. Ji Huanzi thought Kong Qiu's behavior had been strange and asked, "Did he really find offence at my watching those pretty, young dancers of Qi? That he would leave his homeland?" By that time, Ji Huanzi had long grown weary of the erotic Qi dances. His latest fixation was the wolf-like dog that the ruler of Zhao had sent him. He took the duke of Lu with him on daily hunts in the mountains under the guise of training in preparation for war.

Meanwhile Shi Yi thought of Zhongni all the time. He learned that the sage first journeyed to the state of Wei, then arrived in Cao and Zheng and then finally reached Chen. When war broke out later, they were unable to correspond and nothing more was heard of Zhongni's location and welfare. Occasionally Shi Yi distracted himself with the *qin*, first playing "Grievance" and then "A song of Mount Turtle." After he had finished, he would heave one sigh after another. He recalled how Lu had plunged deeper and deeper into turmoil after Zhongni had left. He wished that he could bring the country out of such a desperate state; unfortunately, while the spirit was willing, the flesh was weak. When Zhongni's wife and son died, Shi Yi had helped with funeral preparations. But that had been the only assistance he could offer, given the state and Zhongni' family predicament; he had felt guilty that he had not lived up to his promise to take care of the affairs that his old friend had entrusted him with. He remembered, however, the final request that Zhongni had made and resolved not to let his friend down this time. One day in the year before Zhongni returned to Lu, Shi Yi, long suffering from a disease, felt a little better. He asked his son to bring the *qin* to his sickbed so that he could play a piece of music. He had only just started to play when he fell and died. With his final breath he managed to say, "I'm afraid I will not be able to complete the task Zhongni left with me."

Epilogue The Sage
(479 BC)

Before dawn, Confucius was up. He went out with the walking stick in hand and walked slowly toward the outskirts of the town. In the first rays of the morning sun, he ascended a hill.

The hill was not tall but its terrain stood steep; it was austere and imposing with its precipitous landscape and exuberantly green foliage. Regrettably, the top of the hill was barren with no trees and grass except a smattering of white rocks and rugged stones.

Standing atop the hill, Confucius gazed fixedly at the dark mountain ranges in the distance, dimly visible through the thin fog.

At midnight the previous night, he had dreamed that he was back in the dynasty of zhou. It was the same memorial scene for offering sacrifices that he had dreamed before: the splendid, tranquil sunshine flooded the land like rays of light falling through a blanket of gauze, dazzling but lacking warmth, merely placing his dream into a radiant setting. The ceremony had just started and the civil and military officials were all dressed in formal attire and wearing solemn expressions of respect; they marched quietly and rigidly in an extended procession, up a long, stone flight of stairs. At the head of the procession was the master of the ceremony, a stout ordinary looking man who walked steadily and firmly, with a dignified demeanour. The stone stairs led to the top of the hill where there was a tall temple. Amid the cloud and fog, one could see that the door of the temple stood open; inside, there were large sturdy roof beams and pillars. Between two pillars was a tall altar with figures of dragon, horse, phoenix and kylin carved on the side. Various bronze utensils, carved in the shapes of the fierce beasts, were placed in front of the altar.[1] Fragrant incense smoke lingered in the air, as sounds of the instruments with drumbeats echoed across the building, all the sacred birds, supernatural animals and the fierce beast were brought to life ...

On the altar, sat the figure to which sacrifices were made, its features dimly visible.

Confucius had seen this altar of sacrifice ritual numerous times in dreams but had never seen its sitting figure clearly. Each time he was about to make out its identity, he woke up.

This time he edged closer and closer; until he was within an inch of the altar, the figure sitting there ... The instant his dream was about to disappear, there was a flash of light that illuminated the inside of the temple. He raised his head with a jolt and saw clearly for the first time the figure's identity.

He was both appalled and stupefied.

A thunderbolt flashed across the clear blue skies. Rays of sunlight were shattered, falling in disorderly pieces. The temple trembled before heaven and earth collapsed, and the world was engulfed in darkness.

He woke up and lay in the dark. Unable to completely wake from the nightmare, he drifted between the dream state and reality; the images that appeared in his dream melded together, fragmented but visible. The image he had seen moments before still filled his heart with fear.

The face of the figure whom he had seen and to which sacrifices were offered was none other than his own.

It was past midnight, the surroundings enveloped in darkness and hush keeping a tight rein on the land. He was yet to come to consciousness but his mind was sober. He was still frightened and anxious.

Instantly he felt a chill rising from the soles of his feet and coursing through his veins.

---

[1] The fierce beast: "taotie," a legendary gluttonous beast, the head of which is often decoratively carved on large bronze cooking vessels in ancient China.

The sun came through casting a myriad of colours, distant mountains turning blue and green.

As the sun was rising Zigong found his teacher standing alone at the summit of the hill, leaning on the stick. Confucius faced the morning sun and his figure was outlined in effulgent light that cast a glorious radiance from behind him.

Seeing Zigong, Confucius called to him, "Ci, why have you come so late?"

"At the dawn of the day I searched everywhere but could not find you. I did not know that you had walked so far and had come up this hill." Zigong said. He had been over the age of freeing from perplexities and become more experienced.[1] His apparel was not as ostentatious as it used to be, though he always picked high quality materials. He had just come back from Wei where he had paid his respects to the late Zilu. At learning of his teacher's poor health, he had come to meet with him early in the morning.

Confucius responded, "If you had been a little later, I would not have seen you for the last time."

Shocked, Zigong said, "Why are you saying that?"

Confucius remained silent; he looked far into the distance for a while before turning around and saying, "I'm seventy-three and my days are numbered. Last night I had the same dream I have had before: I saw that I was the figure that was standing between two pillars to which sacrifices were made. The coffins of the Xia dynasty people used to be placed beside the east stairs, coffins of the Zhou dynasty people beside the west stairs, and coffins of the Yin dynasty people between the two pillars. I was born at the wrong time, so my soul is from the Yin dynasty. I probably wouldn't be of the Zhou dynasty."

Zigong added eagerly, "Master, you've always refrained from talking about ghosts, demons, gods and superpowers. Why are you interpreting the dream today?"

---

[1] In *The Analects of Confucius*, Confucius says, "At thirty I was established in career and life; at forty I was free from perplexities; at fifty I was able to understand the heavenly laws; at sixty my ear was attuned; at seventy I had my own way."

With a shake of head, Confucius went on, "Isn't it written in *The Book of Songs*, 'Mount Tai has been crushed! Roof beams and pillars have collapsed! Scholars have shriveled in learning!' Doesn't this reflect my state?"

"Will a man be conscious after he dies?" Zigong raised a philosophical question, attempting to change the topic of conversation so as to distract the master from the issue of death.

Confucius smiled and said, "One will know after he dies." He then pointed to the mountain in the distance and continued, "Look over there."

"The mountains?"

"Beyond the mountains."

"The cloud and mist?"

"Behind the cloud and mist."

"There is more cloud and mist over there." Zigong could not see anything else.

Still pointing into the distance, Confucius squinted into the sunshine, his face lighting up with joy:

"Have you seen those? Beyond the mountains and behind the cloud and mist, on the sunlit land, there are mountains, rivers, villages, houses, fields, ponds, expanses of the white mulberry trees and bamboo groves. Each family raises chicken and pigs in the yard in front of the house and grows mulberry trees and hemp at the rear of the house ... I've seen them. But regrettably I can't walk there."

Zigong looked in the direction Confucius pointed and still nothing was visible except the mountains, cloud and mist. He found his teacher rather eccentric today with some irrelevant remarks, so he casually responded a little more before helping Confucius down the hill.

It was a bright sunny day in the late spring with breezes, thin clouds and verdant plants and trees, all things in full vitality.

Confucius sat in his room, bathed in the sunshine rushing in through the windows. But he hardly felt the warmth of the sun while currents of chill rose from the soles of his feet steadily along his legs and then over his knees. Finally a coldness overran his waist and back before his legs started to be numb.

He recalled a day long ago when, in the same season of the year, he sat in the courtyard with a few disciples talking freely about life goals. He remembered that there were Zilu, Ran Qiu, Gongxi Hua and Zeng Dian. At that time these students were in the bloom of youth. Confucius himself, middle-aged, was handsome, ambitious and vigorous. These young men all cherished lofty aspirations. In Confucius' retrospection Zilu hoped for leading an army of one thousand chariots to gallop across battlefields and fight in the Central Plains; Ran Qiu dreamed of governing a small country successfully by first providing people with food and shelter and then resurrecting the rites and music; Gongxi Hua aimed at becoming a middle-ranking official in charge of ancestral shrines for ruling houses and handling the protocol for allied summits; only the idea of Zeng Dian was a little unusual, the yearning for donning spring clothes in late spring and joining five or six adult friends and seven or eight youngsters to swim in the River Yi, revel on the Rain Altar and return home, singing along at dusk.[1] Listening to their chat Confucius was long engrossed in thoughts of the future.

Now it was late spring again. Looking out of the window he saw the fields carpeted with seedlings, vegetable gardens ablaze with yellow blossom, brooks winding, and mountains undulating in the distance. How he wished he had been able to take a stroll in the field! But he was too feeble to walk, even hardly able to stand up.

After lunch Zeng Dian and Zeng Shen, the father and son, paid a call on Confucius. They saw him seated at the writing desk and leaning against the window, his brows slightly drawn and eyes closed; evidently he was taking the afternoon nap. The sun orbited down in the west, casting a shadow over Confucius, his figure outlined in glimmering light. The room was large and

---

[1] According to "Forefathers" from *The Analects of Confucius*, "I am swimming in the River Yi and enjoying myself at the Rain Altar."

hollow. Thanks to the master's continued suspension of class, short tables, long chairs, long narrow tables and stools were all stacked along the walls, quietly and neatly, as if they were immersed in memories of the hurly-burly that they once knew.

The father and son stood in silence, for fear of disturbing Confucius' sleep.

"Shen, that issue I've thought about for a long time," suddenly Confucius opened his eyes that gleamed with vitality. He went on, looking at Zeng Shen, "Your father's correct. When the father and son cover up things for each other, uprightness is maintained."

Zeng Shen knew Confucius referred to the loss of the sheep in the House of Ye that occurred years before. The House of Ye lost a stray sheep, which Zeng Dian took and ate. As the son Zeng Shen had a heated debate with his father on whether he should report to the local authorities of his father's wrongdoing or cover it up instead. Zeng Shen believed he should lay bare his father's dishonesty, a son though he was. It was an issue of right and wrong in regard to the national laws. To uphold righteousness one must sacrifice ties of blood. However, his father Zeng Dian disagreed. According to him, if a son was unfilial what was the point for him to spouting about upholding righteousness? Zeng Dian was ill-educated and could not come up with more convincing arguments. At that time Confucius did not give tongue on their dispute, but he managed to conceal the dilemma for the Zengs from the public.

"If things were let go this way, how would the national laws be enforced appropriately?" asked Zeng Shen.

"If filial affection were ignored what would you be up to with laws?"

"Would you opt for family ties over laws, sir?"

Smiling Confucius said, "Human nature is universal, isn't it?"

Zeng Shen seemed thoughtful of something when saying, "Should the family be placed before the country, and the father and son before the sovereign and minister, if this is really true?"

Confucius only smiled in response.

Zeng Dian, completely lost for what they were talking about, said promptly, "Don't ask questions any more. What the master said is certainly correct."

As twilight descended sunshine dispersed and was gradually hidden by thin clouds. The sky turned dark and light intermittently, and finally nightfall prevailed.

Now Confucius felt that chill creeping up to his chest and diffusing across his trunk. First the internal organs of his body were submerged in coldness and then his hands felt, inch by inch, invaded by the chilly fluid.

He called Zigong and asked him to summon all his disciples to his front.

When they arrived Confucius was bedridden. The inner room was full of worried students, and the outer room was quickly bursting with crowds, too. Outside a throng of people stood in the yard.

The room was lighted by a bunch of candles. With the prop of Gongye Chang, Confucius sat on the bed, leaning against the head of the bed. He was very feeble and, his eyes, though dim and dull, would glitter from time to time like the flames of the candles.

"The practice of the doctrine has been long discarded under heaven!" Confucius said faintly. "No one but you has been willing to listen to the ideas that I've preached."

Zigong said, "Master, you are like the sun and moon high in the sky. The ordinary man can only look up at you and eat their dust. It's understandable."

Shaking his head Confucius said, "I've exhausted my teaching! I've traveled to the end in my journey of career, but unsuccessfully! What a failure I have suffered in living as an upright person!"

Zigong responded immediately, "You're a sage and the populace under heaven all revere you. How can your life be considered as a failure?"

"A sage? How dare I claim to be a sage?" Confucius sighed and continued, "I'm a *junzi* at best. In reality I only have tried to be an upright man."

Then Confucius asked, "Is Yan Lu around here?"

Yan Lu quickly replied, "Yes, sir. Here I am." Leaning on a stick he tottered to his feet and inched into the room as the men inside made way for him.

Holding Yan Lu's hand Confucius said with emotion, "I've done nothing regrettable in life. But one thing that has bothered me all the time is that I did not sell my chariot and purchase a set of inner and outer coffins for Yan Yuan."

As Yan Lu listened, his eyes were streaming. Wiping the tears he responded, "Master, why should you bring up this matter? You were right. My son, Hui, was not an official. He did not deserve those coffins. I made a foolish request against the rites."

Confucius said, "The rites are based on emotion. Restraining oneself from emotions is against the rites. In my life I have pursued compliance with the rites but ignored accommodating emotional needs. I should be ashamed of what I've done. Yan Yuan looked on me as his father. But I did not make worthy funeral services for him as his father."

The old Yan Lu cried his heart out as he said, "Hui said before he died that he had been greatly honored to be your follower in life. It is a pity that he died young and was unable to see the day when the Great Way prevails under the Sun."

Confucius replied, "I won't be able to see that day, either. Is this fate? One thing that a man cannot overcome in life is his own life (性命). In order to make the great doctrine be practiced under heaven I have relied on and cultivated virtues of benevolence and righteousness and probed into the will of heaven. It's a shame that I did not learn to understand 'life (性命)' these two characters. The doctrine originates in nature (天性). Heaven is fate (命运). All truth in this world is embodied in life. I did not know this truth in the past so I had constantly suffered from setbacks. In the end I've got nowhere. Now I have understood. But it's too late. I won't be able to see the day the great doctrine is implemented across the land."

Confucius paused and closed his eye, overwhelmed with sorrow. It was a long while before he opened his eyes and said to his students, "I have collated and annotated *The Book of Songs*, *The Book of History*, *The Book of Rites*, *The Book of Music*, *The Book of Changes*, and *The Spring and Autumn Annals*. Now I am leaving them with you all. You will have these books available and so will you with the doctrine. After I die please leave me alone."

The disciples inside and outside the room replied in unison, "We'll keep watch by your side for ever."

With great difficulty Confucius shook his head and said, "When you travel to the four corners of the earth the doctrine will be disseminated under heaven."

His students were heartbroken at these words. The spell of silence was quickly pierced by a choked cry bursting out from the crowd.

The night that followed Confucius fell into sleep. Later he lost consciousness as his body gradually turned cold. He never woke up.

The early morning seven days later, the locals of the county of Qufu heard a roar of weep rising from the southwest of the town, the grief shaking earth. When they got out they saw men and women everywhere clad in mourning garments of hemp, white flowers, white wreaths, white funeral streamers, and white banners, half the town turning white overnight. The town folk inquired of each other and learned that Confucius died the night before and his followers were mourning for his death. What struck one as unexpected was that three thousand Confucian followers attended the burial ceremony that day; the enormous funeral procession wound through the town, beating drums and blowing trumpets; those marching at the head of the contingent arrived on the burial ground, while those bringing up the rear were yet to shuffle out of the town. The funeral was so grand that the duke of Lu was present, which confounded the town people for what official position this Confucius had held in life.

After the funeral ceremony was completed the disciples buried Confucius north of the town by the side of the River Si. They kept vigil for three years and then dismissed reluctantly. Zigong stayed behind alone. He built a thatched shack beside Confucius' grave and kept watch for six whole years. One drizzling morning six years later he left sadly. Alone he set out first west and then south; thereafter no news was heard of him since. Later one man said he saw Zigong in the capital town of Wei, Diqiu; another man recounted his encounter with him in a town of Chu, Yingdu; but both were sure that Zigong took up his old profession, business. The word on the street went that each time before Zigong bargained with the customer over the price, he would expound the gist of the *Analects of Confucius*; if the customer showed patience, he would let the customer have quite a bit into the bargain; if he made himself understood, the customer would be allowed to purchase the first piece of his merchandise at the regular price and obtain the second free. This eccentricity of his got known quickly and drew flocks of people around him each day, who just came to listen to his jabber and then obtained silver coins without the sweat of the brow. Zigong never gave thoughts to gains and losses. But his business remained prosperous.

The old residence of Confucius was not occupied after its host was gone. The courtyard was overgrown with weeds and dotted with wild blossoms. Confucius' clothing, hats, chariot and books sat at the places where they used to be, but were coated with a thick dust.

The neighbors said that, though no one had inhabited the house long since, the sound of teaching, reciting and reading aloud was still often heard from inside; occasionally the sound of music, singing, laughter and clamor soared into the air and lingered. The strains rang in bits and danced like a shred and flake; one moment it sank to the ground and the next it shot into the sky; it hit one's ear unexpectedly, but when attention was paid nothing was heard any more; from winter to summer it remained faintly audible. Two hundred and fifty years later the troops of the First Emperor of the Qin dynasty, one million armored horses, swept the states of Qi and Lu in a windy autumn and set fire to the House of Confucius. The flames devoured more than half the residence; then the sound of chatter and music was wiped out. However, the following year when spring returned and plants were in bloom, that sound was reborn and drifted dimly out of that compound.

Today, if you visit the county of Qufu and tour the street in which ancient mansions and historical buildings stand, you may wait until tourists are all gone and then stand by the east wall of the Temple of Confucius and listen attentively with eyes closed. In a hush you may hear indistinct sounds of reciting and reading, strains of the music played on sheng pipe wind instruments and lutes, and songs sung, which hover overhead.

Appendix   Character List

Confucius (551 BC – 479 BC): surnamed Kong, named Qiu and styled Zhongni; a native of Zouyi in the state of Lu.

Family Members

Shuliang He: surnamed Kong, named He and styled Shuliang; father of Confucius.

Yan Zhengzai: mother of Confucius.

Mengpi: styled Boni; elder brother of Confucius by the same father but a different mother.

Qiguan-*shi*: wife of Confucius; a native of the state of Song.

Kong Li: the only son of Confucius; styled Boyu.

Disciples

Yan Yuan: surnamed Yan, named Hui and styled Yuan; a native of Lu, 30 years Confucius' junior.

Zilu: surnamed Zhong, named You and styled Zilu; a native of Lu, 9 years Confucius' junior.

Zigong: surnamed Duanmu, named Ci and styled Zigong; a native of the state of Wei, 31 years Confucius' junior.

Ran Qiu: surnamed Ran, named Qiu and styled Ziyou; a native of Lu, 29 years Confucius' junior.

Yan Lu: surnamed Yan, named Wuyao and styled Lu; one of Confucius' early disciples, father of Yan Yuan, 6 years Confucius' junior.

Zeng Dian: surnamed Zeng, named Dian and styled Zixi; a native of Lu, an early disciple of Confucius, father of Zeng Shen.

Zeng Shen: surnamed Zeng, named Shen and styled Ziyu; 46 years Confucius' junior.

Fan Chi: surnamed Fan, named Xu and styled Zichi, also called Fan Chi; a native of Lu, 36 years Confucius' junior.

Zai Yu: surnamed Zai, named Yu and styled Ziwo; a native of Lu, 29 years Confucius' junior.

Gongye Chang: surnamed Gongye, named Chang and styled Zichang; a native of the state of Qi, son-in-law of Confucius.

Zixia: surnamed Bu, named Shang and styled Zixia; a native of the state of Jin, 44 years Confucius' junior.

Zizhang: surnamed Zhuan, named Shi and styled Zizhang; a native of the state of Chen, 48 years Confucius' junior.

Ziyou: surnamed You, named Yan and styled Ziyou; a native of Wu, 45 years Confucius' junior.

Zhongsun Yue: surnamed Zhongsun, named Yue, also called Nangong Jingshu; son of Lu's minister Meng Xizi, younger brother of Meng Yizi.

Yan Zhuozou: surnamed Yan, named Geng and styled Zhuozou; a native of Wei.

Gongliang Ru: surnamed Gongliang, named Ru and styled Zizheng; a native of Chen.

Yan Ke: surnamed Yan, named Gao and styled Zijiao, also called Yan Ke; a native of Lu.

Gongxi Chi: surnamed Gongxi, named Chi and styled Zihua; a native of Lu, 42 years Confucius' junior.

Sima Niu: surnamed Sima, named Geng and styled Ziniu, also called Sima Niu; a native of Song, widely believed younger brother of Sima Huanliang, Minister of War of Song.

Gao Chai: surnamed Gao, named Chai and styled Zigao; a native of Wei, 30 years Confucius' junior.

Gongbo Liao: surnamed Gongbo, named Liao and styled Zizhou; a native of Lu.

Min Sun: an early disciple of Confucius.

Ran Geng: an early disciple of Confucius.

Qin Zhang: an early disciple of Confucius.

Dukes of Lu

Duke Xiang of Lu: surnamed Ji and named Wu; in reign 572 BC – 542 BC.

Duke Zhao of Lu: named Zhou; son of Duke Xiang by one of his concubines; in reign 541 BC – 510 BC.

Duke Ding of Lu: named Song; son of Duke Xiang, younger brother of Duke Zhao; in reign 509 BC – 495 BC; he once appointed Confucius as Chief Justice acting as Deputy Prime Minister.

Duke Ai of Lu: famous military strategist; in reign 494 BC – 468 BC. Ministers of Lu.

Ji Wuzi: from the Jisun clan, named Su; court minister of Lu; he twice conducted "Carving Up the State Among Three."

Ji Pingzi: named Yiru; grandson of Ji Wuzi.

Ji Huanzi: named Si; son of Ji Pingzi.

Ji Kangzi: named Fei; son of Ji Huanzi by a concubine.

Meng Xizi: senior official of Lu; from the Mengsun clan; father of Meng Yizi and Nangong Jingshu.

Meng Yizi: surnamed Zhongsun, named Heji; son of Meng Xizi, elder brother of Zhongsun Yue (or Nangong Jingshu).

Natives of Lu

Yang Hu: also called Yan Huo; house manager of the Clan of Ji.

Gongshan Furao: house manager of the Clan of Ji, later house manager for Yang Hu.

Wan Fu: carriage driver of the Ji Mansion; he used to teach Confucius carriage driving.

Shi Xiangzi: *qin* musician from Lu; he used to teach Confucius playing *qin*.

Shi Yi: court musician from Lu; friend of Confucius.

Dukes of the States

Duke Jing of Qi: surnamed Jiang, named Chujiu; state head of Qi.

Duke Ling of Wei: state head of Wei.

Duke Zhuang of Wei: named Kuai Kui; state head of Wei, son of Duke Ling.

Duke Chu of Wei: named Zhe; state head of Wei, grandson of Duke Ling and son of Duke Zhuang.

Duke Min of Chen: state head of Chen.

Duke Ye: surnamed Shen, named Zhuliang and styled Zigao; minister of Chu, granted the fief of the region Ye, well known for his "Love of Dragons."

Others

Nanzi: wife of Duke Ling of Wei.

Song Chao: prince of Song, ex-love of Nanzi.

Gongsun Yujia: close subject of Duke Ling of Wei.

Mi Zixia: favorite court official of Wei.

Yong Qu: eunuch of Wei.

Gongshu Xu: minister of Wei; he once rose in rebellion in Puyi.

Kong Kui: minister of Wei; he was once in power.

Huan Liang: high ranking military general of Song.

Laozi, also spelled Lao-tzu: surnamed Li, named Er, also called Dan; historian at the archives room of the Zhou dynasty.

Geng Sangchu: assistant of Laozi.

Yan Ying: Prime Minister of Qi, a man of virtue.

Zhao Yang: minister of Jin.

Fo Xi: magistrate of Zhongmou.

Jie Ni: a recluse.

Chang Ju: a recluse.

Jie Yu: an arrogant man from Chu.

Ji Xian: minister of Chen, a fictional character.

Du Neng: minister of Cai, a fictional character.